HENRI SAINT-SIMON

Henri Saint-Simon
(1760–1825)

Selected writings on science, industry and social organisation

Translated and edited by

KEITH TAYLOR

CROOM HELM LONDON

© 1975 Keith Taylor

Croom Helm Ltd.
2-10 St. John's Road London SW11

ISBN: 0-85664-206-1

Printed by Biddles of Guildford

CONTENTS

Preface 7
Note on the Translation 9
Abbreviations 11

Introduction

1. Saint-Simon's Life and Work 13
2. The Doctrine of Saint-Simon 29
3. The Influence of the Doctrine 49
Notes to the Introduction 55

Selected Writings

PART I SCIENCE AND THE PROGRESS OF THE HUMAN
           MIND (1802-13) 65
1. Letters from an Inhabitant of Geneva to His Contemporaries 66
2. Extract on Social Organisation 83
3. Introduction to the Scientific Studies of the 19th Century 86
4. Second Prospectus for a New Encyclopaedia 105
5. Memoir on the Science of Man 111
6. Study on Universal Gravitation 124

PART II PROPOSALS FOR POST-WAR RECONSTRUCTION
           (1814-15) 129
7. The Reorganisation of European Society, by Saint-Simon
   and Ausgustin Thierry 130
8. On the Establishment of an Opposition Party 137
9. Letter to the Minister of the Interior 141
10. To All Englishmen and Frenchmen Who Are Zealous
    for the Public Good 145

PART III FROM THE GOVERNMENT OF MEN TO THE
           ADMINISTRATION OF THINGS (1817-20) 157
11. Declaration of Principles *(L'Industrie)* 158
12. Letters to an American *(L'Industrie)* 162
13. Letter to the Publicists 169
14. Views on Property and Legislation *(L'Industrie)* 171
15. On the Political History of Industry *(L'Industrie)* 174
16. The Political Interests of Industry 181
17. On M. Barthélemy's Proposal to the House of Peers
    (Le Politique) 183

18.	Comparison between the National (Industrial) Party and the Anti-National Party *(La Politique)*	187
19.	Prospectus for *L'Organisateur*	192
20.	A Political Parable, First Extract from *L'Organisateur*	194
21.	Sketch of the New Political System *(L'Organisateur)*	198
22.	On the Replacement of Government by Administration *(L'organisateur)*	207
23.	Considerations on Measures To Be Taken To End the Revolution *(Du système industriel)*	211
24.	Third Letter to the Farmers, Manufacturers, Merchants, Bankers, and Other Industrials *(Du Système industriel)*	217
25.	Letters on the Bourbons *(Du système industriel)*	219

PART IV THE TRUE CHRISTIANITY (1821-5) 223

26.	Address to Philanthropists *(Du système industriel)*	224
27.	From Feudalism to Industrialism: The Role of the Lawyers and Metaphysicians *(Du système industriel)*	227
28.	On Liberty *(Du système industriel)*	229
29.	Constitutional Proposals to the King *(Du système industriel)*	231
30.	Letter to the Workers *(Du système industriel)*	238
31.	First Letter to the Electors of the Department of the Seine Who Are Producers *(Du système industriel)*	242
32.	Historical Survey of the Progress of French Industry *(Catéchisme des industriels)*	244
33.	On the Intermediate (Bourgeois) Class *(Catéchisme des industriels)*	250
34.	Comparison of the English and French Political Systems *(Catéchisme des industriels)*	253
35.	The Failure of European Liberalism *(Catéchisme des industriels)*	257
36.	The Reorganisation of French Science *(Catéchisme des industriels)*	259
37.	Fragments on Social Organisation *(Opinions littéraires, philosophiques et industrielles)*	262
38.	Social Physiology Applied to the Improvement of Social Institutions: Supplementary Notes *(Opinions littéraires, philosophiques et industrielles)*	272
39.	The Artist, the Scientist, and the Industrial: Dialogue, by Saint-Simon and Léon Halévy *(Opinions littéraires, philosophiques et industrielles)*	279
40.	New Christianity: First Dialogue	289
Notes to the Selected Writings		305
Bibliography		311

PREFACE

When Saint-Simon's writings first appeared, during the first quarter of the nineteenth century, they invariably aroused little more than amusement and mild curiosity. The ideas they contained — ideas concerning, for example, the application of scientific method to the study of man and society, the coming of a new 'scientific-industrial' age in which the State would assume responsibility for promoting social welfare, the prospects for international co-operation and integration in Europe, man's need for a secular religion — were widely dismissed as the eccentric products of a disturbed mind. In view of the boldness and originality of Saint-Simon's thought, such a reaction is not surprising. Today, however, when social science is an established academic discipline, when scientific-industrial society and the Welfare State are realities, when a movement towards European unity is under way, and when the secular religion of Marxist communism is the established basis of social organisation in many parts of the world, his ideas deserve to be treated with more respect.

In view of Saint-Simon's historical importance as a 'founding father' of social science and socialism, and considering the intrinsic interest and continuing relevance of his theory of social organisation, it is surprising to find that in the 150 years since his death (the anniversary falls on 19 May 1975) only a very small proportion of his works has appeared in English. A translation of *Nouveau christianisme*, by J.E. Smith, was published in 1834; and in 1952 a collection of selected writings, edited and translated by F.M.H. Markham, was published. This edition (full details of which are given in the bibliography) certainly provides a valuable introduction to Saint-Simon's thought. However, it is somewhat limited in scope, especially in its coverage of the major writings published during the Restoration Monarchy, in which the full doctrine of *industrialism* is expounded. Three of these works — *Le Politique, Du système industriel,* and the *Catéchisme des industriels* — are not represented at all; while two others — *L'Industrie* and *L'Organisateur* — are represented by only one very brief extract each.

In the present volume my aim is to provide a much more comprehensive and representative selection of texts than that offered by Markham, including extracts from some important less-known works which shed valuable light on Saint-Simon's thought. The texts are presented in chronological order to enable the reader to follow the evolution of their author's doctrine through its several distinct phases.

Certain writings commonly attributed to Saint-Simon, but which are now known to have been the work of Auguste Comte, his collaborator from 1817 to 1824, are not represented in this selection. These are: the whole of volume III and the first part of volume IV of *L'Industrie* (1817); and the eighth and ninth letters of *L'Organisateur* (1820). These writings were originally published in Saint-Simon's name, but research has shown conclusively that Comte was their author. Thus, while Saint-Simon would seem to have approved of their content, it would be taking literary licence too far to include them in a selection intentionally restricted to his own works.

A similar problem is presented by another text: *De la physiologie appliquée à l'amélioration des institutions sociales* (1825), which has usually been attributed to Saint-Simon and regarded as one of his most important works. In fact the bulk of this text (the *Introduction*) was written by his colleague, Dr. E.-M. Bailly; Saint-Simon merely added some additional notes at the end (the *Continuation*). In the present selection, therefore, only the *Continuation* is represented.

It is my hope that this volume will not only help to make Saint-Simon's importance more widely understood, but will also serve to dispel some of the confusion which presently clouds discussion of his thought. His ideas have been subject to so many different interpretations that the student cannot possibly be expected to assess their respective merits without some fairly detailed knowledge of the full range of his writings.

I should like to take this opportunity to thank all those friends and colleagues who were kind enough to comment on the early drafts of my Introduction: Jan Ciechanowski, Georg Iggers, David McLellan, Susan Saunders, Tom Nossiter, William Pickles, and Vincent Wright. Mr. Pickles' linguistic expertise also helped me to improve various sections of the translation.

I am also grateful to the staff of the Bibliothèque Nationale, Paris, the British Library of Political and Economic Science (London School of Economics), the British Museum reading room, the library of the Institut Français du Royaume-Uni, and the University of London Library for their expert and efficient assistance; to Eileen Gregory, who typed a number of sections of the final script; and to Christopher Helm, whose encouragement and advice was much appreciated.

Finally, but by no means least, I have my wife Chris to thank for sharing all the trials and tribulations of authorship with me over the last two years.

Keith Taylor

NOTE ON THE TRANSLATION

Most of the texts included in this selection have been translated from the six-volume *Oeuvres de Claude-Henri de Saint-Simon* (Paris: Éditions Anthropos, 1966), which is the most comprehensive collection of Saint-Simon's writings available. The first five volumes are devoted to a photographic reproduction of the 1868-76 edition of Saint-Simon's works, published as part of the *Oeuvres de Saint-Simon & d'Enfantin* (Paris: E. Dentu, 1865-76; E. Leroux, 1876-78, 47 vols.). The sixth volume contains various texts omitted from that edition, some of them reproduced from the *Oeuvres choisies de C.-H. de Saint-Simon* (Brussels: Van Meenen, 1859, 3 vols.).

Occasionally I have discovered textual discrepancies between the Anthropos edition and other published versions of Saint-Simon's writings. When this has happened I have made every effort to select the most reliable source for translation. In the case of the *Lettres d'un habitant de Genève à ses contemporains*, the Anthropos version is not satisfactory because it is incomplete. The full text was published by Alfred Pereire in 1925 (Paris: Libraire Félix Alcan), and it is this edition which has been used for translation here. For the *Mémoire sur la science de l'homme* and the *Travail sur la gravitation universelle* – two works circulated by Saint-Simon in manuscript in 1813 – I have used the 1859 *Oeuvres choisies*, to which reference has already been made, as the editor of those volumes (Charles Lemonnier) had access to manuscript copies containing a number of passages which do not appear in the Anthropos versions. The latter were reproduced from the *Oeuvres de Saint-Simon & d'Enfantin*, whose texts of the *Mémoire* and *Travail* were based on a different set of manuscripts.

A number of very important works are absent from the Anthropos edition, and for these I have drawn on a variety of sources, including the original first editions of three texts unjustifiably ignored since Saint-Simon's death and never reprinted: *Sur l'établissement du parti de l'opposition*, from *Le Censeur* (1815); *Sur la proposition faite à la Chambre des pairs par M. Barthélemy*, from *Le Politique* (1819); and the series of notes on social physiology, from *Opinions littéraires, philosophiques et industrielles* (1825). In the case of one unpublished work, *Aux Anglais et aux Français qui sont zélés pour le bien public* (1815), I have referred to the text of the original manuscript, kindly made available to me on microfilm by the Bibliothèque Nationale, Paris. Full details of all sources are provided in the references which follow the texts.

In my translation I have attempted to preserve the character of Saint-Simon's literary style as much as possible. It is not an elegant style, but it is concise, direct, and above all passionate. Its appeal was summed up perfectly by Léon Halévy when, in a marvellously evocative phrase, he described Saint-Simon's writings as possessing 'the powerful and graceless allure of the elephant'! ('Souvenirs de Saint-Simon', *La France littéraire*, March 1832, p.531.)

The translation of Saint-Simon's vocabulary raises some problems due to the fact that he made use of a number of technical terms with no precise equivalents in modern English. Such problems are indicated in the texts as they arise, but one case of particular importance must be mentioned here concerning the term *'industriel'* which Saint-Simon claimed to have invented at the beginning of the Bourbon Restoration. He introduced the word to refer to any person engaged in any productive activity, whether in the strictly 'practical' sphere (agriculture, manufacturing, commerce, finance) or the more 'theoretical' sphere (science and art). From about 1820 onwards he modified this usage and usually used the term to refer only to the 'practical' workers; in other words, the scientists and artists became 'non-industrials'. The modern English equivalent for *'industriel'* is 'industrialist', but this word tends to be applied nowadays only to entrepreneurs in the manufacturing sector, and so does not really correspond to Saint-Simon's conception. For this reason I have thought it best to avoid that word and use instead the somewhat old-fashioned, but perfectly proper noun 'industrial'. In my translation, therefore, an 'industrial' is a productive worker in the very broad sense understood by Saint-Simon.

In general I have used Saint-Simon's titles and headings throughout this selection. But where, for editorial reasons, I have provided my own, I have enclosed them within square brackets.

Finally, a word is necessary concerning the arrangement of editorial notes to the translation. These are placed immediately after the selected writings, at pp.305-10, and are indicated in the texts by figures 1, 2, 3, etc. They should not be confused with the footnotes, indicated by asterisks, which are by Saint-Simon. Since many of Saint-Simon's footnotes are of little interest, I have generally included only those which develop points of argument or give essential information.

K.T.

ABBREVIATIONS

Cens. III	*Le Censeur, ou Examen des actes et des ouvrages qui tendent à détruire ou à consolider la constitution de l'état,* ed. Charles Comte and Charles Dunoyer, vol. III, 2nd ed., Paris, Chez Mme Marchant, 1815.
Not. hist.	'Notice historique sur Saint-Simon', in *Oeuvres de Saint-Simon et d'Enfantin,* vol. I, Paris, E. Dentu, 1865, pp.1-133.
O.c.	*Oeuvres choisies de C.-H. de Saint-Simon,* 3 vols., Brussels, Van Meenen, 1859.
Oeuvres	*Oeuvres de Claude-Henri de Saint-Simon,* 6 vols., Paris, Éditions Anthropos, 1966.
Opin. litt.	*Opinions littéraires, philosophiques et industrielles,* Paris, Galerie de Bossange père, 1825.
Pereire (1925)	Comte Henri de Saint-Simon, *Lettres d'un habitant de Genève à ses contemporains (1803), réimprimées conformément à l'édition originale et suivies de deux documents inédits – Lettre aux Européens, [Essai sur l'organisation sociale],* ed. Alfred Pereire, Paris, Libraire Félix Alcan, 1925.
Pol.	*Le Politique,* 12 pts. in 1 vol., Paris, 1819.
S.W.	Refers to the *Selected Writings* section of this book.
T.c.	Saint-Simon, *Textes choisis,* préface, commentaires et notes explicatives par Jean Dautry, Paris, Editions sociales, 1951.

INTRODUCTION

1. SAINT-SIMON'S LIFE AND WORK

(i) 1760-89

Claude-Henri de Saint-Simon belonged to one of France's most distinguished aristocratic families, which claimed, with some justification apparently, to be directly descended from Charlemagne through the comtes de Vermandois. The second child and first son of Balthazar-Henri and Blanche-Elisabeth de Saint-Simon, he was born at Berny in Picardy on 17 October 1760.[1] Balthazar-Henri was the cousin of Louis, duc de Saint-Simon (1675–1755), author of the well-known memoirs of the court of Louis XIV and the Regency; and the brother of Maximilien-Henri, marquis de Saint-Simon (1720–99), a noteworthy military historian and translator of the classics.

Although his parents were not very wealthy (his father's only income derived from various army pensions), Claude-Henri was brought up in impressive comfort. The family owned a château in Berny, with large estates, and also had a winter residence in Paris, which meant that Claude-Henri was introduced at an early age into Parisian social circles. This enabled him in his teens to meet a number of eminent intellectual figures, such as Rousseau and d'Alembert. The latter actually tutored him for a short time; and it seems likely that it was under d'Alembert's influence that his passionate interest in philosophy and the advancement of scientific knowledge first emerged. In later life he acknowledged that d'Alembert had transformed his mind into 'such a tight metaphysical net that not a single important fact could slip through it'.[2]

Very little is known about Saint-Simon's formal education. The most detailed account available is his own, given in a manuscript of 1810 which remained undiscovered until more than a century after his death:

'Let us recall the education we received. They began by fixing our attention on the history of the Greeks and the Romans: they inflamed our young hearts over the virtues of the Gracchi and the Brutuses; they wounded our still tender souls with the dagger of republicanism. They inspired us with democratic sentiments when they took us from the study of classical languages to French. Jean-Jacques, Voltaire, Helvétius, Raynal, all the Encyclopaedists, including Diderot (who desired to hang the last of the kings with the gut of the last of the priests) were the authors they put in our hands. Our education achieved its purpose: it made us revolutionaries.'[3]

Saint-Simon's early intellectual immersion in the philosophy of the French Enlightenment left a lasting impression on him, instilling into him a remarkable independence of mind, especially in religious matters, which remained with him throughout his life. When he was only thirteen he refused to take his first communion, because he considered it to be a meaningless act. However, he was to suffer for this independence, for his father sent him immediately to the Saint-Lazare prison. As if this was not bad enough, he made matters even worse by escaping and seeking refuge with a sympathetic aunt. This incident marked the beginning of a period during which he became increasingly estranged from his father.

In January 1777, at the age of sixteen, Saint-Simon was offered a commission as second lieutenant in the army. His father did not, however, permit him to accept the offer immediately and twelve months elapsed before he found himself in uniform. In June 1779 he was promoted to the rank of captain; but he was not given his first taste of action until April 1780, when he participated in the French attack on the British colonies of St. Lucia and Barbados, which was mounted by Louis XVI to assist the Americans in their struggle for independence. In the summer of 1781 his regiment reinforced the French contingent fighting in America. Under Washington's command they were sent into action against the British at the Battle of Yorktown and acquitted themselves admirably, helping to inflict a decisive defeat on the enemy, thus bringing to an end of the fighting in America.

Saint-Simon hoped that his military career would impress his father and bring about some improvement in their relationship. He was to be disappointed however. Although he was a first-class soldier (he received the Order of Cincinnatus in recognition of his bravery), his father showed little interest in his affairs. The old man died in February 1783, never having responded to his son's offer of friendship.

Saint-Simon spent a total of two months in America. His experiences in the 'New World', although limited in scope, appear to have exerted a profound influence on his intellectual development. Many years later, in 1817, he discussed the nature of this influence in some detail in his *Lettres à un Américain*, published in volume II of the journal *L'Industrie*. His comments in the second letter are particularly illuminating:

'During my stay in America, sir, I occupied myself much more with political science than with military tactics. The war in itself did not interest me, but its aim interested me greatly, and that interest led me willingly to support its cause. I desire the end, I often used to say to myself, I must certainly desire the means.

'When I saw peace approaching I was completely overcome with disgust for the military profession. I perceived clearly what career I had to take up, the career towards which my tastes and natural inclinations called me. It was not my vocation to be a soldier; I was destined for a quite different, and I might say quite contrary kind of activity. To study the advance of the human mind in order subsequently to work for the improvement of civilisation: that was the aim I set myself. From that moment I devoted myself to it totally; I consecrated my entire life to it, and this new task began to absorb all my powers.'[4]

While he was in America, then, Saint-Simon came to realise that his true vocation was to work as a political scientist for 'the improvement of civilisation'. This notion of social improvement was not simply a vague, abstract concept reflecting youthful idealism. He had a very clear idea of what it involved, having observed in America what he considered to be some of its most important manifestations: complete religious toleration, the absence of social privilege, the recognition that patrimony should play no part in politics, and the universal acceptance of a social philosophy based on pacifism, industry, and thrift. In sum, there existed in America the foundations of 'a regime infinitely more liberal and more democratic than the one under which the peoples of Europe lived'.[5] With this vision of a new world firmly in his mind, Saint-Simon bade farewell to America in 1782 and set sail with the French fleet for the West Indies.

In an engagement with the English navy at the battle of Les Saintes (Dominica) he was badly wounded, taken prisoner and transported to Jamaica. However, the end of the war was approaching and following the conclusion of the Treaty of Versailles (September 1783) he was released. From Jamaica he went to Mexico where he presented the Viceroy with a plan for the construction of a canal across the Isthmus of Panama, linking the Pacific and Atlantic Oceans.[6] This was the first manifestation of an interest in transport and communication which was to become one of his chief preoccupations in later years. The plan was rejected, however, and Saint-Simon decided to return to France.

Soon after his arrival he was promoted to the rank of assistant quartermaster. Over the next year or two his life seems to have been dull and uneventful. He found himself virtually unemployed; and with nothing better to do he travelled to Holland in 1785 to

enlist in a Franco-Dutch expeditionary force about to leave for India
in order to challenge the English forces there. But the planned
expedition was never mounted, and the following year found
Saint-Simon back in France. He now decided to advance his
knowledge of science by attending a course at the military school at
Metz, where his regiment was stationed. The course strengthened
his passion for the sciences and convinced him that he should leave
the army as soon as possible. But what else could he do?

An opportunity at last arose in 1787. The Spanish Government
had decided to construct a canal linking the city of Madrid with
the Atlantic Ocean, but it was unable to put its plan into operation
because of lack of money and workers. Since this was a project
close to Saint-Simon's heart — as his own plan for a Panama Canal
had demonstrated — he decided to offer his services and travelled
immediately to Madrid. In collaboration with the chief architect
of the project, Francisco de Cabarrús (director of the Banco de San
Carlos and chief financial adviser to King Charles III) he drew up a
plan of action. The Bank would provide the necessary finance, while
Saint-Simon would assume responsibility for organising a work-force
of 6,000 men. Unfortunately, the execution of this ambitious plan
was made impossible by the outbreak of the French Revolution,
which drew Saint-Simon back to France at the end of 1789.

(ii) 1789-98

It was not long before he found himself at the centre of political
affairs in his home district of Falvy, near Péronne. In February 1790
he was chosen President of the municipal assembly, in which capacity
he was offered his first opportunity to proclaim his faith in the
revolutionary ideals of liberty, equality, and fraternity. At the same
time he emphasised the importance of recognising the inevitable
inequalities of virtue and ability between men:

> 'All citizens are equally eligible for all public honours, offices
> and positions, according to their capacity, and with no
> distinctions other than those of their virtue and talents . . .'[7]

During the early months of the Revolution Saint-Simon was able to
define more precisely the nature of the tasks before him. His
immediate aim was 'to organise a great industrial establishment,
to found a scientific school of improvement'.[8] But he realised that
he could do very little without money. The most urgent need, therefore,
was to acquire funds; and with this aim in view he decided to invest
in the *biens nationaux* (national property) put up for sale by the
new Government. In 1790 he formed a partnership with the comte
de Redern, Prussian Ambassador to England, whom he had first met

in Madrid two years earlier, and who shared his enthusiasm for science and social improvement. He managed to acquire a bank loan of 636,000 francs, and immediately set about launching an extensive investment programme. However, the deteriorating political situation in France soon threatened to put a halt to his financial activities. Under Robespierre's 'reign of terror' it soon became clear that no one was safe from the guillotine. Saint-Simon's fears for his own safety were so great that he actually took the precaution of renouncing his title, which he knew would be regarded with suspicion and hostility. In September 1793, in a ceremony of 'republican baptism'[9] before the *conseil général* of the commune of Péronne, he formally changed his name to Claude-Henri Bonhomme. However, he had acted too late, and in November he was arrested and imprisoned by the secret police on suspicion of being a counter-revolutionary. Fortunately for him, the fall of Robespierre on 27 July 1794 (9 Thermidor in the republican calendar) brought the Terror to an end, and he was released three months later.

Reverting to the name of Henri Saint-Simon, he immediately renewed his financial activities and soon achieved the results for which he was hoping. By 1795 he had purchased over four million francs' worth of property, the income from which more than covered his immediate needs. Under the new Directory regime, established in October 1795, he expanded his business activities, becoming involved in various industrial and commercial enterprises: he manufactured linen and a new set of republican playing cards, in which the Kings, Queens, and Knaves were replaced by symbols representing Genius, Liberty, and Equality; he set up as a wine merchant; he registered as a trader at the Paris corn-exchange; he drew up plans for a coach service from Paris to Calais. He even found himself with some political influence: in 1797 he participated in the Anglo-French peace negotiations as a representative of French financial circles.

In material terms the immediate results of Saint-Simon's business ventures were impressive:

'Hardly out of prison, Saint-Simon rents a residence and the top floors of the two neighbouring houses on the rue Chabanais, near the rue de Richelieu. He settles down there with two of his sisters.

'It is the street where the pompous Cambacérès lived when he was appointed second Consul. Not an aristocratic quarter, but rich, fashionable, with the Palais-Royal at its centre.

'... Saint-Simon manages a princely train of attendants. As house steward he has Monoyer, the former house steward of M. de Choiseul, once famous for his pomp; as chief cook Le Gagneur, who had made the reputation of Marshal de Duras's suppers; as chief butler Tavernier, who had learned his profession in Rome, at the house of Cardinal de Bernis. Twenty servants.'[10]

The Hôtel Chabanais was quickly transformed into a fashionable *salon*, to which the most eminent *savants* of Paris were invited. Among the regular visitors were the mathematicians Lagrange, Monge, and Poisson, who kept their host informed of the progress of the sciences. The *salon* was a great success; it was also a great expense, even for the *nouveau riche* Saint-Simon. It soon became clear to his financial partner, the comte de Redern, that such luxury could not possibly be maintained. So he informed Saint-Simon of his desire to dissolve their partnership (at the end of 1797), the precise terms to be settled by arbitration.

Following this shattering decision, Saint-Simon left the Hôtel Chabanais in 1798 and moved to a house near the École Polytechnique, where he had decided to follow courses in physics and mathematics. Science was now his sole passion, and he was determined to devote the rest of his life to it.

(iii) 1799-1813

The result of the arbitration was announced in August 1799. Saint-Simon was to be bought out for a capital sum of 150,000 francs. Compared with Redern's share — an *annual* income of 100,000 francs — this was not very much. But the arbitrator had come to the conclusion that Saint-Simon had been extravagant, and had adjusted his award accordingly.

Napoleon Bonaparte's assumption of power on 18 Brumaire of the year VIII (9 November 1799) resulted in a major reorganisation of the École Polytechnique; but this did not affect Saint-Simon's plans, and he continued his studies there until 1801. During this time he initiated a remarkable experiment in free education by organising (and financing) public courses in science, taught by some of the most brilliant young scientists in Paris, headed by the mathematician Poisson whose career Saint-Simon was attempting to promote. Because he regarded the encouragement of intellectual ability as of the utmost social importance, Saint-Simon assumed the role of patron of the sciences with great enthusiasm and selflessness. Numerous anecdotes have been recorded which testify to his financial generosity. Typical is one concerning the brilliant young surgeon Guillaume Dupuytren, whom Saint-Simon once had occasion to visit for a scientific discussion. As he departed, Saint-Simon intentionally left behind a thousand francs. Only after repeated protests by Dupuytren was he persuaded to take the money back.[11]

After completing his work at the École Polytechnique in 1801,

Saint-Simon transferred to the École de Médecine in order to follow courses in physiology. The scientific study of organic phenomena interested him greatly, since he considered it offered the most suitable starting-point for the development of a theory of social organisation — a 'social physiology' as he called it. In his view, recent physiological research — for example, the work of Dr Jean Burdin, the influence of whose ideas he explictly acknowledged[12] — clearly pointed to the conclusion that a science of man and society was possible.

While he was pursuing his studies, in August 1801, Saint-Simon was married to Sophie de Champgrand, a talented young writer and musician who had studied under the composer Grétry. According to the bridegroom, this venture was not motivated by romance, but by more mundane considerations. He thought Sophie would be the perfect hostess to help him entertain the scientists of Paris:

'I used marriage as a means of studying scientists, something which seemed necessary to me for the execution of my enterprise; for in order to improve the organisation of the scientific system, it is not enough to be well acquainted with the state of human knowledge; it is necessary besides to know what effect the cultivation of science has on those who are devoted to it; it is necessary to appreciate the influence which this occupation has on their passions, on their minds, on their morality as a whole and in its various parts.'[13]

Not surprisingly, the marriage was totally unsuccessful and was dissolved by mutual consent in June 1802.[14]

It was shortly before the divorce, in March 1802, that Saint-Simon's first known published writings appeared: a set of letters to the administrators of the Lycée Républicain in Paris, in which he criticised their neglect of scientific studies and offered to lecture himself. The letters were published anonymously and were not discovered until 1948.[15] They are of little interest today, except inasmuch as they testify to Saint-Simon's passionate enthusiasm for science and his conviction that he himself had something to teach people on the subject.

After his divorce Saint-Simon decided to further his scientific knowledge by travelling abroad. Napoleon's peace settlements of 1801-2 had greatly facilitated foreign travel, and he began by visiting England. The trip was a disappointment, however. The English, he concluded, 'did not have in hand any new idea of importance'.[16] He next made his way to Geneva in Switzerland, and this visit proved to be much more eventful. While he was there, he met and exchanged ideas with Madame de Staël, who lived at Coppet and whose social philosophy largely coincided with his own. For some years Madame de Staël had held a *salon* in Paris, and it is possible that Saint-Simon had already made her acquaintance there. It is almost certain that he had read her book, *De la littérature considérée dans ses rapports avec les institutions sociales,* published in 1800, in which she had explored the possibility of constructing a science of society. According to Saint-Simonian tradition, Saint-Simon actually proposed marriage to Madame de Staël in Geneva (she had recently been widowed). The story cannot be verified, but we can be certain at least that if a proposal was made, it was not taken seriously.

While he was in Geneva, Saint-Simon took the opportunity to publish a short booklet in which he set down for the first time in systematic form his ideas on social reorganisation: *Lettres d'un habitant de Genève à l'humanité.* A second, expanded edition of this work appeared in Paris in 1803, under a slightly different title: *Lettres d'un habitant de Genève à ses contemporains.*[17] The *Lettres* outlined a scheme for establishing order and stability in society. They were addressed to humanity in general, because, it was argued, the whole of civilisation was threatened by the forces of revolution and anarchy. In Saint-Simon's view this crisis could be overcome only by fundamental reforms in social organisation, based on the recognition that science and industry (in the sense of all productive activity) were the two great agents of progress at the service of man:

'I believe that all social classes would benefit from this organisation: spiritual power in the hands of the *savants;* temporal power in the hands of the property owners; the power to elect the leaders of humanity in the hands of everyone; the reward of the rulers, respect . . . .

'All men will work. They will all regard themselves as workers attached to a workshop . . .'[18]

The most urgent need was to endow the *savants,* the scientists and artists, with the spiritual power previously exercised by the Catholic clergy. The latter's authority had been declining since the Middle Ages because of 'the progress of the human mind', and could no longer serve to hold men together in society. Hence, a totally new religion must be established, in harmony with the level of enlightenment attained by man. Saint-Simon therefore proposed the creation of a 'Religion of Newton', so called in recognition of Isaac Newton's role as a founder of modern science. The new church would be organised on both national and international levels, with the world's most eminent scientists and artists at its head. Its authority would be exercised quite independently of society's temporal power, which would remain in the hands of the property owners. (He did not want another revolution). Such proposals may strike the present-day reader as eccentric and perhaps even ridiculous. It must be remembered, however, that during the French Revolution various attempts were made to institute new religious cults to replace Catholicism — for example, Robespierre's 'Cult of the Supreme Being' and the Theophilanthropic movement under the Directory. Like these experiments the Religion of Newton was a 'cult of reason', and was totally in keeping with revolutionary ideology. Saint-Simon's plan was, however, somewhat untimely; for in 1801 Napoleon had concluded a Concordat with the Vatican which did much to reinstate the Catholic Church in France. In these new circumstances the scheme for a Religion of Newton was bound to be stillborn. The *Lettres* received no serious attention and soon vanished into obscurity.

Following the publication of the first edition of his booklet in Geneva, Saint-Simon continued his scientific investigations abroad. He travelled to Germany, where he observed an impressive enthusiasm for science which he felt sure would lead to remarkable results before very long.[19] From Germany he made his way back to Paris where, during 1803 and 1804, he developed his ideas on social reform in the *Lettre aux Européens* and *Extrait sur l'organisation sociale*. Neither of these works was published, and they remained unknown until the first quarter of the twentieth century.[20] The *Extrait* is an especially interesting text,[21] since in it Saint-Simon acknowledged his debt to Condorcet, author of the *Esquisse d'un tableau historique des progrès de l'esprit humain*, who had died in 1795. Saint-Simon predicted that the nineteenth century would witness the development of a positive science of social organisation, whose theory would be based on Condorcet's observations. He was himself anxious to do everything in his power to promote that development, but his lack of money was proving to be a major obstacle. By 1806 he was virtually a pauper; he had no job and his health was deteriorating. For a while he entertained the hope that Redern would come to his assistance, but no help was forthcoming. One acquaintance did at last take pity on him, and gave him a job as a copyist. He worked for nine hours a day, pursuing his scientific research during the night. After a few weeks in this position, though, he received another offer of help from a man called Diard, whom he had once employed as a servant. He was invited by Diard to stay with him and concentrate on his studies. The offer was gratefully accepted.

In 1807, with Diard's financial assistance, Saint-Simon was able to have his second major work printed: *Introduction aux travaux scientifiques du XIXe siècle*. The text was subsequently improved and expanded, and appeared in a new two-volume edition early the following year. The *Introduction* is a very important work.[22] In it Saint-Simon puts forward the view that the task of nineteenth-century science is to construct a new theoretical system incorporating all the knowledge acquired in the various fields of research. The aim must be to produce an all-embracing philosophical synthesis, such as Bacon and Descartes had achieved in the seventeenth century. This synthesis would deal the death-blow to metaphysics and theology, and furnish the basis for a new, scientifically acceptable religious system.

Convinced of the validity of his ideas, Saint-Simon sent the two volumes of the *Introduction* in June 1808 to the Bureau des Longitudes, one of France's most important scientific institutions, for critical assessment. However, all he received in reply was a brief note informing him that the volumes had been deposited in the Bureau's library. There was not a word of intelligent criticism. Not content to let the matter rest, Saint-Simon entered into correspondence with the Bureau's administrators in an attempt to make them take notice of his work. The letters (which were published in 1808) provoked little response, however, and Saint-Simon finally had to admit defeat. But he was determined not to abandon his scientific work, and before long he was seeking support for another venture: the publication of a new encyclopaedia of knowledge, to supersede the *Encylopêdie* of d'Alembert and Diderot. He prepared various brochures setting out his plans, some of which were printed in 1810.[23] None of these writings was successful, and it was only after his death that they received any serious attention.

At the same time as he was trying to bring his theories to the attention of France's scientific community, Saint-Simon also became involved in an attempt to renegotiate his financial settlement with Redern. It was a tedious and exhausting business, occupying him from 1807 to 1813. During these years he deluged the comte with letters (some of them published at the time) in which he proposed reconciliation and the re-establishment of their partnership. In order to rid himself of this nuisance, during 1807-8 Redern did arrange for a modest monthly allowance to be paid to Saint-Simon. However, the payments were brought to an end in 1811 when Redern became anxious about his own financial situation. This was a crushing blow for Saint-Simon, since he had no other source of income. His loyal friend Diard had died at the end of 1810, and he could think of no one else who might offer help. Not surprisingly, he was by now on the verge of a nervous breakdown. He continued to pester Redern, but to no avail. His condition eventually became so bad that in January 1813 he was sent by his physician to a private sanatorium in Paris. While he was undergoing treatment he received an offer of an allowance from his family in Péronne, which he did not hesitate to accept. This solved his immediate financial problems, and helped to promote his mental recovery. He left the sanatorium in February, his enthusiasm for life and work renewed.

By the end of the year he had written two major texts: the *Mémoire sur la science de l'homme*[24] and *Travail sur la gravitation universelle.*[25] In these works he explored the possibility of constructing a science of man and society. The foundations of such a science, he asserted, had been laid by French physiologists and philosophers, notably Vicq-d'Azyr, Condorcet, Cabanis, and Bichat. The next step was to bring their theories together in one general synthesis. This required the collaboration of Europe's most talented scientists; and he appealed to them to set about their task immediately, since war and social disorder were spreading like the plague across the continent, and would continue to spread until a coherent, scientifically founded philosophy of social organisation was formulated.

Unable to afford the printing costs, Saint-Simon was compelled to make handwritten copies of the *Mémoire* and the *Travail,* which he sent to various scientists in France, Germany, Italy, and England, as well as to some French Ministers. A number of the recipients, including Professors Cuvier (Musée d'Histoire Naturelle), Hallé (École de Médecine), and de Blainville (Université Impériale), responded enthusiastically. Some of them even sent letters of recommendation to Napoleon, stating that in their view Saint-Simon's work was worthy of financial support. At last, after fifteen years of laborious work, Saint-Simon was achieving recognition. Fifty-three years old, in poor health, and with very little money, he felt that his career as a social philosopher was only just beginning.

(iv) 1814-25

The *Mémoire* and the *Travail* not only brought Saint-Simon recognition, but also an offer of secretarial assistance from Augustin Thierry, a brilliant young historian (born in 1795) who was greatly impressed by Saint-Simon's philosophy. Under the first Bourbon Restoration, which followed the abdication of Napoleon in April 1814, Thierry was relieved of his professional post at Compiègne, and in his search for work he asked Saint-Simon if he could assist him in his scientific investigations. The offer was immediately accepted. In October 1814 the first fruits of the new collaboration appeared: a booklet entitled *De la réorganisation de la société européenne,* which outlined a plan for gradually uniting the nations of Europe through parliamentary institutions, commencing with an Anglo-French union.[26] This work, which was intended for the guidance of the delegates at the Congress of Vienna, was hastily written, incomplete, and censored by the Government; but it aroused considerable interest and admiration in liberal circles. Its success encouraged Saint-Simon to concentrate his attention on political affairs, and with the help of Thierry — whom he now regarded as his 'adopted son' — he assumed the role of publicist for the liberal cause. In the journal *Le Censeur* he advocated the formation of a new opposition party of owners of national property.[27] He planned a full-length work on the subject, but his attention was soon diverted to other matters when Napoleon regained power in March 1815.

For a short while during the Hundred Days of Napoleonic rule, Saint-Simon worked as a librarian at the Bibliothèque de l'Arsenal. He was given the post by the Minister of the Interior, Lazare Carnot, who had known him for some years and thought he deserved help.[28] Following the defeat of Napoleon at Waterloo in June, however, Carnot was dismissed from office, and in the ensuing Government reorganisation Saint-Simon lost his job.

Louis XVIII was now given a second opportunity to establish order and stability in France. It was a formidable task, since the nation was fundamentally divided on every major political issue, not least the question of whether the Bourbon monarchy ought to have been restored. In Saint-Simon's view this underlying instability could not be ended until a truly 'positive' political philosophy was formulated. The foundations of such a philosophy, he believed, were to be found in the liberal doctrines of such thinkers as Jean-Baptiste Say, Benjamin Constant, Charles Comte, and Charles Dunoyer. He was particularly impressed by their utilitarian economic theories and their advocacy of a more representative system of government favourable to the needs of industry — an advocacy which he supported wholeheartedly.[29] For their part, liberal writers in Paris respected Saint-Simon's own perceptiveness as a philosopher, and welcomed him into their circles, offering him encouragement and advice, and occasional financial support. Many of them became close friends of Saint-Simon, and these included Say, to whom he submitted manuscripts for appraisal. Say's criticisms were always taken seriously. Thus, one of Saint-Simon's most interesting writings, a project for Anglo-French union entitled *Aux Anglais et aux Français qui sont zélés pour le bien public*,[30] written during the first few weeks of the Second Restoration, was not published because Say considered its underlying philosophy, although admirable, to be beyond the comprehension of the general public.

In 1816 Saint-Simon's support for liberalism found expression in a scheme for a new journal, devoted exclusively to the propagation of what he called 'industrial opinion'. An impressive list of subscribers was drawn up,[31] and the first issue of the journal, entitled *L'Industrie*, appeared in December 1816, devoted exclusively to a long essay *Sur les finances* by Camille Saint-Aubin. No writings by Saint-Simon appeared in the journal until May 1817, when he contributed a number of items to the second volume. These included an introduction, in which he outlined a theory of 'industrial liberty'[32]; and seven letters to an imaginary correspondent in the United States, in which he contrasted the liberalism of American society with the oppressive social systems of Europe, and gave an interesting account of the relationship between economics and politics in the context of an analysis of Say's teachings.[33]

During the first half of 1817, probably before the publication of volume II of *L'Industrie,* Saint-Simon suffered a setback when Augustin Thierry decided to give us his post as secretarial assistant. The 'adopted son' apparently found Saint-Simon's ideas too obscure, and was anxious to concentrate on his own historical studies. The loss of Thierry was a severe blow for Saint-Simon, but within a short while he was able to enlist the services of another brilliant young assistant, Auguste Comte, who was looking for work after his expulsion from the École Polytechnique for insubordination. Comte's first major task was to help prepare volume III of *L'Industrie,* which was published in four parts during September and October 1817. The ideas presented in this volume shocked many readers, for they concerned questions of science, religion, and ethics, with which orthodox liberal philosophy was not directly concerned. A new 'terrestrial morality' was advocated in harmony with positive science and conductive to industrialism, which would replace the outworn theology of Catholicism. The actual writing of this volume was done by Comte,[34] and therefore, strictly speaking, the contents cannot be regarded as the work of Saint-Simon; but it was undoubtedly Saint-Simon who formulated the basic theory of 'terrestrial morality'. In fact, as early as June 1817 he had provided an outline of this theory in a *Lettre à MM. les publicistes,* written as a prospectus for the third volume of *L'Industrie.*[35]

Saint-Simon's anti-Catholic moral theories met with a hostile reception in liberal circles. Some subscribers to *L'Industrie* were so angry that they decided to withdraw their financial support from the enterprise. Saint-Simon subsequently attempted to restore their confidence by devoting the fourth volume to a more orthodox discussion of economic and political issues.[36] But the damage had been done; *L'Industrie* could not continue, and it ceased publication in the summer of 1818.

Not in the least disheartened by this failure, Saint-Simon quickly went ahead with plans for a new periodical publication: *Le Politique,* the first issue of which appeared in January 1819. The main purpose of the new journal was to formulate a political strategy for the 'industrial class'. The contributors, chief among whom were Saint-Simon, Comte, and Alexandre-Louis La Chevardière, undertook a scathing attack on the unproductive class of nobles, idle property owners, clergy, magistrates, and military chiefs. They urged the producers to overcome their apathy and form an active 'industrial party'. In their struggle for political rights they were assured of eventual victory, since they outnumbered their opponents by at least fifty to one.[37]

Le Politique failed to create any impression in industrial circles, and it survived only until May 1819. Saint-Simon was determined, however, not to give up his propaganda campaign, and during the summer months he drew up a prospectus for yet another 'industrial' publication: *L'Organisateur*. The prospectus was issued in August,[38] and the work itself was inaugurated in November with a thirty-two page booklet, *Extraits de l'Organisateur*.[39] The *Extraits* brought Saint-Simon his first major success as a publicist. At first this was no more than a *succès de scandale,* caused by the fact that in a bold attack on the French State Saint-Simon actually named members of the royal family who, he felt, performed no useful service for the nation, and whose loss would therefore do no great harm. The text aroused the suspicions of the police, who duly arrested Saint-Simon in January 1820. While he was in custody, on 13 February 1820, the duc de Berry, one of the members of the royal family included in Saint-Simon's list of useless 'idlers', was stabbed to death by the fanatic Louvel as the first step in his attempt to annihilate the Bourbons. This development made Saint-Simon's predicament extremely serious. Charged with subversion, he issued a series of public letters to the members of the jury in his defence. He denied being at all hostile to the Bourbons, explaining that the purpose of the *Extraits* was merely to draw attention to the fact that the nation's producers could not be expected to remain satisfied for much longer with the inferior political status in which they found themselves. The members of the jury were not impressed, and Saint-Simon was found guilty. However, that was not the end of the matter, for the case subsequently went to the Court of Appeal, and this time Saint-Simon was acquitted.

After regaining his freedom, he immediately resumed his work on *L'Organisateur*. He knew there was no time to be lost, for since the assassination of the duc de Berry a royalist reaction had been gaining strength, making the future of the liberal movement extremely uncertain.[40] *L'Organisateur* proved in fact to be a very successful publication. It even became known outside France, causing a major sensation in Berlin.[41] The key to its success was its startling originality, which is difficult to appreciate today but which was widely recognised at the time. It is undoubtedly one of Saint-Simon's most important works, and includes the first detailed blueprint of the 'industrial society' he wished to see inaugurated, as well as a discussion of the means whereby that society should be established.[42] It also contains an interesting historical analysis of the rise of industry, almost certainly written by Comte.[43]

As one reads through the pages of *L'Organisateur*, Saint-Simon's dissatisfaction with orthodox liberalism becomes increasingly apparent. He was now convinced that the liberals would never achieve success as a political party. They had failed completely to see the inadequacies of the existing parliamentary system, and were totally apathetic when it came to political action. Furthermore, the party contained an aristocratic element whose conservatism severely hindered the progress of industrialism. In his view, the industrials must dissociate themselves thoroughly from this alien element as soon as possible, and form themselves into a new industrial party.

In another set of brochures, published at the end of 1820 and brought together in the first part of *Du système industriel* in February 1821, Saint-Simon made the strategy quite clear. The success of these brochures led to the publication of two more sets at irregular intervals between April 1821 and July 1822 (*Du système industriel*, parts II and III). All these brochures were presented in the form of letters and addresses to various individuals and groups – the King, the industrials, the electorate, the scientists and artists, the philanthropists, the workers, etc. – in an attempt to convince them of the desirability of instituting the new industrial order.[44] His addresses to the King are especially interesting, since they make it quite clear that the new society should preferably be instituted by the monarch, acting as the nation's 'first industrial'.[45] Also noteworthy is Saint-Simon's conception of his doctrine as a new, definitive Christianity,[46] a conception clearly anticipating the *Noveau christianisme* of 1825. Henceforth Saint-Simon was to place considerable emphasis on the *moral* virtues of industrialism, seem primarily in terms of its capacity to improve the standard of living of the poor. These virtues, he argued, corresponded to the ethics of true Christianity, and thus no genuine Christian could deny the validity of his doctrine.

Inasmuch as it aroused widespread interest in liberal circles, *Du système industriel* could be counted a fairly successful publication. But in more practical terms it failed to achieve the results for which Saint-Simon was hoping, and this was for him a severe disappointment. The problem was that his views were simply not being taken seriously enough. He was 'considered only as a clever *original*', as John Stuart Mill, who met Saint-Simon in 1821, put it in his autobiography.[47] For the founder of the industrial doctrine this was not enough; he sought public recognition. Now an old man of over sixty, he began to despair of ever achieving it. Despair gradually turned into severe depression, culminating in attempted suicide on 9 March 1823. Having decided to shoot himself he prepared a final message for his close friend and supporter, Ternaux:

> 'Sir, after a great deal of reflection I have remained convinced that you were right in telling me that it will take longer than I thought for public interest to be disposed towards the work which for so long has been my sole concern. Consequently, I have chosen to bid you farewell. My final sentiments are those of profound esteem for you and exalted affection for your noble and philanthropic character. Allow me to offer my heart to you for the last time . . .'[48]

After finishing the letter Saint-Simon loaded a pistol with seven bullets and fired them at his head in quick succession. Miraculously, the result was not death, but merely a deep wound and the loss of his right eye.

Saint-Simon's recovery, both physical and mental, from this terrible ordeal was remarkably swift. Within a few months he was at work again, launching another periodical, *Catéchisme des industriels*. He was assisted by a group of new supporters, chief among whom was Olinde Rodrigues, a young Jewish intellectual who first met Saint-Simon in May 1823 and was immediately impressed by his doctrine, in particular his conception of 'the true Christianity'. In the *Catéchisme*, which was published in four parts between December 1823 and June 1824, Saint-Simon made complete his break with liberalism, making it absolutely clear that the doctrine of industrialism was quite distinctive.[49] Auguste Comte also made an important contribution to the *Catéchisme*, in book three, which was devoted to his *Système de politique positive*. In a preface Saint-Simon praised this as 'the best work on general politics ever published'.[50] At the same time he made some fundamental criticisms of the *Système* which angered Comte and brought to a head a dispute between the two men which had been developing for some time. During the course of 1824 disagreement between the two men became so intense that Comte finally decided to withdraw his support, and to pursue his own positivist studies.[51]

Following Comte's departure, Rodrigues assumed the role of chief assistant to Saint-Simon. It was largely due to his devoted work that by the end of 1824 the nucleus of a more formal Saint-Simonian organisation was established. Besides Rodrigues the most active supporters were Léon Halévy, Jean-Baptiste Duvergier, and Dr. E.-M. Bailly. The efforts of Saint-Simon and these four disciples were properly united for the first time at the beginning of 1825, when the first volume of a new review, *Opinions littéraires, philosophiques et industrielles*, appeared. This contained articles on various aspects of social organisation, each writer concentrating on subjects of particular personal interest.[52] Preparations for a second volume were in hand when, in April 1825, it was decided to publish separately, because of its importance, a work on the religious question by Saint-Simon: *Nouveau christianisme*.[53] This short book was offered as a contribution to the fierce debate on the relationship between Church and State which had been developing since the accession of Charles X to the throne in September 1824. From a doctrinal point of view, it is notable primarily because of its emphasis on religious sentiment as the most important instrument of social change. A united Christian church, founded not on the principles of Catholicism or Protestantism but on the original teachings of Christ, is now seen by Saint-Simon as the necessary means of promoting a just society. Such a view was not entirely new; it had been presented in its bare essentials four years previously in the *Adresse aux philanthropes*. But on that occasion religious sentiment was still not regarded as the *chief* instrument of change; it was intended to reinforce political reform. Now, in the *Nouveau christianisme*, the whole of Saint-Simon's doctrine is presented in the guise of a social religion. 'New Christianity' becomes the watchword, in place of 'industrialism'.

Nouveau christianisme was intended to be the first of three texts dealing with the reform of religious institutions. However, Saint-Simon's work was suddenly cut short when, soon after the book's publication, he fell seriously ill with gastro-enteritis. For six weeks he was confined to bed in considerable pain. He died on 19 May 1825, at ten o'clock in the evening.

He was buried three days later in the Père-Lachaise cemetery in Paris. The funeral was a purely civil occasion with no elaborate ceremony. In graveside orations Léon Halévy and Dr. Bailly talked at length of Saint-Simon's considerable achievements. But the orientation of their words was to the future, not to the past; for the moment of Saint-Simon's death was recognised by them as the moment of birth of the Saint-Simonian movement. Although no clear strategy had been determined, Saint-Simon's young disciples were resolved to fulfil the mission on which their master had embarked. The first positive steps were taken a few days later, on 1 June, when the journal *Le Producteur* was officially founded in the office of Olinde Rodrigues.

2. THE DOCTRINE OF SAINT-SIMON

This section is devoted to an analytical examination of the doctrine expounded by Saint-Simon in his writings between 1802 and 1825. Consideration will first of all be given to the methodological foundations of that doctrine, that is, the precise nature of Saint-Simon's approach to the study of man and society.

(i) Towards a Science of Social Organisation

Saint-Simon always considered his primary aim as a social theorist to be the promotion of the study of man and society to the level of a truly *positive* science, that is, a science based entirely on empirical observation. He was convinced that the degree of certainty achieved in the natural sciences could also be attained in social science, if the same methodology were adopted; and he founded his entire philosophy on this conviction. Regarding himself as the heir of Bacon and Descartes, he attempted from the start to pursue his investigations according to the 'golden rule' of science: that 'man should believe only those things avowed by reason and confirmed by experience'.[54]

In accordance with contemporary scientific opinion, Saint-Simon considered the science of man to be a branch of physiology, the science of organic phenomena. According to this view human society was seen as an organic entity whose development, like that of any other organic body, was governed by certain natural laws which it was the purpose of scientific inquiry to reveal. From the notion of *organism* it was a short step to that of *organisation*.[55] A healthy society was seen in terms of a well-organised society, a society whose fundamental characteristics were order and stability.

The concept of social organisation came to occupy a central position in French social theory in the years immediately following the Revolution. Because the Revolution offered a clear demonstration of what social *dis*organisation involved, it inevitably encouraged social theorists to turn to the problem of how social reconstruction could be promoted, and how further revolutions and outbreaks of anarchy could be avoided. Saint-Simon was convinced that a positive science of man would reveal the laws of social organisation, that is, a body of rules explaining, on the one hand, the causes of social order, stability, and progress; and, on the other, the causes of revolution and social disintegration. He believed that once these causes had been ascertained with scientific precision, man would be able to promote the construction of the very best form of social organisation. The realisation of utopia thus became a practical possibility.

'A series of observations on the course of civilisation'[56] was regarded by Saint-Simon as the necessary starting-point for the development of the new science. These observations must then be brought together in a general theory of history capable of explaining the fundamental causes of historical change, not only in the past and at the present time, but also in the future; for the causes of future events must already be in existence, and there was no reason why these should not be observed and analysed scientifically.

In stating that it should be possible to forecast the future course of history, Saint-Simon was clearly implying some sort of historical determinism. However, he was not a complete fatalist, for although he was convinced that general historical trends were inevitable, he believed that man could exert some influence over them. Most importantly, man could determine the pace of social change. Thus, if a particular result was shown by scientific investigation to be inevitable, and could also be considered a desirable result, then man could devote his energies to achieving it as quickly and as painlessly as possible.

This belief that a scientific theory could be formulated which would permit man to predict the shape of his historical future was one of Saint-Simon's most important contributions to social thought. It is certainly sufficiently original to justify the view of Saint-Simon as one of the founders of modern historicism.[57] In this respect his importance is matched only by that of his great contemporary, the German idealist philosopher Hegel, with whose works he does not appear to have been familiar. There were thinkers before Saint-Simon who had attempted to develop a scientific analysis of history, notably Montesquieu, Turgot, and Condorcet. But of these only Condorcet, whose influence Saint-Simon readily acknowledged, had suggested that the analysis could be extended to embrace the future.

Saint-Simon's first firm conclusions about what was needed to promote the development of a positive science of man were the result of his studies at the École Polytechnique and the École de Médecine (1798–1802). These studies left him with the conviction that the new science could in fact be developed fairly quickly and without too much difficulty. Such a view was perfectly in keeping with the unbounded confidence in the capacity of science characteristic of the age in which he lived. The natural sciences in general and the life sciences in particular were making rapid, impressive progress in France by the beginning of the nineteenth century, and Saint-Simon was confident that this progress would soon extend to physiology. Indeed, he believed that the most basic physiological principles had already been furnished by French scientists. In order to organise the general theory of physiology, it was asserted in the *Mémoire sur la science de l'homme,* little more was needed than to bring together the works of Vicq-d'Azyr, Cabanis, Bichat, and Condorcet, for these four authors had dealt with nearly all the important physiological questions.[58] The contributions of Vicq-d'Azyr and Condorcet he regarded as the most important; the ideas of Bichat and Cabanis were basically 'appendices' to those of Vicq-d'Azyr.[59] If only the necessary reorganisation of scientific research could be brought about, he felt sure that this synthesis of physiological knowledge could be achieved relatively quickly. As his two major texts on the science of man, the *Mémoire* and the *Travail sur la gravitation universelle,* make clear, he recognised that he could not possibly fulfil the task alone. But he did consider himself capable of contributing something on the subject of 'the progress of the human mind', and he was willing to offer his services to any physiologist who might wish to employ them.

(ii) The Laws of History

Saint-Simon's conviction that a theory of social organisation must take as its basis ' a series of observations on the course of civilisation' has already been mentioned. In accordance with this principle he became an enthusiastic student of history, and devoted much of his written work to historical analysis. His attempt to study history scientifically has often been dismissed as crude,[60] and there can be little doubt that much of the criticism levelled against him is justified. Nevertheless, the quality of his work does at least represent a definite improvement on that of most earlier thinkers. It must be remembered that before Saint-Simon few serious attempts had been made to apply any kind of scientific method to the study of history. His own efforts do therefore deserve some credit. Moreover, his analysis does in fact contain a body of essential argument which is perfectly valid, and which merits serious attention.

As a student of history his chief purpose was to trace the general course of development of human society since ancient times. His perspective was not that of the specialist concerned with every minor detail, but of the philosopher interested in broad historical trends. Directly inspired by Condorcet's *Esquisse d'un tableau historique des progrès de l'esprit humain,* he too aimed to produce *une esquisse historique,* an outline history of social evolution which would serve as a point of departure for an analysis of man's present historical situation.

The results of Saint-Simon's investigations are to be found scattered throughout his writings, but principally in his *Introduction aux travaux scientifiques du XIXe siècle,* the *Mémoire sur la science de l'homme, L'Industrie,* and the *Catéchisme des industriels.* The eighth and ninth letters of *L'Organisateur* also deserve attention in this context, but it must be remembered that they were in fact written by Comte, not Saint-Simon. From these texts a clearly-defined philosophy of history emerges, the validity of which Saint-Simon believed to be a matter of scientific fact. Its starting-point is the observation that changes in social organisation occur, indeed become necessary, because of the development of human intelligence, of knowledge and beliefs. The failure of historians to examine the relationship between ideas and social organisation was, in Saint-Simon's opinion, a serious mistake. He urged them to look beyond 'secondary or local events', that is, 'political, religious, or military facts', and attempt to discover the ideological and doctrinal forces behind them.[61] The development of *moral* ideas deserved particular attention, he argued, since at any particular time in history the form of organisation of a society was a direct reflection of the prevailing moral code. The social order of ancient Greece and Rome was based on one system of moral ideas; that of medieval Europe on another; and the new order which Saint-Simon saw emerging at the beginning of the nineteenth century was being shaped by yet another moral system. Three quite distinctive eras of western civilisation, each based on its own clearly-defined system of morals, were thus identified. They were separated from each other, it was argued, by transitional periods during which one moral system was gradually replaced by another. This process of replacement was made necessary by the advancement of scientific knowledge and the accompanying changes in man's philosophical outlook — changes which eventually became so fundamental that they resulted in the adoption of new moral values.

The values which underpinned the social organisation of ancient Greece and Rome were seen by Saint-Simon to be in harmony with the supernatural, polytheistic beliefs of that age. But with the transition from polytheism to Christian theism, a transition set in motion by Socratic science, a new moral code and with it a new social order were necessitated. This was the major cause of the rise of the theological-feudal system, which reached its zenith under Charlemagne's rule in Europe. In its turn Christian theism was now in decline, being replaced by positivism, which rejected all forms of supernatural belief. This explained the gradual collapse of feudalism since the Middle Ages, culminating in the chaos of the French Revolution.

(iii) The Crisis of European Society

According to Saint-Simon's theory of history, because the social order of feudalism was founded on a theological system of ideas it could survive only as long as theology remained scientifically valid. In actual fact theology gradually lost its validity as a result of the rise of positive sciences of observation, first of all astronomy, then physics and chemistry, and finally physiology. The inevitable consequence of this was first of all that the Catholic Church, which exercised spiritual power under feudalism, began to lose its authority; and then that the military lords, the holders of temporal power, found their superiority challenged more and more by their subjects. This process of disintegration proceeded most rapidly in France, where it reached its climax in the eighteenth century with the collapse of the *ancien régime,* precipitated by the social criticism of Enlightenment philosophy, in particular by the *'antithéologie'* of the Encyclopaedists.[62] The French Revolution represented the final act of this drama. It brought to an end the theological-feudal era, and paved the way for the construction of a new social order appropriate to the level of enlightment attained by man. However, the task of social reorganisation was not at all easy, and could not possibly be accomplished without careful preparation. Before a new system could be inaugurated, it must first of all be conceived, and conceived clearly in all its aspects. The attempts of the revolutionaries in France to establish a new system were totally inadequate, because they were based on vague 'legal-metaphysical' ideas, such as the belief in certain fundamental rights of man, which may have been good enough to destroy the *ancien régime* but which could not possibly serve as the basis of a new form of social organisation because they were too negative.

In Saint-Simon's view, therefore, a major crisis threatened France and its European neighbours. It was a crisis which could be overcome, he believed, only through the concerted efforts of scientists and philosophers, with whom the prime responsibility rested for formulating a positive social theory capable of providing man with a new sense of purpose and direction. By 1814 he had resolved to do everything in his power to promote the necessary work, and he made a start in the same year with his booklet *De la réorganisation de la société européenne,* written with Augustin Thierry. The message of this work was clear and concise: 'The philosophy of the last century was revolutionary; that of the nineteenth century must be organisational.'[63]

(iv) Foundations of Terrestrial Morality

The theological-feudal system had collapsed, Saint-Simon argued, because in the light of advanced scientific reasoning the moral code of which that system was a direct expression had become unacceptable to man. The basis of the old moral code was a conception of man's earthly life as nothing more than 'a passage to a future life in which we shall be rewarded or punished by an all-powerful Being, according to whether we have or have not followed the wishes of this Being as taught to us through the medium of the priests, his direct interpreters.'[64] In accordance with this conception, the teachings of the Catholic Church were acknowledged to be the source of all rights and duties, including political rights and duties. Men were in fact taught to accept a generally authoritarian system of temporal power, to 'render unto Caesar the things that are Caesar's', and to submit to the law of the strongest. They were also instructed to remain content with their situation on earth, spiritual values being regarded as much more important than material living conditions.

As long as the spiritual authority of the Catholic clergy was generally recognised, the theological moral code retained its influence over the minds of men. But this authority did in fact begin to collapse in the fifteenth century, with the beginnings of the modern scientific revolution — a revolution which persuaded man to reject revelation as a source of knowledge, and to rely instead on reasoning based on observation. On the basis of such reasoning the conviction gradually grew among the laity that neither the spiritual power of the clergy nor the temporal power of the feudal lords could be tolerated. Consequently, a process of social upheaval was inaugurated, culminating in the violent revolution of 1789.

The task facing nineteenth-century Europe, Saint-Simon asserted, was one of social reconstruction. And social reconstruction could not possibly be achieved until a new moral code based on scientific reasoning was formulated and accepted as valid by the majority of the people. The 'celestial' morality of theology had been rejected; a new 'terrestrial' morality must be founded — 'terrestrial' because the achievement of happiness on earth must now be man's first priority.

Happiness was defined by Saint-Simon in terms of material and moral well-being. Hence, for him the fundamental purpose of social organisation was the maximisation of that well-being. 'The greatest happiness of the greatest number' was one way of putting this;[65] and since the greatest number in society were the ignorant and impoverished masses, the improvement of their condition became the essential social aim. In moral terms, the validity of this principle was undeniable. It was also defensible in terms of Christian doctrine, since Christ had taught men to treat one another as brothers and devote special attention to the plight of the poor. Catholic theologians may have paid lip-service to this principle, but they had failed completely to give it any meaningful application.

Having arrived at this conclusion, Saint-Simon then considered the question of what social arrangements were necessary to establish a system of social organisation in accordance with 'terrestrial' morality. He was concerned to answer the question: in whose hand should spiritual and temporal power reside? His solution was perfectly straightforward: First, spiritual power must pass into the hands of the most enlightened men, the *savants,* both scientists and artists, since only they could command sufficient respect. Having surpassed theologians, both Catholic and Protestant, in terms of knowledge and understanding, they were the natural intellectual elite of the future. Secondly, temporal power belonged legitimately to the most capable economic administrators, society's most eminent 'industrials',[66] since they alone were qualified to organise the various branches of material production — agriculture, manufacturing, commerce, and banking — so as to fulfil man's material needs. This was what *ought* to happen, Saint-Simon believed. It was also what he believed *would* happen one day, not only in France but throughout Europe, as a consequence of the inevitable progress of the human mind.

(v) Temporal Power Under Industrialism

The scientific-industrial age of the future, Saint-Simon believed, would witness a major transformation in the nature of social power, in both its temporal and spiritual aspects. As far as the temporal power was concerned, Saint-Simon anticipated that with the rise to leadership of the captains of industry, government in the traditional sense of an authoritarian, coercive force, as embodied in the militaristic feudal State, would disappear, to be replaced by a system of administration whose main function would be to supervise productive operations in the national workshop. In the future 'governments will no longer command men; their functions will be limited to ensuring that useful work is not hindered'.[67] Decision-making will be entrusted not to arbitrary rulers, chosen by patronage, but to 'general directors',[68] selected on the basis of their professional ability, for whom politics will be nothing more than 'the science of production'.[69] This conception of a totally new kind of political system was undoubtedly Saint-Simon's most important and most influential contribution to social theory. He himself regarded it as the focal point of his doctrine.[70] Its originality must not be exaggerated, however. The idea of a transition from arbitrary government to scientific administration was almost certainly derived, at least in part, by Saint-Simon from Bacon's argument that a truly scientific society can dispense with power politics.[71] This belief was transmitted to Saint-Simon both through his own reading of Bacon's works and also through the influence of the Encyclopaedists, who were great admirers of Bacon and were largely responsible for introducing his ideas into eighteenth-century France. It also seems likely that Saint-Simon's advocacy of a new system of expert administration owed something to the influence of the classical political economists (both English and French) and Jeremy Bentham, whose faith in 'the professional ideal of a functional society based on expertise and selection by merit'[72] is strikingly similar to Saint-Simon's doctrine.

Saint-Simon did not anticipate that the transition from a governmental to an administrative regime would involve a major upheaval. The Restoration political system of France (a limited parliamentary system, regarded by Saint-Simon as an intermediate, transitional stage between feudalism and industrialism) could, he believed, be transformed quite smoothly, once the industrials overcame their political apathy and mounted an alliance with the Bourbon monarchy against the aristocracy. Their immediate aim, he asserted, should be to secure financial reform: 'The whole of positive politics is incorporated in the financial law'.[73] Public revenue, instead of being squandered on the army, police, courts, and aristocracy, should be invested in science and industry so as to promote social welfare, develop transport and communications, and provide useful employment for all men. Writing in 1821 Saint-Simon pointed out that the potential of France in this respect was enormous. He estimated that of 900 million francs collected in taxes only about 50 millions were spent on socially useful projects.[74] The country's rulers, instead of looking after the welfare of all citizens, were concerned only with their own self-interest: 'Those who are in charge of administering public affairs,' he wrote in *L'Organisateur,* 'share between them every year half the taxes.'[75]

Saint-Simon believed that the process by which public expenditure was allocated stood in urgent need of reform, and he proposed, as his own solution, that control of the national budget should be handed over to those men who knew most about economic affairs, that is, the country's leading producers:

'It is evident that the most certain way to promote the prosperity of agriculture, commerce, and manufacturing is to give to the farmers, merchants, and manufacturers the task of directing the administration of public affairs, that is, of framing the budget . . .'[76]

It is most important to point out that this was just about the only major power Saint-Simon thought necessary to place in the hands of the industrials. He was convinced it would be sufficient to produce the sort of political authority be deemed necessary. He certainly did *not* advocate the establishment of a new all-purpose State structure, as some commentators have suggested, thus giving the impression that he was a nineteenth-century 'totalitarian'. While it is undoubtedly true that Saint-Simon's social theory does have some *authoritarian* implications (which are discussed in this Introduction), the view that he advocated a form of social organisation involving the exercise of a

37

limitless, i.e. *totalitarian,* power over the individual by a repressive elite goes too far. Exponents of this view include F.A. Hayek, who states that Saint-Simon considered freedom of thought to be 'the root-evil of nineteenth-century society', and wanted to establish strong dictatorial government;[77] Peyton V. Lyon, who sees him as an advocate of an organic social system similar to modern communist China and Russia;[78] F.M.H. Markham, who asserts that 'Saint-Simon did not think freedom worth preserving';[79] Giovanni Sartori, who criticises Saint-Simon's belief in the virtues of 'total planning' and the 'abolition of the free market;'[80] Leonard Schapiro, who asserts that Saint-Simon 'despised parliamentary democracy and had little use for freedom of speech or thought', and was preoccupied with ends and indifferent to means;[81] H.G. Schenk, who writes that Saint-Simon 'was fully prepared to jettison the ideal of individual liberty';[82] Walter M. Simon, who states that Saint-Simon was a totalitarian 'philosopher-king, extinguishing any right to dissent on the part of the people', who would be 'forced to be free';[83] and J.L. Talmon, for whom Saint-Simon is a 'totalitarian technocrat', intent to achieve 'total integration' in society.[84] Such views are the result, I would suggest, of a combination of factors: a tendency to confuse the terms 'authoritarian' and 'totalitarian'; a fundamental misinterpretation of Saint-Simon's thought; and also a failure to distinguish carefully enough between his own ideas and those of his disciples, the Saint-Simonians, many of whom were much more authoritarian in outlook than their master. Even for these disciples, however, the designation 'totalitarian' is somewhat inappropriate, since it has obvious connotations of violent repression which cannot be read into the Saint-Simonian literature.[85]

Saint-Simon did in fact believe that the new temporal power should interfere as little as possible in society's affairs, and he constantly reiterated his belief that industrialism would secure the highest degree of liberty for all members of society.[86] He placed particular emphasis on the fact that the economy should be left as free as possible, once the necessary industrial investment had been secured: workers must be allowed to 'exchange with each other directly and with complete freedom the products of their various labours'.[87]

Another essential aspect of Saint-Simon's view of temporal power under industrialism is that he believed public expenditure could actually be *cut* and taxation thereby *reduced* as a consequence of efficient administration. The industrials, he argued, would not need anything like as much money as was then being squandered, as long as they put what they did have to proper use. Thus Saint-Simon could look forward to a day when the functions and expenses of governments were reduced to an absolute minimum, when they would 'no longer have at their disposal more than a small amount of power or money'.[88]

Private enterprise, he believed, could be relied upon to foster economic development, as long as the right incentives were offered:

'The funds required by useful undertakings, whatever their scale, will be provided by voluntary subscriptions, and the subscribers themselves will supervise the use and administration of their money.'[89]

All these conclusions make it perfectly clear that Saint-Simon considered a large degree of economic liberty to be essential under industrialism. He was never an advocate of absolute *laissez-faire*, but he did maintain that as long as the social framework in which they lived and worked was a just one, all men would be capable of achieving self-development through their own efforts. Even the mass of labourers, he confidently asserted in 1822, 'had acquired the necessary capacity to conduct their own affairs'.[90] Only in ensuring that all men were well educated and provided with useful employment did the government have an overriding responsibility:

'The most direct way to bring about an improvement in the moral and physical well-being of the majority of the population is to give priority in State expenditure to the provision of work for all fit men, so as to assure their physical existence; to disseminate as quickly as possible among the proletarian class the positive knowledge which has been acquired; and finally to ensure that the individuals composing this class have forms of leisure and interests which will develop their intelligence.'[91]

Such an outlook may justifiably be regarded as essentially socialist in character, however 'lukewarm' it may appear today. It certainly represents something quite different from orthodox liberalism, a doctrine of which Saint-Simon became increasingly critical during the last few years of his life, primarily because of its totally negative attitude towards social welfare, and its consequent inability to promote a radical improvement in the condition of the working class.

As far as specific proposals for the reorganisation of political institutions were concerned, Saint-Simon was never entirely consistent. Furthermore, he was always concerned primarily with the situation in France, and so it is not always clear whether he considered his proposals to be of universal application. In his first major set of proposals, included in *L'Organisateur*,[92] he emphasised the need to transform the French House of Commons (i.e. the Chamber of Deputies) into a new industrial chamber — composed of industrials and elected by industrials. (This implied an extension of the suffrage, perhaps, but certainly not universal suffrage.) This new chamber was given the name 'Chamber of Execution', and was placed side by side with a 'Chamber of Invention' and a 'Chamber of Examination', composed respectively of 'inventors' (artists and engineers) and 'examiners' (scientists) who would help the industrials to plan a comprehensive programme of economic and social development. This was an impressive, but thoroughly utopian scheme, at least a century ahead of its time, and was never repeated by Saint-Simon. In subsequent years his proposals were much more sober. The emphasis on reforming the House of Commons remained, but recognising the obstacles to reform, Saint-Simon suggested an alternative strategy: the King should appoint councils of industrials, outside the Parliament, to prepare the nation's budget.[93]

Saint-Simon was always anxious to emphasise that the inauguration of this new industrial structure in France would not affect the position of the monarchy as long as the King supported the principles of industrialism. If he failed to do so, however, there was a real danger that the monarchy would eventually be swept away by the mighty and inexorable tide of progress. Thus, while Saint-Simon was convinced that the establishment of new temporal institutions appropriate to a scientific-industrial society could be accomplished smoothly, without violent upheaval, he always admitted that revolution was a possibility. The events in France during 1830 and 1848, while certainly not amounting to the political transformation envisaged by Saint-Simon, were at least to prove how well founded were his fears for the monarchy's future.[94]

(vi) Spiritual Power Under Industrialism

The reorganisation of temporal institutions in the scientific-industrial era would be accompanied, according to Saint-Simon's conception of social change, by a fundamental restructuring of spiritual power. This would involve the elevation of positive scientists and artists to the positions of moral and educational leadership formerly occupied by the Catholic clergy.

Saint-Simon always believed that the passing of spiritual authority from the clergy to the scientists and artists was inevitable. However, he remained uncertain as to whether the latter ought to organise themselves as leaders of a new religion — an alternative to Catholicism — or whether they should leave religion alone and concentrate on achieving influence in secular institutions. In his *Lettres d'un habitant de Genève* and other early works he advocated the first alternative: the Religion of Newton was presented as a new scientific religion to replace Catholicism. This outlook was very much in the tradition of the revolutionary programmes of de-Christianisation. However, once it became clear, under Napoleon, that de-Christianisation was no longer official policy, he suggested that scientists and artists would have to leave the religious question alone and concentrate on increasing their influence in the Academies, Parliament, and other secular institutions.

This outlook was maintained by Saint-Simon throughout the Empire and for the first few years of the Restoration. Thus, in his first major sketch of the new industrial political system, in *L'Organisateur*,[95] the scientists and artists were allotted places in new parliamentary chambers — Chambers of Invention and Examination — and were instructed to leave religious questions alone when preparing their plans for a system of public education. However, from about 1820 onwards Saint-Simon gradually reverted to the idea that the new spiritual heads of society should present themselves as religious leaders, but not as *anti*-Christians (as he had previously suggested), rather as *true* Christians whose morality was in perfect accord with the original teachings of Christ.

Precisely how the New Christian spiritual power would function under industrialism is not perfectly clear from Saint-Simon's writings. However, some basic principles are evident, and these are presented in a convenient summary form in the following paragraph taken from the *Adresse aux philanthropes:*

'I believe that the new spiritual power will be composed at first of all the existing Academies of Science in Europe, and of all persons who deserve to be admitted to these scientific corporations. I believe that once this nucleus is formed, its members will organise themselves. I believe that the direction of education, as well as of public teaching, will be entrusted to this new spiritual power. I believe that the pure morality of the Gospel will serve as the basis of the new public education, and that, for the rest, it will be pushed as far as possible in conformity with positive knowledge, in proportion to the time which children of different levels of wealth will be able to spend at school. Finally, I believe that the new spiritual power will settle a fairly large number of its members throughout all the communes, and that the principal mission of these detached scholars will be to inspire their spiritual charges with a passion for the public good.'[96]

Elsewhere Saint-Simon considered in more detail the question of how the French Academics should be reorganised. In the fourth book of the *Catéchisme des industriels,* for example, he proposed the creation of three new institutions. First, an Academy of Sentiments, consisting of the most distinguished moralists, theologians, lawyers, poets, painters, sculptors, and musicians, who would work together to formulate a code of industrial morality. Secondly, an Academy of Reason, similar in structure to the Academy of Sciences founded by Louis XIV, the main difference being the inclusion of a number of political economists.

The task of this body would be to construct 'the best code of interests' for industrial society, to be embodied in the nation's civil laws. Finally, there would be a third institution, a Royal Scientific College, consisting of the most eminent general scientists, to coordinate the work of the two Academies and synthesise their findings into a national programme of education. So crucial was this educational role in Saint-Simon's view that he actually described the Royal Scientific College as 'the most important of all social institutions'.[97]

The new spiritual power thus conceived was intended by Saint-Simon to be first and foremost a source of moral guidance capable of providing the members of industrial society with a clear sense of direction and common purpose, a new *religious* sense, in other words. (There are clear authoritarian implications here, but the authority in question is based on respect and confidence, not force.) Eventually, towards the end of his life, Saint-Simon came to realise that if it was to be effective this moral guidance must be channelled through the medium of an organised Church, with an appropriate ritual and dogma; and it was for this reason that in 1825 he produced a work dealing specifically with the *Nouveau christianisme*. Unfortunately, this *premier dialogue* provided no guidance at all on the question of what form of worship was to be adopted by the new Church. Saint-Simon expressed his intention to deal with this whole matter in a subsequent work,[98] but owing to his death in May 1825 this work was never written. It was left to the Saint-Simonians to fill this vacuum, after their master's death.

In addition to the role of moral leadership, another task was allotted to the new spiritual power in industrial society: the training of individuals for employment. This was of crucial significance for Saint-Simon, since an industrial society was, by definition, an association of men devoted to useful work in all its forms. The national workshop, like an individual factory, could not be expected to function properly unless work was allocated to individuals on the basis of their particular skills. And this could not be done until all men were given the opportunity, through education, to develop their abilities to the full. Only in this way, too, could the individual achieve any significant measure of self-realisation.[99]

Judged by the standards put forward by Saint-Simon, the educational systems of all west European countries were totally inadequate. In France, for example, the vast majority of children received no formal education at all. For Saint-Simon, therefore, the immediate aim of reform was to extend educational facilities at the primary and secondary levels to all children, irrespective of their social background. This could best be done, he suggested, by means of the Bell-Lancaster system of 'mutual education', which involved the employment of the ablest pupils as teachers. This system was greatly admired by French liberals under the Restoration, and was also supported by Bentham and his followers in England. It is therefore not surprising to find that it gained Saint-Simon's support.[100]

(vii) The Relationship Between the Two Powers

Saint-Simon devoted a considerable amount of attention in his writings to the question of the relationship between the temporal and spiritual powers. He was particularly interested in the historical development of this relationship. He observed that in the social system of ancient Greece and Rome, while both powers were held in the hands of the patrician class, the temporal function assumed the greatest social importance. Subsequently, in the Middle Ages, a formal division between the two powers was established through the influence of Christianity. Spiritual power then achieved predominance, exercising a direct authority over feudalism's temporal rulers. Against this historical background, Saint-Simon gave careful consideration to the issue of what form of relationship between the two powers should be established in industrial society.

As with other aspects of his doctrine, his ideas on this subject changed somewhat between 1802 and 1825. In his earliest writings, and particularly in the *Lettres d'un habitant de Genève,* society's spiritual leaders are accorded supremacy over the temporal rulers, who are reduced to a position of secondary importance.[101] Here Saint-Simon is simply transposing the feudal relationship between the two powers to the post-feudal situation. This theory was maintained by Saint-Simon during the Empire, but under the new political circumstances of the Restoration it was eventually rejected in favour of a new conception according to which the temporal-spiritual relationship was reversed, with the industrials being granted predominance over the new priesthood of scientists and artists. This new theory is made perfectly clear in the fourth book of the *Catéchisme des industriels,* in the context of a discussion of the role of scientists in the industrial system:

'The scientists render very important services to the industrial
class; but they receive from it even more important services;
they receive from it their *existence.* It is the industrial class which
satisfies their primary needs, as well as their physical tastes
of all kinds, and which provides them with all the instruments
of use to them in the execution of their work.

'The industrial class is the fundamental class, the nourishing
class of all society, without which no other class could exist. Thus, it
has the right to say to the scientists, and with even greater
reason to all other non-industrials: We wish to feed you, house you,

clothe you, and generally satisfy your physical tastes only on certain conditions'.[102]

The same point had earlier been made by Saint-Simon in his *IIIe lettre à messieurs les cultivateurs, fabricants, négociants, banquiers et autres industriels*[103] and in his preface to Comte's *Système de politique positive,* published as the third book of the *Catéchisme.* In this preface Saint-Simon criticised his 'pupil' for advocating the supremacy of the spiritual power rather than the temporal under industrialism:

> 'In the system which we have conceived, the industrial capacity is that which should find itself in the first rank; it is that which should judge the value of all other capacities, and make them all work for its greatest advantage.'[104]

In stating this principle Saint-Simon believed he was being thoroughly realistic in the face of the undeniable historical fact that 'the power of the industrials in society has become entirely preponderant'.[105] Where would the scientists and artists be, asked Saint-Simon, if the satisfaction of their basic material needs were not made possible by the efforts of the producers? The answer was obvious: they could not possibly survive; and it was this basic economic fact which made their social subordination inevitable in the industrial society of the future. This did not mean, Saint-Simon emphasised, that the autonomy of the spiritual power, in the performance of its social function, would be impaired but merely that the material conditions of its existence must be determined by the temporal rulers.

(viii) International Relations

Industrialism, as Saint-Simon conceived it, was a social system with an international dimension as well as a national one. For the decline of theological-feudal institutions caused by the development of scientific thought and industrialisation was a truly international phenomenon, embracing the whole of western Europe. The destinies of the individual nations composing that region had always been closely interrelated, and they were bound to become even more so with the improvement of systems of transport and communication which industrialism would promote.

Eventually, Saint-Simon believed, all the western European nations would complete the transition from feudal to industrial society. He saw the adoption of a parliamentary system of government as a half-way stage in this transition, and was encouraged to see, in the early 1820s, that such a system had in fact been established in all of the countries with which he was concerned. This augured well for industrialism. The recent adoption of the parliamentary regime by the Spanish, the Neapolitans, and the Portuguese, he argued in 1820, had brought to an end the preliminary work which must precede the preparation of the industrial system.[106] To a large extent the nations of western Europe were actually interdependent: the policies of one government invariably had a direct impact on neighbouring states, especially in the military sphere. And it was for this reason, in Saint-Simon's view, that no individual country could proceed to the establishment of the industrial system of social organisation without a movement in the same direction by all its neighbours. The spread of parliamentary government throughout western Europe was the first unmistakable sign that such a common movement was in progress. It at last made it possible for the most enlightened west European nation — France — to embark on the final transition to industrialism, thus setting the example for its politically less developed neighbours, chief among which Saint-Simon ranked England.

If industrialism could achieve full development only within the framework of a peace-loving, non-military social system, then clearly it could not possibly make very much progress until some measure of pan-European cooperation was promoted, to provide for the peaceful resolution of any international disputes which might arise. Such cooperation, Saint-Simon suggested, could best be fostered through the medium of a system of international institutions — both temporal and spiritual — through which the countries of western Europe would be able to work together towards the goal of a free association of industrial communities in which war was no longer a possibility. Ultimately, perhaps, a formal European federation might be created, such as that envisaged by Saint-Simon and Thierry in 1814 in their booklet *De la réorganisation de la société européenne*. Until that stage was reached, however, a more loosely-knit arrangement would be acceptable, as loosely-knit it would seem as the Holy Alliance, for which Saint-Simon frequently expressed admiration.[107]

In the broad context of European unity, the relationship between England and France was considered to be of crucial importance. An *entente cordiale* between these two countries, extending perhaps as far as an actual political union, would, he believed, provide the best starting-point for the creation of a wider European solidarity, by making a major continental war virtually impossible. For Saint-Simon and Thierry to present such a proposal on the eve of the battle of Waterloo was bold indeed; to reiterate it in the aftermath of that conflict was even bolder.[108] It is not surprising to learn that at the time the French public regarded Saint-Simon as somewhat foolish and unpatriotic.[109]

The vision of a union of European nations, it was argued, was no mere utopia, for the simple reason that in the Middle Ages 'for six centuries such a state of affairs existed, and for six centuries wars were more rare and less terrible'.[110] The kind of cohesion which then characterised relations between the nations of Europe must, Saint-Simon believed, be recreated if the disintegration of the continent through nationalistic rivalries was to be prevented.

Although his discussion of international relations was always focused on western Europe, Saint-Simon emphasised that the spread of industrialism was bound, eventually, to have an impact on the rest of the world too. The industrially advanced nations of Europe could, he believed, do a great deal to promote the economic and social progress of the less developed parts of the globe, once their own social reorganisation was completed. It was their historical destiny to extend the boundaries of civilisation to the farthest corners of the earth. In the performance of this task the chiefs of industry and the ministers of the New Christian religion would work together, revealing to the world, in both word and deed, the social benefits afforded by the industrial system. Always their essential aim would be to eradicate poverty, both material and spiritual:

'The direct aim of my enterprise is to improve as much as possible the condition of the class which has no other means of existence but the labour of its hands. My aim is to improve the condition of this class not only in France, but in England, Belgium, Portugal, Spain, Italy, throughout the rest of Europe, and the whole world.'[111]

As far as the other branch of modern society, North America, was concerned, Saint-Simon frequently expressed the opinion that in that part of the world much progress had already been made in the direction of industrialism, so that the United States was well equipped for the role of partner with western Europe in the future programme of social advancement. Relations between the Old World and the New were bound to be friendly and cooperative in the industrial age. On the basis of such a solid association, Saint-Simon was confident that the ancient dream of perpetual and universal peace would one day become a reality.

(ix) Social Classes and The Constitution of Property

So far, Saint-Simon's industrial doctrine has been examined chiefly from the standpoint of changes in the nature of temporal and spiritual power, on both the national and international levels. Consideration must now be given to his conception of the kind of social structure which he saw emerging under industrialism, for clearly, in order to support the new arrangement of temporal and spiritual power, that structure would have to be very different from the one prevailing under the feudal system.

Saint-Simon saw social structure essentially in terms of a network of class relationships. In this context he used the term 'class' to refer to any distinctive functional, occupational group. The focal point of his analysis is the very fundamental distinction between the productive classes — the 'workers' in the broadest sense of that term, including all farmers, manufacturers, merchants, bankers, scientists, artists, etc. — and the idle classes (chiefly the nobility and the clergy), who enjoyed the benefits provided by the workers without themselves contributing to production. In the early years of the Restoration Saint-Simon introduced the term 'industrial' (*'industriel'*) to refer to any member of any of the productive classes.[112] From about 1820, however, he modified this usage and applied the term only to members of the 'practical' classes, i.e. in particular the farmers, manufacturers, merchants, and bankers. In other words, the scientists and artists were excluded and regarded henceforth as 'non-industrials', although they were still considered to be useful 'theoretical' workers.[113] A further complication which must be mentioned is that towards the end of his life Saint-Simon introduced the concept of an intermediate, 'bourgeois' class consisting of those idle lawyers, soldiers, and landowners who came originally from the industrial class and were granted their privileges by the nobility.[114] It was this bourgeois class, Saint-Simon believed, which had gained power in France during the Revolution, and which was attempting to establish a new social system on the basic of its negative 'legal-metaphysical' reasoning.

According to Saint-Simon the social significance of these various classes could be understood only in historical terms. The whole of human history had to be seen as a perpetual struggle between the productive and idle classes. At first, in ancient times, the advantage in this struggle lay with the idlers, who maintained their social supremacy through the institution of slavery. Under the theological-feudal system, however, the producers achieved successive measures of emancipation: the replacement of slavery by serfdom, the enfranchisement of the commons, and finally the establishment of the parliamentary system of government, first of all in England and then, after the French Revolution, in France and other European countries. Strictly speaking, this parliamentary system represented a transitional phase between feudalism and industrialism. It was no more than a partial success for the producers: it gave them a share in political power, but not the whole of political power, because parliaments continued to be dominated by idlers. In the case of France these idlers were the bourgeois lawyers, landowners, and soldiers referred to above. However, Saint-Simon was convinced that it could only be a matter of time

47

before the producers gained the absolute supremacy they deserved. The spread of enlightenment and the numerical superiority of the productive classes would ensure that.

Saint-Simon full recognised the division within the productive classes between those men who were employers and managers of labour ('directing industrials') and those who were employees – proletarians – doing the bulk of the physical work ('executive industrials'). However, unlike Marx and Engels, who were to stress the inevitability of class conflict between capitalists and the proletariat, Saint-Simon believed that these two groups shared a common interest in production, and that consequently there was no reason why relations between them should be anything but friendly and cooperative.[115] At the same time he pointed out that the precise degree of unity would vary from country to country. It was much stronger in France, he believed, than in England, where the proletariat were likely to take advantage of the first opportunity to begin the war of the poor against the rich.[116] This makes it quite clear that Saint-Simon did not rule out altogether the possibility of a 'class war'. However, he was convinced that such conflict could be avoided, or at least kept to a minimum, if two conditions were fulfilled: first, society's leaders must provide for the basic moral and physical needs of the whole population; and secondly, society must be organised so as to give all men equal opportunities for advancement on the basis of their proven ability.

Saint-Simon believed, then, that the final demise of the unproductive idlers, and the rise to social supremacy of the workers – the practical industrials in the temporal sphere, and the scientists and artists in the spiritual sphere – was an historical inevitability. He also recognised, however, that positive action must be taken to establish the industrial system as smoothly and as rapidly as possible. With this aim in mind he stressed the crucial importance of increasing the parliamentary representation of the country's leading industrials *vis-à-vis* the idlers,[117] and of reforming the laws governing the actual constitution of landed property. It was chiefly on the basis of these laws, he argued, that the privileged social position of the idle property owners rested. Hence, as long as the laws remained unchanged, no real progress was likely to be made towards a truly egalitarian society. In Saint-Simon's view the chief purpose of property law reform should be 'to render it [property] most favourable to production'.[118] A start had been made in France with the sale of *biens nationaux* during the Revolution.[119] But further measures were needed: at least the abolition of entail;[120] and preferably the 'mobilisation' of all landed property, that is, the granting of full entrepreneurial rights to farmers.[121] These measures – which have obvious socialistic implications — would surely be sufficient to rid society for ever of all idlers who believed they had a natural right to live off unearned income.

Saint-Simon's vision of a future society in which all men would be workers has often been interpreted as a theory of the 'classless' society, similar to that subsequently developed by Marx and Engels.[122] However, such an interpretation is erroneous, for the simple reason that Saint-Simon frequently emphasised the inevitability of some class divisions in all societies, including industrial society.[123] Indeed, the notion of a classless society would have been regarded by Saint-Simon as absurd, since for him the basic meaning of the word 'class' was 'occupational group', and naturally in industrial society, as in any other society, there would be fundamental group distinctions corresponding to the division of labour: for example, on the broadest level, between industrials, scientists, and artists; and *within* the industrial class between farmers, manufacturers, merchants, and bankers. Thus industrial society would in no sense be a classless society. It would, however, be a *homogeneous* society in which all classes would share a common interest in production, and from which all class conflict would thereby be eliminated, or at least reduced to an acceptable minimum.

3. THE INFLUENCE OF THE DOCTRINE

During his lifetime Saint-Simon never achieved the public recognition for which he was hoping. It was not until later in the century that his ideas began to exert any significant measure of influence, and this was due largely to the efforts of those disciples who immediately after their master's death resolved to devote themselves to the cause of social reconstruction which he had pioneered.

At first the disciples did not constitute a properly organised group; they were merely a collection of young intellectuals who shared a common social philosophy. They came together to found a new journal which Saint-Simon had been planning shortly before he died: *Le Producteur,* the first issue of which appeared at the beginning of October 1825, and included contributions by Antoine Cerclet (the general editor), Saint-Amand Bazard, Auguste Comte,[124] Barthélemy-Prosper Enfantin, Olinde Rodrigues, and Pierre-Isidore Rouen. *Le Producteur* suffered a setback in November 1826 when it had to be suspended because of lack of funds; but before long the financial difficulties were overcome, and through the medium of public lectures and published writings a systematic exposition of Saint-Simon's doctrine was undertaken. During 1828 and 1829 the teachings of the disciples — who now regarded themselves as a Saint-Simonian 'School' —

aroused widespread interest, and as a result Saint-Simon's ideas began to reach a large audience for the first time, not only in France, but also in neighbouring countries. A weekly publication, *L'Organisateur*, founded in July 1829 by Laurent de l'Ardèche, devoted itself exclusively to the propagation of the doctrine and succeeded in attracting many new supporters to the movement.

In the course of their exposition the Saint-Simonians introduced many of their own views, with the result that in some respects the doctrine they elaborated was significantly different from that of their master. Especially important was their critique of the existing economic system, and in particular the institution of private property. This critique was much more radical than that contained in the writings of Saint-Simon, and is justifiably regarded as totally collectivist in character.[125] The disciples also introduced into their exposition, very tentatively at first, a theory of female emancipation which was not present in Saint-Simon's works. These modifications to the original doctrine of Saint-Simon were largely due to the influence of Enfantin, who by 1829 was emerging as the leading Saint-Simonian theorist. And it was also mainly due to his efforts that at the end of 1829 the School was formally transformed into a 'Church', with himself and Bazard as 'Supreme Fathers' of the Saint-Simonian 'Family' (by election). This change was made, it was stated, in recognition of the religious character of Saint-Simon's teachings. A number of disciples and associates did not approve and left the group. Among them was Auguste Comte, whose links with the Saint-Simonians had always been tenuous, and who now proceeded to found a rival 'positivist' school in Paris, the main purpose of which was to promote the development of a science of society or 'sociology', to use the term later invented by Comte. In subsequent years he went to great lengths to dissociate himself from the doctrine of Saint-Simon and his followers; but the fact remains that his positivist theories owed a great deal to the influence of Saint-Simon's ideas on the possibility of developing a 'positive science of man' or 'social physiology'.[126]

The loss of support resulting from the formation of the new Church at the end of 1829 did not seriously hinder the success of Saint-Simonism, and by July 1830, when revolution broke out in France, it had established itself as one of the country's most important reformist movements. In a number of respects the July Revolution represented the fulfilment of Saint-Simonian prophecies. During the last ten years of his life Saint-Simon had issued numerous warnings to the Bourbons, declaring that unless the monarchy dissociated itself from the feudal aristocracy and embraced the principles of industrialism, its downfall was inevitable. When the downfall of the

Bourbons came in July 1830, the Saint-Simonian doctrine was inevitably taken much more seriously than ever before. Inspired by success, the Church mounted a major effort to spread the Saint-Simonian gospel through educational 'missions' sent from Paris to various parts of France and neighbouring countries, including Belgium, Germany, and England, where they received a considerable amount of support from two of their most fervent admirers, John Stuart Mill and Thomas Carlyle.[127] Progress was made in another direction, too, with the conversion to Saint-Simonism of Pierre Leroux, editor of *Le Globe*, one of the most important Paris newspapers, which Leroux had helped to found in 1824. In November 1830 the paper announced its support for Saint-Simonism, and the following August it formally adopted the sub-title 'Journal of the Saint-Simonian Religion'.

These combined efforts soon produced remarkable results. By mid-1831 some 40,000 persons had joined the sect.[128] Among them were many of France's most eminent intellectuals. The doctrine was especially popular among the literary and artistic community, whose members were greatly impressed by the Saint-Simonian conception of the artist's role in society. Such major writers as Maxime du Camp, Renouvier, Renan, Sainte-Beuve, Lamennais, Georges Sand, and Béranger, and the composers Berlioz, Liszt, and Félicien David were attracted to the new religion. And Saint-Simonism was also the main inspiration behind the Young German school of literature which flourished during the early 1830s (with Heinrich Heine as one of its most active members), and which soon succeeded in arousing widespread enthusiasm for the Saint-Simonian doctrine among German radicals.[129]

So rapidly did the Church's influence spread that in February 1832 one of the leading Saint-Simonians, Charles Duveyrier, felt assured enough to predict that 'within the next few years the whole of France will be Saint-Simonian'.[130] But Duveyrier's confidence was soon to be shaken; for just as the Saint-Simonian movement appeared to be going from strength to strength, its very existence was seriously threatened by a dispute which arose among its members concerning the status of women and the whole question of relations between the sexes. By the end of 1831 Enfantin was making an overt attempt to steer the movement towards advocacy of a much freer form of relations than was sanctioned by orthodox Christian doctrine. It was a move which achieved little besides the loss of a considerable amount of support, both within the Church's hierarchy and among the general public. Many leading members, including Bazard, Rodrigues, and Leroux, withdrew from the movement and proceeded to mount an attack on Enfantin and his followers.

51

After such a serious split within its ranks, the Church totally lost its sense of direction. Enfantin, now the sole Supreme Father of the Family, attempted to restore its vitality, but he faced severe opposition from the Government of Louis Philippe which, suspicious of the sect's philosophy and frightened of its potential influence, first of all initiated a prosecution against its leaders (in April 1832), and then declared it to be an illegal association (August 1832). After a trial at the Assize Court, Enfantin, Duveyrier, and Michel Chevalier (formerly co-editor of *Le Globe*) were each sentenced to a year's imprisonment for offences against public order and morality. The Saint-Simonian religion thus found itself reduced to impotence. Its dissolution on 15 December 1832 by the Supreme Father, shortly before he was taken to prison, was a mere formality.

The Government was now confident that the spread of Saint-Simonian ideas would quickly abate. But it was to be proved wrong, for they continued to exert a strong influence throughout the country after 1832. The first collected edition of Saint-Simon's writings, prepared by Olinde Rodrigues and published in 1832,[131] received widespread attention; and it performed a considerable service by enabling the public to study the original social doctrine of Saint-Simon, freed from the controversial theories introduced by Enfantin. The Government could at least find some cause for satisfaction in this, since Rodrigues' book made it quite clear that Saint-Simon had never sanctioned the new moral code advocated by Enfantin and his followers.

The appeal of Saint-Simon's ideas broadened during the 1830s and 1840s with the emergence of socialism as a distinctive ideology, first of all in Paris, and subsequently throughout France and the rest of Europe. For proponents of the new creed of social revolution, Saint-Simon's vision of a society organised by and for the workers — the producers — was an inspiration. Although in matters of detail they often disagreed with that vision, they frequently acknowledged it to be a starting-point for their own theories. Of the numerous thinkers who assimilated Saint-Simonian ideas in this way the most important were undoubtedly Proudhon, Marx and Engels, and the Russian socialist circle led by Herzen and Ogarev. Proudhon admitted that his whole view of the relationship between economics and politics was derived directly from Saint-Simon.[132] In terms strikingly reminiscent of those used by his predecessor, he predicted the eventual replacement of 'the feudal, governmental or military regime' by an 'economic or industrial regime'.[133] Marx and Engels were less explicit about their indebtedness, but it is known that the doctrine of Saint-Simon played a formative role in their early intellectual development, especially during the late 1830s, when they were members of the Young Hegelian circle in Berlin;[134] and it is clear from the numerous references to Saint-Simon scattered throughout their subsequent writings that his doctrine eventually became one of the most important sources of their own 'scientific socialism'. Although they regarded him as a fundamentally 'utopian' thinker, because of his belief in a harmony of interests between capitalists and proletarians, they nevertheless greatly admired many aspects of his social theory, in particular his concern for the welfare of 'the poorest and most numerous class', his theory of the class struggle (even though, in their view, he did not take this theory to its logical conclusion), his realisation that economic conditions are the basis of political institutions, and his internationalism. Perhaps most importantly, it was from Saint-Simon that Marx and Engels derived the idea that the government of men must be replaced by the administration of things — an idea which was a central feature of their own vision of future society.[135]

In Russia the ideas of Saint-Simon and his disciples began to exert a profound influence in radical circles after 1830. This may have been due in part to the efforts of a group of Saint-Simonian 'missionaries' who visited St. Petersburg in 1829. But a much more important factor was the Polish Revolution of 1830-31, which inspired a new wave of revolutionary fervour in Russia itself. Interest in Saint-Simonian ideas now spread quickly among the young intelligentesia. According to Herzen, he and his followers based all their fundamental conceptions on the Saint-Simonian doctrine.[136] They were especially receptive to its underlying philosophy of history and the vision of social regeneration through a New Christian religion. Largely due to the efforts of the Herzen-Ogarev circle Saint-Simonian ideas continued to exert a direct influence in Russia during the 1830s and '40s. They are known to have been studied by the Petrashevsky group, which included Dostoevsky, in 1848; and it seems likely that Dostoevsky's own conception of socialism as a new religion owed something to the Saint-Simonian influence.[137]

During the 1830s many prominent ex-Saint-Simonians became enthusiastic supporters of the socialist cause. Among them were Leroux, Cabet, Reynaud, Buchez, Pecqueur, Blanqui, and Louis Blanc, all of whose writings reveal the unmistakable influence of the Saint-Simonian doctrine. At the same time there were other ex-leaders who regarded socialism as too revolutionary an ideology, and who preferred to work for change within the existing social framework. They included Enfantin and his supporters, many of whom entered new careers in industry in order to help promote the creation of large-scale enterprises such as Saint-Simon had advocated in his writings on industrialism. They regarded the construction of railways and the organisation of credit facilities to be especially important, and devoted themselves to these tasks with an almost maniacal enthusiasm. They were guided in their work by an ambitious plan for industrial development outlined by Michel Chevalier in *Le Globe* during February 1832 under the title *Exposition du système de la Méditerranée*. This plan proposed nothing less than the creation of a 'universal association' of the peoples of Europe and the Orient through a comprehensive network of railways, rivers, and canals, the finance for which would be provided by new industrial banks. These ideas, which were subsequently elaborated by Chevalier in numerous writings and also in his lectures at the Collège de France (where he was made Professor of Political Economy in 1840), inspired many of his colleagues, and in particular Émile and Isaac Pereire, who soon emerged as two of Europe's most able bankers and entrepreneurs. During the 1830s and '40s, together with associates such as Henri Fournel, Léon and Edmond Talabot, and Enfantin, they pioneered the construction of railways in France and other countries, including Switzerland, Austria, Hungary, Spain, Italy, and Russia. Later, under the Second Empire of Napoleon III (1852-70), himself an enthusiastic admirer of Saint-Simon, they founded the Crédit Mobilier bank — capitalised at sixty million francs — which did much to foster economic expansion and industrialisation in France, and which in subsequent years served as a model for new commercial banks in the majority of continental countries.

The Second Empire also witnessed the realisation of another major Saint-Simonian enterprise: the Suez Canal, advocated by Chevalier in 1832 as an essential part of the *système de la Méditerranée*. The first positive steps towards the realisation of the project were taken in 1846 when Enfantin founded a *Société d'études pour le canal de Suez;* and it was the preparatory work done by this society which made it possible for de Lesseps to embark on the actual construction of the canal in 1854.

Finally, the Anglo-French free trade treaty of 1869 also deserves to be included in the list of major Saint-Simonian achievements, since its chief architect on the French side was Chevalier, who had been a passionate advocate of free trade since his association with the original Saint-Simonian movement forty years earlier.

By the end of the Second Empire most of the original group of disciples, including Enfantin, were dead, and the last remnants of the movement they had founded were rapidly withering away. By any standards its achievements had been impressive. It had certainly succeeded brilliantly in its essential aim of disseminating the doctrine of Saint-Simon; so brilliantly in fact that by 1870 there were few social theories propounded in Europe which were not in some way indebted to that doctrine. The doctrine had, in fact, over the space of fifty years, provided an impetus for the development of philosophical and sociological positivism, socialist thought in all its varieties, the ideology of industrialism, and secular religious thinking — in short, for 'all the great intellectual currents produced during the nineteenth century.'[138] Today, when the social and political consequences of those intellectual currents are still in the process of working themselves out, it is surely more necessary than ever to study Saint-Simon's thought and to understand why it exerted such a profound influence in nineteenth-century Europe.

NOTES

1. His full name and title: Claude-Henri de Rouvroy, comte de Saint-Simon. Most biographers state that he was born in Paris; but documentary evidence exists to show that Berny was the actual birthplace. See Mathurin Dondo, *The French Faust, Henri de Saint-Simon*, New York, 1955, p.10.
2. Letter to M. Boissy-d'Anglas, 2 November 1807, in *Oeuvres*, vol. I, pt. 1, p.69(fn.). Some commentators have expressed disbelief at Saint-Simon's claim to have been tutored by such an eminent figure as d'Alembert. In my own view, the possibility should not be so readily dismissed, since it is known that during the 1770s d'Alembert held regular literary and philosophical meetings in Paris which attracted numerous young students. His close friend Charles Pougens once remarked that 'According to some perhaps too many young people . . . were admitted to our evenings, but the famous academician could not be unaware that this was for them a kind of encouragement.' (Quoted by Ronald Grimsley, *Jean d'Alembert [1717-83]*, Oxford, 1963, p.288.) It is certainly not inconceivable that the young Saint-Simon attended such meetings.
3. *Projet d'encyclopédie. Second prospectus. Avertissement*, in *Oeuvres*, vol. VI, p.281.
4. *S.W.*, p.162. It has often been suggested that with the benefit of hindsight Saint-Simon exaggerated the extent of his passion for science at this time. But in a letter to his father, written while he was in America, he expressed sentiments very similar to those contained in the second *Lettre à un Américain* of 1817: 'If I was in a calm situation I would clarify my ideas. They are still undigested, but I see clearly that after ripening them I would be in a position to do scientific work useful to humanity, which is the chief aim I set myself in life.' Quoted by Georges Weill, *Saint-Simon et son oeuvre*, Paris, 1894, p.5.
5. *S.W.*, p.163.
6. *Lettres au Bureau des Longitudes. Préface* (1808), in *Oeuvres*, vol. I, pt.1, p.64.
7. From a speech of May 1790, in *Not. hist.*, pp.15-16.
8. *Lettres au Bureau des Longitudes. Préface*, in *Oeuvres*, vol. I, pt.1, p.67.
9. From the official record of the proceedings. Quoted by Frank E. Manuel, *The New World of Henri Saint-Simon*, Notre Dame, Ind., 1963, p.32.
10. Maxime Leroy, *La vie véritable du comte Henri de Saint-Simon*, Paris, 1925, pp.181-2.
11. Pierre Leroux, *La grève de Samarez*, 2 vols., Paris, 1863, vol. I, ch. IV.
12. *S.W.*, pp.112-15.

13. *Not. hist.*, p.26, quoting from one of Saint-Simon's autobiographical manuscripts.
14. Sophie lived until 1860, by which time, as Baroness de Bawr, she had become a well-known authoress.
15. See Jean Dautry, 'Sur un imprimé retrouvé du comte de Saint-Simon', *Annales historiques de la révolution française*, vol. XX, 1948, pp.289-321. One of the reasons why these letters, as well as other early works, remained undiscovered for such a long time is that Saint-Simon never referred to them himself in later life.
16. *Lettres au Bureau de Longitudes. Préface*, in *Oeuvres*, vol. I, pt.1, p.70.
17. *S.W.*, ch.1. Both editions were published anonymously and were not discovered until after Saint-Simon's death. The Paris edition was traced by Olinde Rodrigues in 1826; the Geneva edition was found by Paul E. Martin in the 1920s. See his article 'Saint-Simon et sa Lettre d'un habitant de Genève à l'humanité (1802-1803). Étude bibliographique', *Zeitschrift für Schweizerische Geschichte*, vol. V, no.4, 1925, pp.477-97.
18. *S.W.*, pp.77,80.
19. *Lettres au Bureau des Longitudes. Préface*, in *Oeuvres*, vol. I, pt.1, p.70.
20. Georges and Hubert Bourgin included some passages from the *Extrait* in their book *Le socialisme français de 1789 à 1848*, Paris, 1912, pp.26-7. The complete text first appeared in Pereire (1925), pp.87-93, together with the *Lettre aux Européens*, pp.72-83.
21. *S.W.*, ch.2.
22. *S.W.*, ch.3.
23. The most important of these texts is the *Projet d'encyclopédie. Second prospectus, S.W.*, ch.4.
24. *S.W.*, ch.5.
25. *S.W.*, ch.6.
26. *S.W.*, ch.7.
27. *S.W.*, ch.8.
28. For the text of a remarkable letter from Saint-Simon to Carnot, written during the 'Hundred Days', see *S.W.*, ch.9.
29. The parliamentary institutions established by Louis XVIII — a Chamber of Deputies and a Chamber of Peers — failed to satisfy liberal demands in this respect. The requirement that only men who paid over 1,000 francs in direct taxes could be admitted to the Chamber of Deputies favoured the landowning class, as did the system of indirect election to that Chamber, through electoral colleges whose members also had to meet stringent financial requirements.
30. *S.W.*, ch.10.
31. The list is reproduced in Alfred Pereire, *Autour de Saint-Simon. Documents originaux,* Paris, 1912, pp.4-9, and makes fascinating reading. It contains the names of 134 subscribers of various sums ranging from 100 to 1,000 francs, giving a total subscription of 24,400 francs. Included in the list are the names of the Minister of Finance (Roy), four peers, and twenty-four deputies. Most of the other contributors were prominent businessmen.
32. *S.W.*, ch.11.
33. *S.W.*, ch.12.
34. This is confirmed by Henri Fournel in his *Bibliographie Saint-Simonienne,* Paris, 1833, p.17, and by Comte's own statements to his friend Pierre Laffitte. See further Auguste Comte, *Écrits de jeunesse 1816-1828,* ed. Paulo E. de Berrêdo Carneiro and Pierre Arnaud, Paris, 1970, pp.33-8.

35. *S. W.*, ch.13. See also the extracts from one of Saint-Simon's unpublished manuscripts, *Des intérêts politiques de l'industrie*, *S. W.*, ch.16, probably written some time during 1818.
36. *S. W.*, chs.14-15.
37. *S. W.*, chs.17-18.
38. *S. W.*, ch.19.
39. *S. W.*, ch.20.
40. Shortly after the murder one journalist, Charles Nodier, wrote: 'I have seen the knife. It is a liberal doctrine.' (Quoted by John R. Hall, *The Bourbon Restoration*, London, 1909, p.251.) This attitude towards liberalism quickly gained currency during the next few weeks.
41. M.G. Hubbard, *Saint-Simon, sa vie et ses travaux*, Paris, 1857, p.84.
42. *S. W.*, chs.21-2.
43. 8th and 9th Letters. In 1854 Comte published six of his earliest essays, originally written between 1819 and 1828, as an appendix to volume IV of his *Système de politique positive*. These included the 8th and 9th Letters of *L'Organisateur*. An English translation of these Letters, by Henry Dix Hutton and originally published in 1877, has recently been reprinted in *The Crisis of Industrial Civilization. The Early Essays of Auguste Comte*, ed. Ronald Fletcher, London, 1974, pp.79-110.
44. *S. W.*, chs.23-31.
45. *S. W.*, p.237.
46. *S. W.*, ch.26.
47. John Stuart Mill, *Autobiography*, London, 1873, p.61. The meeting took place in the house of Jean-Baptiste Say. The accuracy of Mill's view is confirmed by contemporary French sources, such as the *Biographie nouvelle des contemporains*, Paris, 1824, pp.374-5, which emphasises Saint-Simon's originality, with particular reference to *L'Organisateur*, but offers no systematic analysis of his doctrine.
48. Leroy, op. cit., pp.314-15.
49. *S. W.*, chs.32-6.
50. *Oeuvres*, vol. IV, pt.2, p.5.
51. See further below, p.50.
52. *S. W.*, chs.37-9.
53. *S. W.*, ch.40.
54. *S. W.*, pp.88,90.
55. The French word *'organisation'* can mean both 'organisation' and 'organic structure'. (Hence, *'organisé'* may mean either 'organised' or 'organic'.) In the *Mémoire sur la science de l'homme* Saint-Simon used the term *'organisation'* to refer to the organic structure of man and other animals. See *S. W.*, pp.114-15.
56. *L'Organisateur*, in *Oeuvres*, vol. II, pt.2, p.72.
57. See Peyton V. Lyon, 'Saint-Simon and the Origins of Scientism and Historicism', *Canadian Journal of Economics and Political Science*, vol. XXVII, no.1, February 1961, pp.55-63.
58. *S. W.*, p.112.
59. *S. W.*, p.112.
60. See, for example, W.M. Simon, 'Ignorance is Bliss: Saint-Simon and the Writing of History', *Revue internationale de philosophie*, vol.14, nos.3-4, 1960, pp.357-83.
61. *S. W.*, p.94.
62. *S. W.*, p.170.
63. *Oeuvres*, vol. I, pt.1, p.158.

64. *S.W.*, p.181.
65. Although this precise expression was never actually used by Saint-Simon, it does sum up his moral outlook, which was basically utilitarian in the Benthamite sense. Whether this was due to the direct influence of Bentham's ideas is not definitely known. But the supposition does seem reasonable in view of the widespread popularity enjoyed by Bentham in France during the first quarter of the nineteenth century. Cf. W. Stark, 'The Realism of Saint-Simon's Spiritual Program', *The Journal of Economic History*, vol. V, no.1, May 1945, pp.24-42 *passim*. See also J.-B. Duvergier, *De la législation*, in *Opin. litt.*, pp.199-225. In this illuminating but hitherto neglected essay, the relationship between the ideas of Bentham and Saint-Simon is discussed in some detail.
66. For an explanation of this term see my note on the translation, p.10.
67. *S.W.*, p.165.
68. *Nouveau christianisne*, in *Oeuvres*, vol. III, pt.3, p.164.
69. *S.W.*, p.168
70. *S.W.*, p.267
71. See further Joseph Haberer, *Politics and the Community of Science*, New York, 1969, ch.3. In *Novum Organum* Bacon predicted that the progress of the arts and sciences would result in the replacement of dominion over man by 'the empire of man over things'. Quoted by Benjamin Farrington, *Francis Bacon, Philosopher of Industrial Science*, London, 1951, p.7.
72. Harold Perkin, *The Origins of Modern English Society 1780-1880*, London, 1969, p.320. See also note 65.
73. *Considérations sur les mesures à prendre pour terminer la révolution, Du système industriel*, pt.1, in *Oeuvres*, vol. III, pt.1, p.118. Cf. *S.W.*, p.150(fn.).
74. *Première adresse au Roi, Du système industriel*, pt.2, in *Oeuvres*, vol. III, pt.2, p.171.
75. *S.W.*, p.196.
76. *Deuxième correspondence avec messieurs les industriels, Du système industriel*, pt.1, in *Oeuvres*, vol. III, pt.1, pp.131-2.
77. F.A. Hayek, *The Road to Serfdom*, London, 1944, p.18.
78. Lyon, op. cit., p.62.
79. F.M.H. Markham, 'Saint-Simon. A Nineteenth-Century Prophet', *History Today*, vol. IV, no.8, August 1954, p.547. Cf. the same author's introduction to Henri de Saint-Simon, *Social Organization, the Science of Man and Other Writings*, New York, 1964, pp.xlviii-xlix.
80. Giovanni Sartori, *Democratic Theory*, New York, 1965, p.389.
81. Leonard Schapiro, *Totalitarianism*, London, 1972, p.89.
82. H.G. Schenk, 'Revolutionary Influences and Conservatism in Literature and Thought', in *The New Cambridge Modern History*, vol. IX, ed. C.W. Crawley, Cambridge, 1965, p.112.
83. Walter M. Simon, 'History for Utopia: Saint-Simon and the Idea of Progress', *Journal of the History of Ideas*, vol. XVII, no.3, June 1956, p.329.
84. J.L. Talmon, *Political Messianism. The Romantic Phase*, New York, 1960, pp.35-70 *passim*.
85. For an illuminating examination of this whole complex issue see Georg G. Iggers, 'Le Saint-Simonisme et la pensée autoritaire' (in English), *Économies et sociétés*, vol. IV, no.4, April 1970, pp.673-91. Iggers quite rightly points out (p.673, note 3) that 'the major studies dealing with

Saint-Simonian affinities to totalitarianism have first appeared in the English language', reflecting the fact that 'the major centre of research into the nature of totalitarianism has been the English-speaking world.' It is certainly interesting to note that French commentators have not demonstrated the same preoccupation.
86. *S.W.*, p.210, 229.
87. *S.W.*, p.165.
88. *S.W.*, p.165.
89. *S.W.*, p.165.
90. *Suite à la brochure: Des Bourbons et des Stuarts*, in *Oeuvres*, vol. VI, p.518, Cf. *S.W.*, ch.37 *passim*.
91. *S.W.*, p.266.
92. *S.W.*, ch.21.
93. *S.W.*, chs. 23, 29.
94. In July 1830 the Bourbons were overthrown and a new Orleanist monarchy was established with the support of the anti-Bourbon bourgeoisie. The new King, Louis Philippe (the duc D'Orléans), was himself forced to abdicate in the face of revolutionary protest in 1848. But this time the monarchy did not survive, and France's Second Republic was established.
95. *S.W.*, ch.21.
96. *S.W.*, p.224.
97. *S.W.*, p.260.
98. *Nouveau christianisme*, in *Oeuvres*, vol. III, pt.3, pp.185-6.
99. 'The essence of my life's work', Saint-Simon declared shortly before his death, 'is to afford all members of society the greatest possible opportunity for the development of their faculties.' Quoted by Manuel, op. cit., p.365.
100. *S.W.*, p.231.
101. *S.W.*, p.81(fn.).
102. *Catéchisme des industriels, 4e cahier*, in *Oeuvres*, vol. V, pt.1., p.25.
103. *S.W.*, ch.24.
104. *Catéchisme des industriels, 3e cahier*, in *Oeuvres*, vol. IV, pt.2, p.4.
105. *Considérations sur les mesures à prendre pour terminer la révolution, Du système industriel*, pt.1, in *Oeuvres*, vol. III, pt.1, p.122.
106. *S.W.*, p.222.
107. See, for example, *Quelques opinions philosophiques à l'usage du XIXe siècle* (from *Opin. litt.)*, in *Oeuvres*, vol. V, pt.1, pp.99-101.
108. See H. Saint-Simon and A. Thierry, *Opinion sur les mesures à prendre contre la coalition de 1815* (dated 18 May 1815), in *Oeuvres*, vol. VI, pp.355-79. Cf. Saint-Simon's unpublished manuscript of 1815, *Aux Anglais et aux Français qui sont zélés pour le bien public, S.W.*, ch.10.
109. Hubbard, op. cit., p.75.
110. Saint-Simon and Thierry, *De la réorganisation de la société européenne*, in *Oeuvres*, vol. I, pt.1, p.175.
111. *Lettres sur les Bourbons, Du système industriel*, pt.1, in *Oeuvres*, vol. III, pt.2, p.81.
112. See *S.W.*, chs.11, 18.
113. Saint-Simon did in fact use the term *'industriel'* in this more restricted sense as early as 1815, in *Aux Anglais et aux Français qui sont zélés pour le bien public (S.W.*, ch.10). However, this work remained in manuscript. The public first encountered the term in *L'Industrie* and *Le Politique*, when it was used in the much broader sense.
114. *S.W.*, ch.33. Cf. ch.27.

115. The actual term 'capitalist' *('capitaliste')* was used by Saint-Simon to mean 'financier' or 'money-lender'. *(S. W.,* p.247). This is, of course, a much more restricted definition than that adopted by Marx.
116. *S. W.,* p.265.
117. In France this could only be done, in Saint-Simon's view, through reforms of the taxation system, since only the country's chief taxpayers were given the vote. See *S. W.,* ch.14.
118. *S. W.,* p.206.
119. *S. W.,* pp.262-3.
120. *S. W.,* p.255.
121. See *S. W.,* ch.14 and p.151(fn.).
122. Most recently by Anthony Giddens, *The Class Structure of the Advanced Societies,* London, 1973, pp.23-4, 64, 135-6, 287.
123. *S. W.,* pp.212, 251-2.
124. Comte, naturally enough, did not regard himself in any sense as a 'Saint-Simonian', but was willing to contribute to the journal as it offered him an opportunity to expound his own views.
125. For enthusiastic comments on this aspect of Saint-Simonism see Karl Marx and Friedrich Engels, *The German Ideology,* ed. R. Pascal, London, 1938, pp.145, 147-8, 150.
126. He had, after all, worked with Saint-Simon from 1817 to 1824, during which time he made no secret of his intellectual debt to 'the master': 'Intellectually, I certainly owe a lot to Saint-Simon,' he told one close friend in 1824, 'he contributed powerfully to launching me on the philosophical course which I have clearly created for myself today, and which I will follow unhesitatingly all my life.' (Letter to Valat, quoted by Weill, op. cit., p.207.) And in the preface to his *Système de politique positive,* published as the third book of the *Catéchisme des industriels* in 1824, he praised Saint-Simon at some length, 'so that if my works seem to merit some approval, it may go to the founder of the philosophical school of which I am honoured to be part.' *(Oeuvres,* vol. IV, pt.2, p.9.)
127. Mill and Carlyle were particularly impressed by the Saint-Simonian philosophy of history. In his autobiography Mill stated that 'The writers by whom, more than by any others, a new mode of political thinking was brought home to me, were those of the Saint-Simonian school in France . . . I was greatly struck with the connected view which they for the first time presented to me, of the natural order of human progress; and especially with their division of all history into organic periods and critical periods . . .' (op. cit., p.163) Carlyle considered Saint-Simon's *Nouveau christianisme* to be so important that he actually translated it into English with a view to publication, but the plan never materialised. See further David Brooks Cofer, *Saint-Simonism in the Radicalism of Thomas Carlyle,* London, 1957; Richard K.P. Pankhurst, *The Saint-Simonians, Mill and Carlyle,* London, 1957.
128. Georg G. Iggers, Introduction to *The Doctrine of Saint-Simon: An Exposition. First Year, 1828-1829,* New York, 1972, p.xxiv.
129. See E.M. Butler, *The Saint-Simonian Religion in Germany. A Study of the Young German Movement,* Cambridge, 1926.
130. Letter to Enfantin, 10 February 1832. Quoted by Pankhurst, op. cit., p.63.
131. *Oeuvres complètes de Saint-Simon,* 2 pts. in 1 vol., Paris, 1832. Despite its title this volume is far from being a complete edition of Saint-Simon's works.

132. 'For authority and politics I substituted the notion of *Economics* — a positive, synthetic idea which, as I see it, is alone capable of leading to a rational, practical conception of social order. Moreover, in this I was simply taking up Saint-Simon's thesis ... This thesis consists of saying, in the light of history and of the incompatibility of the notions of authority and progress, that society is in the process of completing the governmental cycle for the last time; that the public reason has become convinced that politics is powerless to improve the lot of the masses; that the notions of power and authority are being replaced in people's minds, as in the course of history, by the notions of labor and exchange; and that the end result is the substitution of economic organisations for political machinery, etc., etc.' *Philosophie du Progrès* (1853), in *Selected Writings of Pierre-Joseph Proudhon*, ed. Stewart Edwards, London, 1970, pp.90-91.
133. *Idée générale de la révolution au XIXe siècle* (1851), quoted by John Plamenatz, *Man and Society*, vol.2, London, 1963, p.52 (fn.).
134. See Georges Gurvitch, 'La Sociologie du jeune Marx', *La Vocation actuelle de la sociologie*, Paris, 1950, ch.10; and the same author's 'Saint-Simon et Karl Marx', *Revue internationale de philosophie*, vol.14, nos.3-4, 1960, pp.399-416.
135. See Friedrich Engels, *Socialism: Utopian and Scientific*, Moscow, 1968, pp.35-6. Here Engels states that the Marxist theory of the 'abolition of the state' was derived directly from Saint-Simon's idea of 'the future conversion of political rule over men into an administration of things and a direction of processes of production'.
136. See Rouchdi Fakkar, *L'influence internationale de Saint-Simon et de ses disciples. Bilan en Europe et portée extraeuropéenne*, Geneva, 1967, pp.170-71.
137. Cf. Felix Markham, Introduction to Henri de Saint-Simon, *Social Organization, the Science of Man and Other Writings*, op. cit., pp.xlvii-xlix.
138. Émile Durkheim, *Socialism*, ed. Alvin W. Gouldner, New York, 1962, p.235.

SELECTED WRITINGS 1802–25

PART I   SCIENCE AND THE PROGRESS OF THE HUMAN MIND   (1802–13)

I wanted to try, like everybody else, to systematise the philosophy of God. I wanted to descend in succession from the phenomenon universe to the phenomenon solar system, from there to the terrestrial phenomenon, and finally to the study of the species, considered as a dependency of the sublunar phenomenon, and to deduce from this study the laws of social organisation, the original and essential object of my research.

Saint-Simon to Olinde Rodrigues,
Not. hist., p.49.

1. LETTERS FROM AN INHABITANT OF GENEVA TO HIS CONTEMPORARIES

(Extracts from *Lettres d'un habitant de Genève à ses contemporains,* 1802-3)

FIRST LETTER

I am no longer young. I have observed and reflected actively throughout my life, and your happiness has been the object of my labours. I have conceived a plan which I think may be of use to you. I shall present it to you.

Open a subscription at the tomb of Newton. Subscribe, all of you, without distinction, whatever sum you wish.

Let each subscriber nominate three mathematicians, three physicists, three chemists, three physiologists, three authors, three painters, three musicians.

Renew both the subscription and the nomination each year, giving everyone complete freedom to nominate the same persons again.

Divide the proceeds of the subscription between the three mathematicians, three physicists, etc., who receive the most votes.

Invite the President of the Royal Society of London to receive this year's subscriptions.

In subsequent years entrust this honourable task to the donor of the largest subscription.

Instruct your nominees not to accept posts, honours, or money from any of you. Allow them complete freedom to employ their powers as they think fit.

Men of genius will then enjoy a reward worthy of themselves and of you. This reward alone can enable them to render all the services of which they are capable. It will become the ambition of the most energetic minds, diverting them from those activities which disturb your peace. Finally, by means of this measure, you will give leaders to those who work for the progress of your enlightenment. You will invest those leaders with enormous importance, and place at their disposal great financial power.

I have read this plan to a friend of mine who is a sensible man. I shall invite him to state in writing what he thinks of it, and shall let you know his opinion. It seems to me, my dear contemporaries, that this is the best way of making it easy for you to examine the idea.

Opinion of my Friend

You have invited me to give you my views on the plan you have presented. I shall do so with particular pleasure, since no attentive reader can fail to be struck by the purity of the author's mind, because the intention is sublime, and because it deserves to be favourably received by all sensible and thoughtful beings. Finally, the author's object is the happiness of humanity. He is working for it, and I admire him.

His ideas are both new and philanthropic. He is right to consider men of genius as the torches which illuminate humanity, the rulers as well as the ruled. And it is on the basis of a sound principle of justice that he urges humanity to act collectively to reward them. His plan is just as good in another respect: it is clear that by acting collectively to reward men of genius, humanity will divert them from their concern with the sectional interests of that group of men who by rewarding them paralyse a part of their power.

This plan creates the finest posts there have ever been, posts which will raise the man of genius to his true rank, that is to say, above all other men, even those with the greatest authority. The sight of these posts will stimulate genius. At last there will be prizes worthy of the love of glory, that passion which makes the hardships of study and deep thought tolerable, which provides the stamina needed to achieve fame in the sciences and the arts . . .

If I compare the elevated position in which humanity would place the man of genius with an academic chair, I see that the elect of humanity will find himself in a much more advantageous position than the academician. He will enjoy much greater independence, and will be able to develop his powers to the full without being hindered by any sectional interest. No false caution will be able to slow down the progress of his genius, or impede his work and happiness. He will be stimulated by the desire to retain his post. He will look anxiously at the work of his predecessors; he will want to surpass them, to abandon the beaten track and explore new ones. His enthusiasm will steadily increase until he attains his true goal, that of furthering the progress of the human mind.

Such will be the course followed by the genius when he is placed in a position of independence, whereas the academic mind will continue along quite a different path. It will always tend to maintain the views it has already established, regarding itself as the depository of truth. It would be attacking its own claim to infallibility if it changed its opinion. It will continue to cry heresy and remain intolerant rather than take a retrograde step for the sake of enlightenment and the happiness of humanity. With what fury the academies have persecuted men of genius who contested their opinions! Observe the progress of the academic mind: you will see how fierce and rampant it has been, how skilfully it has stifled debates which might have illuminated humanity whenever they threatened its own existence. This has been due to two causes: academicians are nominated for life, and they are dependent on the Government.

If you survey the history of the progress of the human mind, you will see that nearly all its great achievements have been due to isolated, often persecuted men. Invariably, those who have been made academicians have fallen asleep in their armchairs; and if they have written anything it has been with trepidation, only to produce fables of the truth. Only independence can foster the love of humanity and the desire for glory, the two forces which motivate the man of genius. Since the academician is a slave, is it surprising that he never produces anything? In spite of his slavery he thinks he is at the height of his glory. He is frightened to climb down, and this is precisely what prevents him from ascending.

If I look at the history of academies, I see that in England there has never been an academy, and only two societies have resembled academic institutions; whereas they have abounded in monarchies and even in states ruled by superstition and ignorance. But what country has produced more great men in every sphere than England? Where have more truths been discovered? Where have they been published more courageously or adopted more quickly? Where have useful discoveries been rewarded more generously? Love of corporal liberty and independence of thought have led this island to scorn and debar academies. As a citizen the Englishman recognises the dignity of his being. As a scientist he would be enraged if he had to prostitute himself in the service of men of power, and join a body which existed only under their protection . . .

I must admit, however, that the academies have been of some use. Their establishment, however imperfect, has been of some advantage to the sciences and the arts. I also recognise that some academicians have managed to preserve their vigour. But the academic method is too far behind current philosophical views to be preserved any longer. Now that the human mind has started to advance more boldly, it should be possible to abolish completely every kind of chain that restricts even the most learned academies. Humanity should not lose sight of the fact that it ought to reward collectively those torches which are so brilliant that they give light to the whole earth. It is the only way it can prevent them employing some of their power in the interests of a particular group who are prepared to reward them — a use of their power which not only has the disadvantage of restricting their views, but which also turns them into low adulators and dull pawns, which inspires them with a spirit of rivalry and unjustified suspicion of all other bodies which make useful discoveries, discoveries which are often abandoned immediately for fear of criticism and jealous persecution.

The plan strikes me as excellent from another point of view. What obstacles men of genius have had to surmount in the past! Invariably they are diverted from good ideas right at the start, because of work they have to do in order to survive. What experiments and travels necessary for the development of their ideas they have had to do without! How often they have been deprived of the collaborators they required in order to fully develop their work! How many good ideas have not been developed simply because they were not nurtured by help, encouragement, and rewards!

And if, in spite of all these difficulties, some men of genius have managed to become known and obtain a reward, that reward has never been adequate to cover the full cost of their work, to enable them to encourage young people with the necessary ability, and to provide for their needs when they have no money...

Any post or reward obtained by the man of genius invariably involves him in duties which distract him from his work, and, by confining him to one place, prevents him from travelling to see those things or those persons who might help him to make new discoveries. The inconstancy of the government which rewards him makes him worry about his future, and often obliges him to devote his attention simply to maintaining his post and securing his own position in it. And in spite of all foresight, often a war or some financial crisis results in the suppression of his fee or at least the suspension of its payment.

Finally, the man of genius, whose work requires absolute independence, is always to some extent dependent on the government which rewards him. He has to adopt its point of view, submit to the forms and usages it condones, and therefore relegate his own ideas to a secondary position instead of giving free rein to his imagination. He has to timidly contrive a way of bringing his ideas to light, showing himself in the end not so much as he really is, but as he is required to be. In short, he is made to pay dearly for his paltry reward.

As for the man of genius who agrees to accept the benevolence of one particular ruler, or of any other individual, his position is even more unfortunate because of the degradation to which he succumbs...

The plan contains one elementary idea which can serve as the basis of a general organisation. It thus presents humanity with a conception which will enable it to safely ascend one step on the ladder of abstraction.

How fortunate it is that the tomb of Newton, the seat of the assembly, should be in England, the country which has always been the refuge of men of genius and scientists persecuted in other countries; whose inhabitants have long been accustomed to opposing the Government's crimes against the independence of individuals and the liberty of the press.

We cannot speak of Newton without observing that the Government rewarded him with the post of Master of the Mint. Henceforth this citizen of the world was merely an Englishman applying himself to his job. This radiant star was presented to the multitude as an opaque body employed to reflect the rays of royal light.

Let us stress the fact that all men of genius who are given governmental posts lose their reality and their respectability. For in order to fulfil their duties they neglect the work of importance to humanity. And if they cannot resist the call of genius they often neglect their duties.

One can only avoid this dual hazard, troublesome for humanity, for the rulers, and for men of genius, by placing the latter in the one position which will satisfy the interests of all. They must remain *themselves,* and humanity must fully recognise this truth: these men are destined to be its torches, and not to be sold to particular interests which debase them and divert them from their true role . . .

I approve of the annual election and the provision for re-election. It will enable men of superior genius to remain for life, and provide their closest rivals with the greatest incentive.

The method of election is such that it will be impossible for particular prejudices to become strong enough to dominate the general interest.

There, my friend, you have my immediate reactions to your letter. Now I want to ask you two questions:

Will the plan be adopted?

If so, will it remedy humanity's present troubles, troubles which prudence prevents me from mentioning?

Reply

Thank you, my friend, for all the kind things you have said concerning my qualities as author of the plan which I have presented to you. The vigour with which you justified your approval, in the views which you bothered to put into writing, should have a considerable effect on the readers. This observation will, I hope, allay your fear that my plan will not be adopted. I have addressed this plan directly to humanity because it interests humanity collectively. But I have not succumbed to the mad hope of seeing it suddenly put into effect. I have always thought that success would depend on the efforts made by persons of great influence on this occasion. The best way to win their approval is to clarify the question as much as possible. That is the purpose of my addressing the different sections of humanity, which I divide into three classes: the first (to which you and I are honoured to belong) marches under the standard of the progress of the human mind, and is composed of the scientists, artists, and all men of liberal ideas; on the banner of the second is written 'no *innovation*' – all the property owners who do not belong to the first class are attached to the second.

The third class, which rallies to the word *equality*, comprises the rest of humanity.

To the first class I shall say: everyone with whom I have discussed my plan for humanity has approved it in the end, usually after quite a short discussion. The have all told me that they wish it success, but at the same time they have all revealed a fear that the plan will not succeed.

In view of the unanimity of their opinion, it seems likely that I shall find all men, or at least the majority, similarly disposed. If this prediction is correct, only the force of inertia will stand in the way of my ideas.

Scientists, artists, and also those of you who devote some of your power and resources to the progress of enlightenment: you are the section of humanity with the greatest intellectual energy, the section most able to appreciate a new idea, and most directly interested in the subscription's success. It is up to you to defeat the force of inertia. So, mathematicians; as you are the vanguard, begin!

Scientists, artists: look with your eye of genius at the present condition of the human mind. You will see that the sceptre of public opinion is in your hands. Seize it vigorously! You can secure your own happiness as well as that of your contemporaries. You can protect posterity against the evils which we have suffered and those which we still endure. Subscribe, all of you.

I shall then speak as follows to the property owners of the second class:

Gentlemen,

Compared with those who do not own property you are numerically very small. Why, then, are they willing to obey you? It is because your superior enlightenment enables you to combine your powers against them, and this is usually enough to give you the advantage in the natural and inevitable struggle which always exists between you and them.

Once this principle has been established, it is clearly in your interest to admit to your ranks all the non-proprietors who prove their intellectual superiority through their important discoveries. It is equally clear that as this is in the interest of the whole of your class, every member should contribute ...

As long as you do not adopt my proposal, gentlemen, each of you will be exposed, in your own particular country, to such calamities as have befallen those members of your class living in France. You need only reflect upon the course of events in that country since 1789 to be convinced of what I am saying. The first popular movement there was secretly stirred up by the scientists and artists. As soon as the insurrection assumed legitimacy, through its success, they declared themselves to be its leaders. When their attempt to destroy every institution which offended their self-esteem met with resistance, they aroused the ignorant even more, breaking all the links of subordination which checked the fiery passions of the non-proprietors. They succeeded in their aim: all the institutions they originally intended to destroy were inevitably overthrown. In short, they won the battle and you lost it. The cost of victory was high; but you who were defeated suffered even more. Some scientists and artists, victims of their army's insubordination, were massacred by their own soldiers. From the moral point of view they all had to endure your reproaches, as they appeared to be responsible for the atrocities committed against you, and for all the disorder their mob had caused through the savage impulse of their ignorance.

Once the misfortunes had reached their height, the remedy became possible. You offered no more resistance. The scientists and artists, having learned from experience, and recognising your superiority in enlightenment over the non-proprietors,* wanted you to be given the necessary power to regulate the organisation of society. The non-proprietors had to suffer almost the whole burden of the famine, which was the outcome of the extravagant measures to which they had been led. They were curbed.

The French population, although forced by circumstances to seek a return to order, could only be reorganised socially by a man of genius. Bonaparte undertook the task and succeeded.

In the course of presenting my ideas to you, I have expressed the view that you lost the battle. If you still have any doubts on this score, compare the esteem and the comforts enjoyed by French scientists and artists today with their situation before 1789.

Avoid a quarrel with these men, gentlemen, for you will be defeated in every war you allow them to fight against you. You will suffer more than they will during the hostilities, and peace will be to your disadvantage. Show your worth and do with a good grace what sooner or later the scientists, artists, and men of liberal ideas, reunited with

---

*I invite the reader to consider this idea: The property owners rule the non-proprietors, not because they are property owners; they have property and rule because they are collectively more enlightened than the non-proprietors.

the non-proprietors, would compel you to do. Subscribe, all of you. It is the only way to prevent the misfortunes I now see threatening you.

Now that this matter has been broached, let us have the courage not to leave it until we have glanced at the political situation in the most enlightened part of the globe.

In Europe the activity of governments is not at present troubled by any ostensible opposition from the governed. But in view of the climate of opinion in England, Germany, and Italy, it is easy to see that this calm will not last for long unless the necessary precautions are taken in time. For, gentlemen, the fact does not have to be concealed from you that the present crisis of the human mind is common to all enlightened peoples. The symptoms that were to be observed in France during that country's terrible explosion are now visible (to the intelligent observer) among the English and even the Germans.

Gentlemen, by adopting my proposal, you will reduce the crises which these peoples must undergo (and which no power on earth can prevent) to simple governmental and financial changes, and you will save them from the kind of general upheaval experienced by the French, an upheaval which upsets social relations so that anarchy, the greatest of all scourges, is free to play havoc until it finally plunges the whole nation into such misery that the souls of the most ignorant are filled with the desire to see order restored . . .

I now take pleasure in presenting this plan from a point of view which will appeal to your self-esteem. Think of yourselves as men who control the progress of the human mind. You can play this role, because through the subscription you can give the men of genius esteem and ease, and since it is a provision of this subscription that those who are elected should not occupy any governmental posts, you will thereby be protecting yourselves and the rest of humanity from the danger which would arise if they were given direct power.

Experience has proved that new, powerful, and just conceptions which serve as a basis for discoveries are, to begin with, usually mixed up with false ideas. In spite of this the inventor, if he had his way, would often apply these conceptions. This is one particular example of the kind of danger involved, but there is another which is absolutely general: Every time that a discovery, in order to be put into practice, requires a change in people's habits, it is a treasure which the existing generation should enjoy only through its affection for the generation destined to benefit from it. I shall end this short discourse, which I venture to address to you, gentlemen, by saying that if you remain in the second class it is only because you choose to do so, for you have the power to rise to the first.

Finally, I speak to the third class:

My Friends,

In England there are many scientists. Educated Englishmen have more respect for scientists than for kings. In England everyone knows how to read, write, and count. And, my friends, in this country the workers in the towns and even in the country eat meat every day!

In Russia, when a scientist displeases the Emperor, they cut off his nose and ears, and send him to Siberia. In Russia the peasants are as ignorant as their horses. And, my friends, the Russian peasants are badly fed, badly clothed, and badly beaten!

Hitherto the rich have done nothing except order you about. Force them to educate themselves and instruct you. They make you put your hands to work for them; make them put their heads to work for you. Do them a service by relieving them of the heavy weight of their boredom. They pay you with money; pay them with respect. Respect is a very precious currency. Fortunately, even the poorest man possesses some of it. If you spend what you have sensibly, your condition will quickly improve. So that you can judge my advice, and can appreciate the possible advantages of executing my plan for humanity, I shall have to elaborate it. I shall concentrate on those details which seem to me to be most essential.

A scientist, my friends, is a man who predicts. It is because science provides the means of making predictions that it is useful, and that scientists are superior to all other men. All known phenomena have been divided into different classes. Here is one classification which has been adopted: astronomical, physical, chemical, and physiological phenomena. Every man engaged in scientific work has a particular interest in one of these fields. Some of the predictions which astronomers make are known to you. For example, you know that they announce eclipses. But they make many other predictions with which you are not concerned, and which I shall not bother to discuss now. I just want to say a few words about the applications of this knowledge, the usefulness of which is well known to you. Astronomical predictions have enabled us to determine the exact positions of different points on the earth. They have also provided a means of navigating on the largest seas. You are familiar with some of the predictions of chemists. A chemist tells you what stone to use to make lime, and what stone not to use. He tells you how you can bleach your linen by using a certain quantity of ashes from one kind of tree, or a larger quantity from another tree. He tells you what to expect, by way of appearance and quality, when you mix two substances together.

When you are ill the physiologist (who is concerned with organic phenomena) tells you: you will try such a thing today, and tomorrow you will be in such a condition.

Do not think I am suggesting that scientists can predict everything.

They certainly cannot. I am indeed certain that they can predict accurately only a very small number of things. But you will agree that it is the scientists, working in their various fields, who are able to make the most predictions. We can be certain of that, since they only acquired their scientific reputations through the verifications which were made of their predictions. That, at least, is how things stand today; but it has not always been so. This requires us to look at the progress of the human mind . . .

The first phenomena to be observed systematically were astronomical phenomena. There is a good reason for this: they are the simplest phenomena. When astronomical studies first began, man confused the facts he observed with those he imagined, and through this elementary rigmarole he made the best calculations he could in order to satisfy all the demands of prediction. He then successively relinquished those facts created by his imagination, and finally, after a great deal of work, he was able to adopt a certain method of perfecting this science. Astronomers no longer accepted any facts which were not verified by observation. They chose the best system of linking these facts, and they have not put a foot wrong in science since then . . .

Because chemical phenomena are more complex than astronomical phenomena, it was a long time before man began to study them. In chemistry he repeated the same mistakes he had made in the study of astronomy. Finally, however, the chemists rid themselves of the alchemists.

Physiology is still at the undeveloped stage through which the astronomical[1] and chemical sciences have passed. The physiologists must expel the philosophers, moralists, and metaphysicians, just as the astronomers expelled the astrologers, and the chemists expelled the alchemists.

My friends, we ourselves are organic bodies. It is by considering our social relations as physiological phenomena that I have conceived the present plan; and by using ideas borrowed from the system of linking physiological facts I shall prove that the plan is a good one.

A fact proved by a long series of observations is that every man experiences to a certain extent the desire to dominate all other men.*
Reason clearly confirms one thing: every man who is not isolated is both actively and passively involved in relations of domination with other men. I urge you to make use of the small degree of domination you exercise over the rich. But before going any further I must examine a fact which grieves you greatly. You may say:

*There are two ways for a man to achieve superiority. One of these is in accordance with the general interest as well as his self-interest. My aim is to adorn this route and to scatter thorns along the other one.

we are ten, twenty, a hundred times more numerous than the property owners; yet the property owners dominate us much more than we dominate them. I concede, my friends, that it is most vexing. But you must observe that the property owners, although inferior in numbers, are more enlightened than you, and that for the sake of the general good, domination should be proportionate to enlightenment. Look at what happened in France when your comrades were in control: they caused a famine.

Let me return to my proposal. By adopting and then executing it, you will place permanently in the hands of humanity's twenty-one most enlightened men the two great instruments of domination: respect and money. For a thousand reasons the result will be rapid progress in the sciences. It is recognised that every scientific advance makes the study of the sciences that much easier. Thus, those who, like yourselves, can devote only a small amount of time to their education will be able to learn more, and by becoming more educated they will lessen the domination exercised over them by the rich. You will not have to wait long, my friends, for favourable results . . .

Let us now consider the artists.

On Sundays eloquence charms you. It gives you pleasure to read a well-written book, to see beautiful paintings and statues, or to listen to a captivating piece of music. It takes a great deal of work to speak or write in an entertaining manner, to create a pleasing painting or statue, or to compose interesting music. Is it not perfectly fair, my friends, that you should reward the artists who fill your leisure time with the most intellectually satisfying pleasures by stimulating the most delicate aspects of your feelings?

Subscribe, all of you, my friends. However small your individual subscriptions, there are so many of you that the total sum will be considerable. Besides, those who are elected will be held in such great esteem that their strength will be incalculable. The rich, you will see, will strive to distinguish themselves in the sciences and the arts when that is the route which leads to the highest degree of respect . . .

If you accept my plan you will have only one problem to face: the choice. I shall tell you, my friends, what I would do. I would ask all the mathematicians I know, who, in their opinion, are the three best mathematicians, and I would nominate the three mathematicians who received the most votes from those persons I consulted. I would do the same for the physicists, etc.

My friend,

After dividing humanity into three sections, and presenting each of them with the arguments in favour of my plan, I shall now address my contemporaries collectively, and present them with my reflections on the French Revolution.

The suppression of the privileges of birth, the strain of which broke the bonds of social organisation, was not an obstacle to social reorganisation; but the frequent appeal to all members of society to assume the functions of a deliberate assembly was unsuccessful. Apart from the terrible atrocities to which such an application of the principle of equality* naturally led, by placing power in the hands of the ignorant, it finally gave rise to an absolutely impracticable form of government under which there were so many rulers (including, in the end, the non-proprietors) that the labour of the governed was insufficient to maintain them. This led to a result which was absolutely contrary to the most steadfast desire of the non-proprietors: to pay low taxes.

Here is an idea which seems sound: The primary needs of life are the most important. The non-proprietors cannot satisfy them completely. To a physiologist it is clear that their most steadfast desire should be to decrease taxation or increase wages, which amounts to the same thing.

I believe that all social classes would benefit from this organisation: spiritual power in the hands of the *savants*; temporal power in the hands of the property owners; the power to elect the leaders of humanity in the hands of everyone; the reward of the rulers, respect.

Let us continue tomorrow, my friend. I think that is enough for today.

Is it an apparition? Is it only a dream? I do not know; but I am certain that I did experience what I am now about to recount.

Last night I heard these words:

'Rome will renounce its claim to be the headquarters of my Church. The Pope, the cardinals, bishops, and priests will cease speaking in my name. Man will be filled with shame for his ungodliness in recognising such improvident men as my representatives.

'I forbade Adam to make the distinction between good and evil. He disobeyed me. I expelled him from paradise, but I provided his descendants with the means of appeasing my wrath: If they work to perfect themselves through the knowledge of good and evil, I shall improve their condition. The day will come when I shall make a paradise of the earth.

'All men who have founded religions received their power from me,

---

*The revolutionaries applied the principle of equality to the Negroes. If they had consulted the physiologists, they would have learned that the Negro, because of his organic structure, is not capable of achieving the same educational level, of becoming as intelligent as the European.

but they did not clearly understand my instructions. They all believed that I shared my divine knowledge with them. Their self-esteem led them to draw a dividing-line between good and evil in the most trifling aspects of man's life. But they all neglected the most essential part of their mission: to found an establishment which will provide human intelligence with the quickest way of returning indefinitely to the care of my divine providence. They all forgot to warn my priests that I would take away from them the power to speak in my name once they were no longer more learned than their flock, and allowed themselves to be dominated by the temporal power.

'Hear this: I have placed *Newton* at my side, to control enlightenment and command the inhabitants of all planets. Hear this also: the man who proved himself to be the greatest enemy of enlightenment *(Robespierre)* has been hurled into darkness, and is destined to remain there for eternity, agent and object of my vengeance.

'The assembly of the twenty-one elect of humanity will be called the Council of Newton. The Council of Newton will represent me on earth. It will divide humanity into four divisions: English, French, German, Italian. Each division will have its own council, with the same composition as the council-in-chief. Every man, in whatever part of the globe he lives, will be associated with one of these divisions, and will subscribe for both the council-in-chief and his own divisional council. Every man who fails to obey this commandment will be regarded and treated by others as an animal. Women will be allowed to subscribe and stand for election. After their deaths the faithful will receive the treatment they earned for themselves during their lives.

'Members of the divisional councils will have to be approved by the council-in-chief, which will admit only those men who have demonstrated the most superior knowledge, each in the particular field for which he has been elected.

'The inhabitants of any part of the globe, whatever its location and size, may at any time establish their own section within a particular division, and elect their own Council of Newton. The members of this council will have to be approved by the divisional council. Permanent delegations from the divisional councils will attend the council-in-chief. Similarly, delegations from the sectional councils will attend their divisional council. These delegations will consist of seven members, one from each class.[2]

'In every council the mathematician who receives the most votes will be president.

'Every council will be divided into two divisions: the first will be composed of the first four classes, and the second of the last three classes. When the second division assembles separately, its president will be the author who receives the most votes.

'Every council will have a temple built containing a mausoleum in honour of Newton. This temple will be divided into two parts: the one containing the mausoleum will be decorated by the artists, who should use all the resources at their disposal; the other part will be constructed and decorated so as to give men an idea of the eternal fate which awaits all those who hinder the progress of the sciences and the arts. The mausoleum of Newton will lead down into an underground temple.

'The first division will control the form of worship inside the mausoleum. No human beings other than members of the first divisions of the councils will be allowed to enter the underground temple without the president's express permission.

'The second division of the council will control the form of worship outside the mausoleum, making sure that a majestic and brilliant spectacle is presented. Every distinguished service to humanity, every action which has been of great use to the propagation of the faith will be honoured. The assembled council will decide what honours are to be awarded.

'All the faithful who live at least one day's walk away from a temple will go down into the mausoleum of Newton once each year through an entrance consecrated for that purpose. Children will be brought there by their parents as soon as possible after their birth. Everyone who fails to obey this commandment will be regarded by the faithful as an enemy of the religion.

'Any mortal who enters the mausoleum may be transported to another planet if Newton considers it to be necessary for my purpose.

'Laboratories, workshops, and a college will be built in the vicinity of the temple. All magnificence will be confined to the temple. The laboratories and workshops, the college, and the residences of councillors and council delegations will be built and decorated in a simple fashion. The library will never contain more than five hundred volumes.

'Each year every councillor will nominate five persons:

'First, a deputy who will have the right to a seat and a deliberative vote when the councillor who nominates him is absent.

'Secondly, a minister, chosen from the five hundred most generous subscribers, who will officiate at major ceremonies.

'Thirdly, one person whose work has contributed to the progress of the sciences and the arts.

'Fourthly, one person who has made useful applications of the sciences and the arts.

'Fifthly, one person for whom the councillor has a particular affection.

'These nominations will not be valid until they have been approved by a majority of the council, and they will be renewed each year. Nominees will hold office for one year only, after which they will be eligible for re-election.

'The president of each council will nominate a guardian of the holy territory on which the temple and its out-buildings stand. The guardian will be an agent of the police. He will be the treasurer, administering all expenses according to the orders of the council. He will be chosen from the hundred most generous subscribers, and will have the right to a council seat. His nomination will not be valid until it has been approved by a majority of the council.

'Distinctive badges will be made for the councillors and their nominees. They will be made in such a way that they can be shown or hidden according to the wishes of those who wear them.

'The council-in-chief will have an office in every division, and will reside in a different division each year.

'The founder of this religion will be a man of great power.[3] As a reward he will have the right to join all the councils and preside over them. He will retain this right for life, and after his death he will be buried in the tomb of Newton. The faithful will give him the title Captain of the Newtonian Guard.

'All men will work. They will all regard themselves as workers attached to a workshop whose task is to raise human intelligence to the level of my divine providence. The Council-in-Chief of Newton will supervise this work, and will do its best to achieve a thorough understanding of the effects of universal gravitation, which is the single law to which I have subjected the universe.

'The council-in-chief will have the right to increase or decrease the number of divisional councils.

'All the Councils of Newton will respect the division between spiritual and temporal power.

'As soon as elections for the council-in-chief and the divisional councils have taken place, Europe will be for ever rid of the scourge of war.

'Hear this: Europeans are the children of Abel. Asia and Africa are inhabited by the descendants of Cain. Just observe how bloodthirsty these Africans are. Look at the indolence of the Asians. These impure men gave up their first attempt to raise themselves to the level of my divine providence. Europeans will unite their forces and free their Greek brothers from the domination of the Turks. The founder of the religion will be commander-in-chief of the armies of the faithful. These armies will subject the children of Cain to the religion, and cover the entire earth with defences for the protection of the members of the Councils of Newton, who will make all the

journeys they consider necessary for the progress of the human mind.'
Sleep.
When I awoke I found what you have just read engraved quite clearly on my memory.

SECOND LETTER

It was God who had spoken to me. Could a man have invented a religion superior to all those that have ever existed? It would first of all have to be supposed that none of them was of divine origin. Look at the religion revealed to me! See how clear its basic principle is, and how certain it is to be executed. The obligation is imposed on everyone to constantly use their personal powers for the benefit of humanity. The hands of the poor will continue to nourish the rich, but the rich man is commanded to put his brain to work, and if his brain is not up to the task, he will then have to work with his hands. For Newton will certainly not allow any workers to remain useless on this planet (which is one of the nearest to the sun).

We shall no longer have a religion whose ministers have the right to elect the leaders of humanity. All the faithful will nominate their guides, every year. And the qualities by which they will recognise God's chosen representatives will no longer be insignificant virtues such as chastity and continence; they will be real talents, the *greatest* talents.

I shall not prolong this subject. Every man who believes in revelation will inevitably be convinced that only God could have provided humanity with a means of forcing each of its members to follow the rule of brotherly love.

P.S. I intend to write you a letter in which I shall consider religion as a human invention, as the only kind of political institution which promotes the general organisation of humanity. Because of the risks involved in inviting you to reduce the rulers to a position of secondary importance,* I shall take the precaution of telling you here and now of the most important idea which will be put forward in my work.

Just suppose that you had acquired the knowledge of how matter is distributed at some particular time, and that you had made a plan of the universe, using numbers to show the quantity of matter in each of its parts. It should then be clear to you that by applying the law of universal gravitation to this plan you could predict (as exactly as the state of mathematical knowledge would allow) all subsequent

*Temporal power will naturally be reduced to a position of secondary importance when spiritual power is placed in the hands of the scientists.

evolution within the universe.

This supposition will enable your intelligence to consider all phenomena from the same point of view; for if you examine, on your plan of the universe, that part of space which you occupy, you will not see any difference between those phenomena which you call moral and those you call physical.

The information I have just given you is sufficient to enable the mathematicians to develop the idea.

I am happy to say, my dear contemporaries, that the most important part of my work has reached a successful conclusion now that I have placed it in your hands. You now have a plan of general organisation requiring only minor changes of habit for its execution, since every part of it proposes only modifications to accepted ideas. I have just told the scientists of the viewpoint I adopted in order to formulate this plan; so whatever happens to me, if my conception is good, you will be able to make use of it. Should a major obstacle prevent me from quickly putting down these intermediate ideas, it will be easy for any man with a clear understanding of the concept of universal gravitation, and a knowledge of physiology (including its observations on the progress of the human mind) to complete the task.

[Pereire (1925), pp.3-42, 45-69.]

2. EXTRACT ON SOCIAL ORGANISATION

(*Extrait d'un ouvrage sur l'organisation sociale*, 1804)

The aim of this work is to apply the idea of Condorcet.[4]

Let us suppose that an enlightened people inhabits an island with a radius of ten leagues, and let us give this ideal society the following organisation.

I

The nation's members vote each year, as individuals, to elect the five best physicists, mathematicians, astronomers, chemists, physiologists, and authors.

These thirty scientists are joined by five artists and ten persons chosen from industry.

The assembly of these forty-five men of genius will be called *Parliament of Improvement*. The mathematician who receives the most votes will be its president.

When making his nomination every member of the nation will donate a sum of money proportionate to his means, which will then be placed at the disposal of those who are elected.

Parliament will dismiss from office any functionaries who abuse their authority. It will control public education. It will reward those who further the progress of the sciences, the arts, and industry. It will make regulations to govern the exercise of these powers.

There will be three grades of salary for Members of Parliament. The artists will receive twice as much as the scientists. The persons chosen from industry will receive twice as much as the artists. The scientists will be given low salaries, the exact amount to be decided by Parliament.

Parliament will use the money placed at its disposal, first, to maintain and improve educational institutions, and increase their number; and secondly, to give financial rewards to those who make discoveries useful to the sciences, the arts, and industry. The financial rewards given by Parliament to those who make discoveries will be small.

Parliament will have a list printed giving details of the various kinds of work useful to society. Upon completion of their education young people will be required to enlist in one class of employment.

Every year all individuals will nominate the five persons who have made most progress in their class of employment. The five who are elected will divide their class into three grades, placing each person in the first, second, or third grade according to his ability.

It will be the duty of those who are elected to wear a distinctive badge showing the class in which they have made progress. Each of them may authorise his wife to wear a similar insignia.

Men and women will belong to separate classes.

Everyone will be free to move from one class to another.

II

Those property owners who are self-sufficient will be collectively invested with governmental power, which they will be obliged to sub-divide into legislative, executive, and judicial branches. They will exercise these three powers as they think fit.

Property owners will fill every post nominated by the governmental power, but will not receive any salary. Those who squander public money will have their property confiscated by the national treasury.

No property owner will be eligible for office who, upon completion of his education, does not receive a *Certificate of Ability* from the board of his school.

III

If the island were twice as large and had double the population, the inhabitants would be divided into two societies, each with the organisation outlined above.

Each year the two societies would elect a parliament chosen from their combined populations, which would exercise in the general interest of the island the same powers exercised in matters of more local interest by the parliaments of each society.

This arrangement could be applied to three, four, five, in fact to a number of societies which need not be specified here. But beyond this number two divisions would have to be formed. There would then have to be a general election for a supreme parliament, an election in each division for the chief divisional parliament, and an election for the parliament of each society.

* * * *

After a long respite the human mind is once again moving forward.

The seventeenth century produced men of genius in every field. It gave birth to Newton.

In the eighteenth century the exact sciences made great progress; superstitious ideas were crushed.

What will happen in the nineteenth century? The science of social organisation will become a positive science. Its theory will be based on the general observations of *Condorcet*.

All enlightened peoples will adopt the view that men of genius should be given the highest social standing.

[Pereire (1925), pp.87-93.]

3. INTRODUCTION TO THE SCIENTIFIC STUDIES OF THE 19th CENTURY

(Extracts from *Introduction aux travaux scientifiques du XIXe siècle,* 2 vols., 1807-8)

PREFACE

... I have conceived a plan which, if put into effect, will bring glory to the French nation. Its rival[5] will be compelled to recognise that France has earned the title of great nation, and that it is worthy of marching under the orders of the great *Napoleon.*

Descartes tore the world's sceptre out of the hands of imagination and placed it in the hands of reason. He said: *'Give me matter and motion, I will make you a world.'* He dared to attempt an explanation of the mechanism of the universe. The system of vortices is admirable, considered from the standpoint one must adopt in order to envisage it. This system had the inestimable merit of being the first purely general observation. It did not involve a single theological idea.[6]

Newton must not be considered superior to Descartes; he must not even be thought his equal. He never progressed beyond the world of science discovered by that great man whom the French have the good fortune to number among their forefathers.

There are two kinds of scientific study: *The Search for Facts,* and *Reasoning Based on Facts,* that is, the improvement of general theories. The improvement of scientific theory was Descartes' chief concern. The School[7] extended the approach bequeathed to it by Descartes beyond its natural limits. It lost its way in the labyrinths of metaphysics. It was totally neglecting the search for facts when Locke and Newton appeared.

Locke and Newton assumed a new approach: they looked for facts and found them in abundance. One discovered the fact of gravitation; the other the fact of the human mind's perfectibility.

The School became Newtonian-Lockeian. For almost a century it has utilised the approach bequeathed to it by those two great men. It has been preoccupied with the search for facts, and has neglected theory.

For the sake of scientific progress, the happiness of humanity, and the glory of the French nation, the Institute[8] must work to improve theory. It must resume the approach of Descartes...

My first two volumes should be regarded only as an introduction. Only after reading them will the reader be able to make a first judgement of my plan. I shall begin by giving a summary of the human mind's advance from Descartes to the establishment of the new dynasty. I shall identify the general ideas produced by the most notable men of the last two centuries. Citations of this kind cannot be abridged; I shall therefore give them in their entirety. I may be criticised at first; but I will be commended later. People will appreciate how useful it is to have a collection of the general ideas which now possess the force of law in the School. They will realise how important it is, for the progress of science, to link these ideas, and will recognise that it is impossible to create this link in a satisfactory manner without reconciling the ideas, without presenting them from a common point of view, without including them in the same work, in the same volume . . .

SURVEY OF THE SCIENTIFIC STUDIES OF THE SEVENTEENTH CENTURY

In the first years of the seventeenth century men began to think rationally about the mechanism of their intelligence, basing their reasoning on observations. It was in these circumstances that Bacon took up his pen. His works mark the most recent great age in the history of science. He had an understanding of good method. He was particularly interested in observing the workings of intelligence. He knew how to distinguish between the synthetic and analytic approaches, and through the use of ingenious comparisons he brought this abstract observation to the attention of the most ordinary minds.

Bacon followed the synthetic course: he adopted the viewpoint of general science; he embraced the whole of science at a single glance; he methodically divided and sub-divided the whole of acquired knowledge; he developed, in his own words, a new organ[9] of our intelligence.

Finally, Bacon grasped and presented in outline these two ideas:

1. That it was necessary to proceed to the organisation of a new scientific system.

2. That it was necessary to proceed synthetically to the organisation of this system.

Descartes began to write shortly after Bacon. He followed the impulse given by that innovator in general philosophy; he clarified his sketches; he perfected his plan and put it into effect; he proceeded, by means of *Synthesis,* to the organisation of a new scientific system; he created the system of vortices, a sublime conception to which we owe the rise of the positive sciences.*

It was Descartes who organised the scientific revolution. It was he who drew the dividing-line between ancient and modern sciences, and who planted the flag around which the physicists rallied to attack the theologians. He tore the world's sceptre out of the hands of imagination, and placed it in the hands of reason. He established the famous principle: *Man should believe only those things avowed by reason and confirmed by experience* — a principle which crushed superstition and changed the moral face of our planet.

Descartes began by proving that all knowledge acquired before him had only a material value. He gave this proof the modest title of *Methodical Doubt*. He then demonstrated, with great vigour, the boldness of his own attitude of mind: *Give me* (he said) *matter and movement, I will make you a world.*

Descartes, who was as shrewd as he was strong, knew how to shelter himself from the persecutions of the clergy without restricting the development of his thought, without cramping his output. He formally declared that he recognised the existence of God, but allotted no role to revealed ideas. He did not base any of his beliefs on them, since

*Many people regard Descartes and Bacon as two rival philosophers, inventors— each in his own way — of projects for the organisation of a new scientific system. These people draw a parallel between the works of these two authors. They compare their writings and accord superiority to the one who seems to them to have best dealt with the question.

This approach, adopted by the School, does not seem to me to be a good one.

Bacon was born on 22 January 1561; Descartes on 2 April 1596. Thus, Bacon was 35 years old when Descartes was born; and 51 when Descartes reached his sixteenth year.[10]

I now ask:

1. Is it possible that Descartes conceived the project for changing the scientific system before he reached the age of sixteen?

2. Can one conceive of the possibility that Descartes, during the course of his education, had no knowledge of the ideas expounded by Bacon?

To the first question I reply:

The project for organising a new scientific system was the greatest result achieved by combining the most abstract ideas. In the nature of things the first formation of such a plan could not possibly have taken place in the brain of an individual under sixteen years of age.

I reply to the second question:

Bacon's principal works had been published for more than ten years when Descartes left the college at La Flèche; and I believe that every sensible person who takes the trouble to think about it will agree that the young Descartes, before leaving college, eager as he was for grand ideas, could not possibly have ignored the project conceived by Bacon, the latter having appealed to all the world's scientists to execute that project.

General ideas may be compared to musk: It is not necessary either to see or touch musk in order to perceive its smell. As soon as a new general idea is expounded, human thought is subject to its influence.

he regarded them as mere scientific sketches produced by men of genius at a time when humanity was still in its infancy and therefore ignorant.

Until the end of the seventeenth century the School followed the impulse given to it by Bacon and Descartes. If one takes a general view of its work during these hundred years one finds:

1. That it revealed the most essential faults of the old system, that is, the religious system.

2. That it constructed the first scaffolding for the erection of a new system.

SURVEY OF THE SCIENTIFIC STUDIES OF THE EIGHTEENTH CENTURY

Our eyes grow tired when we look at things for a long time from the same point of view. Then we no longer discover new relations between them, or even see clearly the relations we have already observed.

The School had been examining things *a priori* for nearly a century. It was tired. The scientific eyes of humanity were no longer able to see new relations; science was no longer progressing. Any number of principles were laid down, but no consequence was drawn from them; systems multiplied. The scientific workshop laboured spiritedly to organise an ideal world, and neglected the study of the real one. Metaphysics was its sole concern; physics had been totally lost from view; facts were no longer observed. It was in these circumstances that Locke and Newton took up their pens. In observing the scientific method they adopted, one is inclined to think that they argued and agreed as follows, before embarking on their careers:

Argument which I imagine took place between Locke and Newton

The *Enterprise* undertaken by Descartes could not be completed by a single man, or by a single generation, or even by the combined efforts of several generations during one century. It is the most important, the most immense enterprise that the human mind could undertake. Consequently, it will require the greatest amount of time for its execution. The organisation of a new scientific system demands various kinds of operations. It requires the same operations to be repeated, for each particular operation can at first serve only as an outline. A general outline was the first operation that was required, and Descartes carried it out. He made a very good job of it: his system of vortices is an admirable general outline of the new scientific system.

Descartes fixed, with great precision, the goal towards which the organisers of the new system must move, by saying: *Man should believe only those things avowed by reason and confirmed by experience.*

Descartes advanced directly towards the goal he had determined. He got as far as he could along the route which led in that direction. The system of vortices contains nothing offensive to reason. Descartes thus fulfilled the first condition he had laid down.

The system of vortices does not give a satisfactory explanation of particular facts; that is to say, this system is not confirmed by experience. Thus, Descartes did not satisfy his second condition. This imperfection in the system of vortices should not astonish us. It is a result of the rule of nature which does not allow experience to precede invention.

The treasury of human knowledge was still not sufficiently stocked with observed facts. There was not yet sufficient acquired material for the building of a new scientific structure when Descartes tried to erect one. Thus, it was not possible for this philosopher to be completely successful in his enterprise.

The structure built by Descartes must be demolished, but the materials used in its construction must be carefully preserved. New materials must be added to them: it is necessary to work for the discovery of new facts, and to postpone the building of the structure until all the materials are available. In short, it is necessary to stop looking at things *a priori* and to examine them *a posteriori*. It is necessary to abandon the synthetic approach for the moment, and to adopt the analytic approach . . .

Locke and Newton left the beaten path to open up a new route. They abandoned the scientific heights to descend to the plain, which they took as their point of departure.

Newton saw an apple fall, and from this single fact he rose by degrees to the idea of universal gravitation.

Locke's attention was fixed first of all on our most direct sensations, those derived immediately from our primary needs. He then ascended from abstraction to abstraction until he reached the conception of the human mind's perfectibility . . .

FIRST CATEGORY OF SCIENTIFIC STUDIES OF THE EIGHTEENTH CENTURY

In my view the four most noteworthy scientific works of the eighteenth century (written and published after those of Locke and Newton) were:

On the one hand, the *Theory of Functions* and the *Celestial*

Mechanics;

On the other hand, the *Treatise on Sensations* and the *Sketch of an Historical Picture of the Progress of the Human Mind.*

The first two works form a sequel to those of Newton. The other two are a continuation of Locke's.

Theory of Functions[11]

The new, powerful, and sound conceptions which form in the brains of men of genius are always mixed up with false ideas. The length of time needed for purification is proportionate to the discovery's importance. Newton based his fine invention of the calculus of fluxions on the idea of infinite smallness, so combining in a very faulty manner ideas from physics and pure mathematics.

M. de la Grange succeeded in separating the tares from the wheat: he organised a theory of the calculus of fluxions not involving a single idea from physics . . .

Celestial Mechanics[12]

M. de la Grange perfected the mechanism of the calculus invented by Newton. M. de la Place generalised and perfected the applications of this calculus . . .

M. de la Place's work on the theory of the moon was sufficient to earn him a place in the temple of glory.

The theory of the moon was incomplete. Astronomers had long since established, through numerous observations, an irregularity in the mean movement of this satellite. But none of them had determined the cause of this irregularity or its exact size. It was M. de la Place who filled this important gap.

I am constantly filled with admiration for the way M. de la Place proved that the apparently irregular movement of the moon was in fact a very regular movement; that this movement was a direct result of universal gravitation; and that this fact, usually regarded as an exception to Newton's theory, should on the contrary be seen as the one fact on which that theory was most firmly based . . .

Treatise on Sensations[13]

A careful reading of Locke's works shows that this scientist made a thorough study of anatomy, medicine, and physiology, and that he raised himself to the level of knowledge reached in every branch of organic physics. Locke clearly set out to incorporate phenomena of the so-called moral order, that is, intellectual phenomena, into the category of physical ideas. That Locke set himself this aim is clear from the way he attacked, fought, and vanquished animal automatism and all innate, revealed, inspired ideas. He even attempted to link the last series of observations on animals with the first series on vegetables.

In Locke's time the number of believers in revealed ideas was still very large. The clergy, although divided into two groups which made unmerciful war on each other, was still very powerful. The Protestant and Catholic clergies were united through their common interest in opposition to the establishment of the new scientific system. Both believed that the laity should be under their subjection. In short, theologians (considering laymen as their subjects) wanted to prohibit them from examining fundamental ideas. They wanted them to continue believing that the priests had received from a supernatural, that is, incomprehensible power the ability to solve all the great scientific questions.

Locke, whose major aim was the establishment of the new scientific system, and who worked to collect materials for this great edifice, was forced to use his ingenuity. He could not give free rein to his thought; he was forced (in order to protect himself from the persecutions of the clergy) to begin each part of his proof of the non-existence of revealed ideas with a formal declaration of his belief in those same ideas . . .

By the time Condillac took up his pen, the clergy had lost much of the power they enjoyed in Locke's time. Condillac, exposed to fewer dangers, was bolder. Following in Locke's footsteps he was able to grasp details which had escaped that transcendent genius when he first followed that route. Condillac was less ambiguous than Locke.

Condillac's attitude at the moment of his greatest intellectual erethism is well portrayed in the first pages of the analytic abstract of his *Treatise on Sensations,* which is at the beginning of this treatise in Ch. Houée's edition. I shall quote it. Condillac deceived himself about its value. He considered himself to be a genius of the highest order, whereas he was really only a commentator on Locke . . .

Sketch of an Historical Picture of the Progress of the Human Mind[14]

In his philosophical essays Locke discussed the development of individual intelligence and the advancement of the human mind.

Condillac commented on Locke's views concerning individual intelligence.

Condorcet attempted to base a system on the idea of advancement. He developed Locke's sketch on unlimited perfectibility . . .*

*Doctors Price and Priestley[15] began to clarify Locke's ideas on the perfectibility of the human mind. Condorcet profited from their work.

I shall often mention Condorcet's study, and shall examine it in depth in the first part of my second work. This study, although faulty in all its details, is one of the finest creations of the human mind.

Locke's observation, clarified by Doctors Price and Priestley, became an instrument of observation in the hands of Condorcet...

SECOND CATEGORY OF SCIENTIFIC STUDIES OF THE EIGHTEENTH CENTURY

The School is not only engaged in studies to further the progress of science. There is a law to which scientists, like all other men, are subject. *All men, every group of men, whatever their nature, aspire to increase their power.* The soldier with his sabre, the diplomat with his cunning, the geometer with his compasses, the chemist with his retorts, the physiologist with his scalpel, the hero through his deeds, the philosopher through his calculations: all strive to achieve command. From different sides they scale the plateau at the summit of which is to be found the fantastic being who commands all nature, and whom every strongly constituted man aspires to replace.

I have included in the first category those studies which aim directly to further scientific progress. In this second category I include the attempts made by the new School to improve its social existence.

I shall now discuss the great struggle which took place in the old School, and the splendid victory won by the scientists, who were innovators, over the clergy who defended the old system, the system conceived by humanity when its imagination was at the height of its power, and its capacity for reason at its lowest ebb.

Towards the middle of the eighteenth century *Diderot* and *d'Alembert* appealed to all supporters of the ideas of Bacon, Descartes, Locke, and Newton. They united them, placing themselves at the head of this army of physicists for an attack on the theologians.

Let us look at the situation when the preliminary discourse to the Encyclopaedia was published.[16] Let us undertake a new examination of the development of science since Bacon. Let us consider the facts we have summarised from a new point of view. So far we have been plotting the progress of science. Let us now consider the successes of those scientists who worked for the organisation of the new system.

At the end of the sixteenth century Bacon provoked a revolt of lay scholars against the established scientific college, that is, the clergy. Bacon planted a flag in new scientific terrain, and the physicists rallied round it.

At the beginning of the seventeenth century Descartes, by providing the system of physics with a provisional organisation, raised a tall beacon on this same land, and all those born after him who were privileged to be involved in organisation gathered around this beacon.

A few years after the death of Descartes, Louis XIV established an Academy of Sciences composed solely of physicists and geometers.[17]

From the moment of its creation the Academy of Sciences began a siege of the fortress which held the theologians.

I imagine the principles of the theological system, transformed into solids, to be the ramparts of this fortification, with the refugee clergy enclosed within. I see the physicists as an army attempting to breach the ramparts. Finally, I see Diderot and d'Alembert as the generals under whose orders the physicists made a general assault on the fortress defended by the theologians.

Leaving aside all metaphor, it is certain that since the appearance of Bacon the importance of the physicists has been continually increasing, while that of the theologians has suffered a continual decline. But it is equally certain that in 1750, which is the period I am discussing, the clergy still enjoyed great power and enormous wealth. The Sorbonne was still the only established scientific tribunal;[18] the clergy were still in charge of public education . . .

I picture this old system as a huge building crowned by a tall edifice, just as a steeple towers over a church. They physicists began by demolishing the steeple; but in 1750 all the lower part of the old system remained intact. It was this lower part in which the masses lived, and into which the clergy descended, continuing to exert control over the common people. It was this part that the physicists attempted to demolish under the guidance of Diderot and d'Alembert.

The Encyclopaedists, I am saying, worked much more effectively for the demolition of the old system than for the construction of the new one . . .

ON THE DIVISION OF HISTORY

Hitherto, *history* has been badly divided. The different successive periods recognised by the School are very unequal in length, and the epochs to which these divisions correspond are not based on the general series of the development of human intelligence, but are always determined according to secondary or local events. Historians have fixed their attention on political, religious, or military facts; they have not adopted a sufficiently elevated point of view. Condorcet was the first writer to sketch the history of the human mind, and the philanthropic passion which dominated him fascinated his eyes. He did not provide us with the outline of a history; he sketched a novel. He did not see things as they are, but as he wanted them to be.

Until the age of Socrates none of the four peoples descended from the plateau of Tartary achieved any great superiority over the others. Each of them made similar progress. Each used its own powers to rise to the conception of divinity, but none conceived this idea very clearly. Socrates was the first known man to firmly imprint a unitary character on this idea, the first to proclaim that the idea of *God* should be regarded as an instrument of scientific calculation. He was the founder of general science. Before Socrates ideas were only bundled together. He was the first to begin to link them systematically.

Since Socrates scientific study has been pursued without interruption. The seventh, eighth, ninth, tenth, eleventh, and twelfth centuries, which collectively have been called the Middle Ages, were not centuries of general barbarity. Certain peoples which we call barbarian were in fact very civilised, and cleared the scientific ground which we cultivate today.

As Socrates was the first man to rise to a general point of view, his works clearly mark the division between ancient history and modern history.

Thus, history may be divided into two major parts:
The history of the human race until Socrates... *Ancient History*
From Socrates to the present... *Modern History*
... I propose to divide ancient history into two parts: the first from the origins of the human race to Moses; the second from Moses to Socrates.

For the historian what happened before Moses is hidden behind an impenetrable veil, a thick veil which only the eye of the physicist-physiologist can pierce.

A very weak light illuminates the historical events from Moses to Socrates. Tradition leaves large gaps. The chronicle is very incomplete. However, the historian could present quite an interesting picture of these ten centuries during which the Egyptians paved the way for the artistic successes of the Greeks. But there will never be a good account of this period, since any man who thinks he has sufficient ability is bound to prefer to study modern history. The best painters always put their brushes to work on the most interesting subjects.

I propose a division of modern history into two parts:
First part: From Socrates to Muhammad.
Second part: From Muhammad to the present.

I want to point out first that these divisions are equal in length. 2,200 years have passed since Socrates: 1,100 from Socrates to

Muhammad, and 1,100 from Muhammad to the present.

I would not have been persuaded to adopt this division because of its mathematical exactness had it not also corresponded to a major turning-point in the development of the human mind.

The vein discovered by Socrates was exhausted after a thousand years of exploitation. In the fifth century the last fervent deist with real oratorical talents, Augustine, died, and the Roman Empire came to an end.

The colonies of the western peoples, those established both in Europe and Africa, were plunged into a deep coma. The human mind appeared to be stagnating; intelligence seemed to have reached its limits. But these appearances were misleading. The Arabs were in ferment; and at the end of the tenth century they brought to light two major ideas, one political and the other scientific. They changed the course of the human mind's development.

During the seventh, eighth, ninth, tenth, eleventh, and twelfth centuries the Arabs were the foremost nation both politically and scientifically. Only since the thirteenth century have they ceased to be the vanguard of humanity.

It was in the thirteenth century that Roger Bacon appeared. He was the first European to demonstrate a superiority over the Arabs in physics and mathematics.

Since Roger Bacon Europeans have made continual progress in the physical and mathematical sciences.

Since the thirteenth century, in Europe, the physical and mathematical sciences have steadily increased their predominance over the theological sciences.

Since the thirteenth century Europeans have pursued the study of physics more carefully than the Asians and Africans, and their ascendancy over those peoples has steadily increased.

It was due to the progress of physics and mathematics that Europeans were able to discover America.

It was the discovery of America which made Europe the world's metropolis.

For 1,100 years there has been a steady development of physicism, while deism has been increasingly abandoned. That seems to me sufficient to justify the break I am proposing in modern history.

A well-constructed modern history would fix the reader's prime attention on the works of the deists from Socrates to Muhammad, and the works of physicists from Muhammad to the present day . . .

* * *

ON THE PROGRESS OF THE GENERAL IDEA

It is to the system of vortices that we owe the advance of the physical sciences and the superiority they have acquired over the theological sciences.

How fine, clear, and satisfactory the system organised by Descartes would have been if he had known the law of gravitation!

With what energy this philosopher expressed the independence of his conceptions! *Give me,* he said, *matter and movement, I will make a world.*

How wisely Descartes conducted his research! He saw that positive philosophy was divided into two equally important parts: the physics of inorganic bodies, and the physics of organic bodies. He concluded that ideas of the highest order could only be worked out in a brain enriched by knowledge gained in these two fields. He studied anatomy, zoology, pathology, hygiene — in short, every branch of physiology. His *Treatise on Man* is more profound than any other work previously written on the subject.

The Egyptians worshipped the stars, rivers, mountains, certain vegetables, some animals. They believed the world to be ruled by those beings which seemed to have the greatest influence over events. They regarded these beings as first causes.

Among the Greeks Homer deified each of the various moral qualities. Olympus was a supreme council entrusted with the task of ruling the universe.

Socrates then conceived the idea of confiding the power of Olympus in a single being. He proclaimed that there was one God, and that this God ruled everything, both as a whole and in its separate parts.

Descartes finally said: God created the universe, and subjected it to one immutable law.

Descartes excluded all idea of revelation, all blind belief. He urged men to educate themselves and condemned only the idle to belief.

Thus, in general science the human mind at first believed in the existence of a large number of independent causes.

It then adopted the idea of several causes considered as parts of a single whole, intelligence.

Afterwards it rose to the idea of one universal and unique intelligence, *God.*

Finally, it saw that as the relations between God and the universe were incomprehensible and unimportant (unimportant since God, having foreseen all that would happen, could change nothing in his established order), it ought to concentrate on the search for facts and regard the most general fact it could discover as the unique cause of all phenomena.

In the case of each of its advances the general idea first of all assumed a philosophical character, next a scientific character, and then became religious. Having thus become superstitious it fell into debasement.

Shortly after Cicero stated that he could not understand how two soothsayers could look at each other without laughing, deism replaced paganism.

The idea of divine unity was purely philosophical in the brain of its inventor. Plato and Aristotle started to give it a scientific form, a character which became increasingly pronounced until the establishment of the Christian religion.

Descartes, I would say, replaced belief by reasoning and observation. He established the system of ideas on this basis, but lacked the facts required to organise this system. I would say that he did not discover one general fact.

Since Descartes the two most notable scientists have been Locke and Newton. They collected excellent materials, but did not know how to make use of them.

The change in the general idea which the human mind is presently striving to complete was introduced by Bacon, in whose works it has a purely philosophical character. As I have just said, Locke and Newton discovered a way of indelibly imprinting this character on it. Circumstances are favourable for the organisation of the new system.

Great ideas, great scientific revolutions are the result of great moral ferments. It is the most severe moral crises which produce the greatest men. The human mind was still recovering from the shock it had received from Luther, when Descartes organised his system. The revolutionary turmoil had hardly ended in England, when Locke and Newton appeared. What stupendous scientific result must we expect from the ferment caused by the French Revolution!

ON RELIGION

All the authors I have encountered have adopted one of the four opinions I shall now expound, and on which I shall afterwards give my own thoughts.

First Opinion

A fairly large and very energetic party is working to restore the original strength of the Christian religion. MM. de Bonald and de Chateaubriand are its leaders; they are the ones who have expressed the opinion in question, who have developed and supported it, the one with much force and reasoning, the other with great ability.[19] I shall refute what they have said, and reveal the major error which taints all their ideas ...

There has been a religious system since the time when human intelligence first distinguished between cause and effect. It would be futile to examine history for details of the first religion, since it originated at the same time as the system of signs, and historians could not begin to write until the formation of that system was complete.

We do not have any satisfactory information on the origins of the Egyptians, or on the customs of the peoples preceding them; but history does provide us with a way of tracing the filiation of religious ideas from the Egyptians to the present day.

The Egyptians worshipped the stars, rivers, mountains, certain vegetables, some animals. From these beings they chose the ones which impressed them most, and acknowledged them to be rulers of the world.

Some time afterwards, among the Greeks, Homer appeared. He improved the religious system. His powerful imagination personified each of the faculties of man, and his talent enabled him to deify every one.

Socrates then conceived the idea of forming one being through the union of all those created by Homer. He invented God. This philosopher taught his disciples that men should regard all existing things as the consequence of a single cause.

The idea of Socrates spread and had been adopted by all enlightened men by the time Jesus appeared.

Jesus appeared five hundred years after Socrates. Jesus was good; he had energy, enthusiasm; he was inspired for a fine and good cause. But Jesus was ignorant. He founded the Christian religion and based it on deism. He passed on his inspiration to his disciples but did not leave them a body of doctrine.

Paul, disciple of Jesus, man of genius, an educated man who knew the philosophy of Socrates so well, and who was also familiar with the knowledge acquired since his death by the Academicians and the Peripatetics,[20] organised the Christian doctrine.

Paul's disciples went out in all directions to teach the new religion. They concentrated in particular on converting the inhabitants of the world's capital. It was in Rome that they established their most important school. These teachers of deism (called by the name of clergy, which means body of scientists) vigorously opposed the decline in Roman moral standards and the ferocious practices of the barbarians who invaded Italy.

The clergy were the link which united the European confederation and which enabled it to achieve supremacy by subjugating the inhabitants of every part of the globe.

It was under Pope Hildebrand that the clergy reached the height of their power. Henceforth their power declined; but this decline was slow, and they relinquished their supremacy over humanity in the same way that the tide goes out: sometimes they suffered great losses, but the next moment they retrieved them almost completely. Only since the fifteenth century has their collapse been rapid.

In the fifteenth century a new scientific era, whose dawn had been observed in Baghdad under Caliph Al-Mamoun, made a visible appearance in Italy. The fine arts assumed a new life. Raphael, Michelangelo, Leonardo da Vinci provided it, and all three were laymen. Shortly afterwards Machiavelli drew back the curtain which concealed the operations of the Sacred College. He explained its political workings. He demonstrated that it was not the principles taught by the clergy which enabled them to maintain their power. He proved that the clergy were no longer concerned with anything except their own interests, and that their work no longer contributed to the progress of science.

Then Copernicus arrived on the scene. He presented a new view of the respective positions and movements of the stars dependent on the solar system. Kepler provided geometers with laws which they could use to calculate changes in the positions of the stars. And Galileo, applying the ideas of Copernicus and Kepler, stated: *The Earth revolves.*

At these words the Sacred College took up arms against the innovator: the blow had struck at its heart. It summoned all its strength to repel it. 'The earth,' it said, 'cannot revolve, for it was the sun which Joshua stopped, not the earth. The Holy Scriptures contain abundant proof that the earth is the centre of the world, and that everything which exists was created for man, etc.' Since this period the downfall of the deist clergy has approached with such speed that the most mediocre thinkers can link the chain of events which has brought about their present state of anguish. It is obvious that Jesus and his commentators had no clear idea of the workings of the universe. It has also been proved that the clergy, guardians of the holy law, did not know how to improve the materials placed in their trust.

At the end of the sixteenth century two new stars appeared on the scientific horizon: Bacon and Descartes shook the whole weight of the old temple of wisdom. They seized human understanding and returned it to the crucible. They proclaimed this anti-Christian truth: *Man should believe only those things avowed by reason and confirmed by experience.*

Soon, in every secondary sphere, these men of genius were opening up new routes for thought. Academies were formed. The association of lay scholars, although still very imperfectly organised, struggled with advantage against the clergy, surpassing them in every scientific field.

At the end of the seventeenth century Bossuet raised the Sacred College's hopes of regaining the authority it had lost.[21] He waged a terrible war on unbelievers, but in so doing he emptied the Holy See's arsenal. The theologians did not hold the advantage for long; the physicists quickly regained the upper hand.

Bacon and Descartes had said that physicists should concentrate on the quest for a general fact.

Newton discovered that general fact.

When knowledge of Newton's discovery was sufficiently widespread in Europe, the French lay scholars united in a general assault on the Christian religion. They constructed an Encyclopaedia in which they proved that in every branch of human knowledge the work completed after the impetus provided by Descartes was infinitely superior to the work based on the system of belief invented by Jesus. They showed that the idea of universal gravitation should serve as the basis of the new scientific system, and *consequently of the new religious system.*

The respectability and wealth of the Catholic clergy were destroyed by the Revolution. Today they lead only a subordinate and precarious existence. They are entirely dependent on the Government.

In my view this recapitulation of the human mind's advancement proves completely that M. de Bonald is wrong. However, in spite of this major fault, his works seem to me to be the best that have appeared for several years. In one respect they are admirable: they are full of life; they are designed to inspire scientists and authors with enthusiasm; they are what is needed to revive science and literature.

After reading and thinking about the work of M. de Bonald I am convinced that this author has a profound sense of the utility of systematic unity, since he sets out to show his compatriots that in the present state of enlightenment such unity should serve as the basis of scientific and literary studies.

In this respect I entirely agree with M. de Bonald; but I do not share his enthusiasm for deism. The concept does not seem to me to have the strongest unitary character. Only the idea of universal gravitation has such unity. I shall develop my opinion on this subject in an article entitled *On the Unity of Causes.*[22]

Second Opinion on Religion

I know several persons who believe in the necessity of religion for the maintenance of the social order, and who are convinced that deism is outworn, that the religion founded on deism cannot be revived, and who are consequently working to organise a religion founded on physicism. These persons are wrong on one essential point: the organisation of a new religion is not yet possible. All that can be done is what the Government is doing: concluding concordats between the various deist sects . . .

Third Opinion

The two opinions which I have just discussed are the most noteworthy, but they are not the ones which have gained most support. The vast majority of the School have little time for religious ideas. Their recklessness in this respect proves the truth of the proposition I have advanced in my own work.

The human mind concentrates alternately on general science and the particular sciences.

The School is presently concentrating on the particular sciences.

Religion is the collection of applications of general science by means of which enlightened men rule the ignorant.

Every age has its own character, every institution its life-span.

Religion ages like all other institutions, and also like them it needs to be revived after a certain time.

At first every religion is beneficent. The priests abuse it when they are no longer held in check by opposition, when there are no more discoveries to be made along the scientific route indicated by their founder. It then becomes oppressive. When religion is oppressive it falls into contempt, and its ministers lose the respect and the wealth they have acquired.

What I have just said clearly refutes a common prejudice in the School: Many scientists believe that the priests will gradually regain the power they have lost. This belief is certainly groundless. It would be much more reasonable to believe that the Catholic priests will not lose the small amount of respect granted them by the Government until the human mind has made sufficient progress to develop the new scientific system into the basis of a new religion.

My Opinion

My opinion is simply the summary of my thoughts concerning the Emperor's policies.

I believe in the necessity of a religion for the maintenance of the social order. I believe that deism is outworn, but that physicism is not sufficiently developed to serve as the basis of a new religion.

I believe that there have to be two distinct doctrines: physicism for educated men, and deism for the ignorant.

The human mind found itself in a similar situation during its transition from polytheism to deism, a transition which lasted from *Socrates* to *Paul,* that is, more than five centuries.[23] Throughout this period there were two doctrines: the scientists were deists, the ignorant believed in several gods.

I practice what I preach. I am working to improve physicism, but I do not publish my ideas; I communicate them only to those persons enlightened enough to see things from this point of view, so that society will not suffer any inconvenience. I am not putting my work on sale; I am not having it discussed in the journals. I am having it printed, but only in a very small number of copies, and I shall only place these in reliable hands. Finally, I profess my respect for deism as the necessary public doctrine for a long time to come . . .

ON MORALITY

The most generally taught moral principle is that of the Gospel:
Do unto others as you would have others do unto you.
I observe:
1. That this principle is negative and therefore only indirectly binding.
2. That it does not impose any obligation on the individual towards himself. What use would this principle be to an individual isolated from society?[24]

I propose to substitute the following principle for that of the Gospel:
Man must work.

The happiest man is the worker. The happiest family is the one whose members all employ their time usefully. The happiest nation is the one with the fewest idlers. Humanity would enjoy all the happiness to which it can lay claim if there were no idlers at all.

I must observe that it is absolutely essential to give the idea of work as much latitude as possible. Any functionary, any person involved in the sciences, the fine arts, in manufacturing or agricultural industry works as positively as the labourer digging the earth or the porter carrying his load. But a *rentier,* a property owner who has no profession and who does not personally direct the work necessary to render his property productive, is a burden on society, even if he gives alms.

Those engaged in science are the most moral and also the happiest men because their work is useful to the whole of humanity.

The legislator must guarantee the free exercise of property.
The moralist must urge public opinion to punish the idle property

owner by depriving him of all respect . . .

ON THE CLERGY

Alexandre Farnèse[25] rightly said that he knew of nothing more intolerable than a cowardly soldier or an ignorant priest.

If the clergy are to be useful they must be respected. If they are to be respected they must be learned, they must include the most learned men.

Suppose for a moment that the priesthood were placed in the hands of lay mathematicians and physicists. It can be seen that a clergy so composed would be highly respected and very useful.

A country parson with a knowledge of geometry, physics, and physiology could undoubtedly be of great use to his parishioners. A quarrel can often be brought to an end by a land survey. A physicist does not ring bells when the clouds are charged with electricity. A chemist who wants to clean a well with a suspect atmosphere lowers a lighted candle into it before sending a man down. A physiologist often finds he can put his knowledge of hygiene to good use.

It is not enought for the clergy to be learned; they must also have morals. Anyone who has observed the different classes in society will have noticed that those persons engaged in the physical and mathematical sciences constitute the social class with the purest morals.

I see quite clearly that the power of theologians will pass into the hands of the physicists, and that it will then take on a new life. But I am not in a position to say when this transition will take place or how it will be brought about.

I shall wait until the master of the human mind, the great Napoleon, has spoken. His intentions will be like a ray of light, illuminating my research.

[*Oeuvres,* vol. VI, pp.13-14, 16-17, 22-8, 31, 34-6, 40-42, 47-50, 54-5, 65, 99-102, 147-52, 154-8, 162-71, 176-7, 181-2.]

4. SECOND PROSPECTUS FOR A NEW ENCYCLOPAEDIA

(Extracts from *Projet d'enyclopédie, Second prospectus*, 1810)

PREFACE

... The common interest of France and England requires the Royal Society of London and the Imperial Institute of France to work together on a new encyclopaedia.

The encyclopaedia of the eighteenth century[26] was written in a spirit good for its own time but bad for present circumstances. It was constructed according to a plan proportionate to the enlightenment of that time but quite inferior to what has since been made possible by the subsequent progress of enlightenment ...

The encyclopaedia of the nineteenth century must be founded on the principle that science, as a whole as well as in its various branches, should be based on observation. Thus, the basis of the encyclopaedia must be an analysis of the history of the human mind's progress. It is this analysis which should determine how the great scientific work is to be divided.

The effects produced by science are certain but slow. Also, few people show any interest in them, so that I would have little hope of seeing my plan for an encyclopaedia realised during my lifetime if its only major goal were to promote the progress of human knowledge. But this plan can be looked at from another point of view: it can be considered in political terms, and in this respect it can and should be of real and general interest to all enlightened men in France and England, for the evils of war afflict everyone, and everyone who suffers them inevitably has a desire for peace. Now, I would ask every sensible man who cares to think about it for a moment, whether it is not clear to him that the association of the Imperial Institute of France and the Royal Society of London for the purpose of constructing a new encyclopaedia is bound to result in a union of the governments and peoples of France and England. Yes, I predict — and in the course of my work I shall state the reasons for my prediction — that once the Imperial Institute of France and the Royal Society of London begin to work together on the construction of a new encyclopaedia it will take less than a year to achieve a lasting peace between France and England.

Practice makes perfect. Just a short time ago, this very day in fact, I realised what course I must follow. Hitherto I have adopted a bad strategy: my main concern has been to clarify the ideas which ought to be included in the preliminary discourse to the future encyclopaedia, and to encourage discussion of some of them.

What has happened to me? The persons who paid attention to my ideas were not clever enough to understand them, so that their observations could not provide sufficient material for a debate; while the persons able to understand them raised no objection to them. Only the positive scientists are capable of understanding them. Now, at present none of these scholars is studying positive general science. Each one is involved in one of the specialised fields of physical and mathematical science, and consequently none of them takes a direct interest in my work.

In order to change this situation the scientists have to be encouraged to work on an encyclopaedia. Once this work is under way a jury, composed of all scientists, will earnestly examine the plans submitted to it, that is, the preliminary discourses.

I have learned from experience, and reason has convinced me, that I should concentrate all my efforts on bringing together English and French scientists to work on an encyclopaedia. This new approach satisfies me; it gives me courage and hope. I hope that it has the same effect on those persons who wish me success . . .

PROSPECTUS: PART ONE

. . . It was Bacon who founded general positive science, just as Moses founded sacred and superstitious science. Bacon's superiority over Moses has been proved by experience: the two peoples which have adopted his doctrine have risen above the rest of humanity. The English and the French, through force of arms and the accuracy of their political and military calculations, have subjected all the inhabitants of the universe, so that today there are virtually only two national powers on the globe, the French and the English.

The English and the French are superior to other peoples in both their domestic and foreign policies. These two nations have the best constitutions, or rather they are the only nations which enjoy the benefit of a constitution. If one compares the English and the French with the other peoples of the earth, one finds that they have obtained national happiness and positive superiority. Their two scientific communities are superior to every other national scientific community. Their highest political class, that is, their great property owners and functionaries, are better educated and more liberal than any of their foreign counterparts. Physical well-being and enlightenment are more widespread among their non-proprietors than among the non-proprietors of the rest of the globe. France and England are the two countries in which the mass of the population has the best housing, the best clothes, and the best food. And the number of men able to read, write, and count in these two countries, as a proportion of their populations, is higher than anywhere else.

Until 1789 the English were superior in every respect, in physics and mathematics as well as in morals and policies. But since then things have certainly changed . . .

Conduct of the English since 1789

If Bacon had risen from his tomb in 1789 he would have spoken to his fellow countrymen as follows:

'Perfect the theory and practice of general positive science. Replace the uncertain and superstitious doctrine which you call religion with a doctrine based on observation. No longer promise men happiness in another life; show them the way to achieve it in this life. Reveal this great truth: that the man who employs his powers for the public good, who contributes to public happiness by fulfilling the duties of his position, will obtain every possible happiness throughout his life.

Parliamentary Reform

'Proceed immediately with your parliamentary reform. Destroy your rotten boroughs. Rid your elections of the mobs. Base your representation on the population, industry, and wealth of each part of the country. Give the vote to two classes: on the one hand owners of financial and commercial property, on the other hand those non-proprietors who distinguish themselves through their ability in the sciences, the arts, or industry.* Ensure that no one becomes a Member of Parliament who does not enjoy an income of at least a thousand pounds.

Royal Power

'Increase your royal power considerably. You are wrong to fear it.

*This admirable political idea was discovered by the Emperor Napoleon, who used it as the basis of his constitution for the kingdom of Italy. This immortal discovery must be regarded as the solution to the most important political problem. Such a constitutional basis protects a people for ever against revolution by ensuring that it always has the best possible social order. According to this constitutional arrangement the ruling class always and inevitably consists of the most important men as well as all educated men.

The limitations which you place on it complicate your political machinery; they clog and slow down the process of government, and expose you to window-breaking and other brutal disturbances by ignorant non-proprietors. A single safeguard is sufficient to contain the royal power within those limits necessary to prevent it from troubling the social order. This safeguard involves the formation of a clear conception of how monarchy ought to be regarded. It requires a general ability on the part of the nation's ruling class to consider monarchy from two different points of view.

Passive Monarchy

'Passive monarchy consists of the civil list, the honours bestowed upon the person of the King, and his inviolability, and should be heriditary. If it were elective the ambition of those mediocre people who are always in the majority would be continually encouraged by the desire to gain the only kind of advantage they can appreciate.

Active Monarchy

'Active monarchy should be elective. By active monarchy I mean monarchy's governmental role. You are already used to electing your active King, who is your Prime Minister. Your nomination, although indirect, is no less positive, since you only vote taxation when the King appoints as Prime Minister the man whom you regard as the most capable ruler. You use the same means to force the King to change his Prime Minister whenever it suits you.

Observation

'It can happen that the hereditary King is also the active King. It happens when the heir to the throne is also England's most capable ruler. In such a case you should guard against the discontent of those men whose ability deserves your greatest esteem. These men, deprived of the hope of being elected to active monarchy, will lapse into a kind of melancholy. You should make sure that you know how to enjoy the valuable advantage which results from this concentration of royal powers, namely, a great increase in your supremacy over humanity, which alone can enable you to pursue your politics with the vigour which your glory requires.

The Demands of the Irish Catholics

'The demands of the Irish Catholics[27] should open your eyes to the dangers which threaten your liberty. Only the balance of power can guarantee a people's liberty. There are two major divisions of political power: spiritual and temporal. The two should be separated, in effect if not in name, and should balance each other. The spiritual and temporal powers are both in the hands of your King. This is a monstrous situation which ought not to last. Your most important political task is to bring it to an end. This is how you can re-establish the balance between these two forces, by organising your spiritual power:

'All your positive scientists should be brought together in a workshop to prepare an encyclopaedia. This encyclopaedia should establish a general doctrine and particular doctrines for each social class. Your clergy should be composed of two classes: improvers and teachers. The class of improvers should always concentrate on improving the theory of general science. The class of teachers should concentrate on disseminating acquired knowledge in every class to the degree permitted by the work and education of each. So that the clergy may be as happy and as useful as possible, its members must be obliged:

'1. to remain unmarried;

'2. to own no landed or commercial property, and even to renounce all rights of inheritance . . .

Foreign Policy

'Your foreign policy should aim to ensure that your political doctrine and your scientific institutions are adopted by all the peoples of the globe. The French, who have already adopted your scientific doctrine and whose School, just like your own, teaches that science should be based on observation, both as a whole and in its parts, have already revealed their intention to establish a national organisation similar to yours. Propose to the French:

'1. That the scientists of the two nations should join together in a single association.

'2. That this association should be given the task of organising the positive doctrine, that is, of basing general science, commonly called religion, on observation.

'3. That this association should be made permanent and given the title of Anglo-French clergy. At the same time it should be declared that this clergy, this Church, represents God on earth, and that its decisions are divine.

'4. The clergy should be divided into two classes: the first in charge of improvement, the second in charge of education.

'Also, in the temporal sphere, you should propose an offensive and defensive alliance to the French in order to promote the adoption of your scientific doctrine and political institutions by all the peoples of the globe.'

What Actually Happened

Bacon did not rise from his tomb. No Englishman had studied the series of the human mind's progress in sufficient depth to predict the political and religious crisis, a crisis made inevitable by the scientific supremacy achieved by the laity over the priests, and by the decline in the clergy's morality. No man was capable of allaying, shortening, or ending this crisis by reorganising the temporal power, reconstituting the clergy with the most educated positive scientists, and establishing seminaries in which teaching, as a whole and in its parts, would be based on observation, in which moral discipline would be severe, and in which the teachers would inspire the novices with a passion for self-sacrifice and renunciation of wealth and sensual pleasure, a passion which would be seen as the means of obtaining the greatest respect and happiness in science and religion.

In 1789 the greatest political mind in England was that of Mr. Pitt.[28]

Mr. Pitt was . . . a great administrator and minister of finance, but he was not a great politician. He did not doubt that humanity had reached a climacteric; but he had no clear idea of the political relations between the continental powers.*

Because of his administrative ability and his inability in foreign policy and knowledge of the human mind's advancement, Mr. Pitt naturally reasoned as follows:

'The French have started a revolution. Their political crisis will inevitably cause them to neglect industry and commerce. We must take advantage of the opportunity to expand English industry and commerce.'

This reasoning led Mr. Pitt, on the one hand, furtively to increase the revolutionary crisis through his secret agents in France, and, on the other hand, to do all he could to promote English industry and commerce . . .

He conceived the idea of overwhelming and annihilating the French nation. He sent emissaries to the continent in order to unite all European nations against France. He made himself the head of a first coalition which failed, and of a second which was no more successful . . .

[*Oeuvres*, vol. VI, pp.282-5, 290-300.]

*Mr. Pitt's ignorance of the military forces and political relations of the various European states was attested to me by Mr. George Ellis, one of his closest friends, whom I saw frequently in Paris.[29]

5. MEMOIR ON THE SCIENCE OF MAN

(Extracts from *Mémoire sur la science de l'homme,* 1813)

PREFACE

... Inspired by the desire to do what is of most use to the progress of the *science of man* ... I began by examining with the most scrupulous attention the present situation of that science. Here is the result of my examination:

The four most noteworthy works relating to that science are, it seems to me, those of Vicq-d'Azyr, Cabanis, Bichat, and Condorcet.[30] Comparing the works of these four authors with those of their predecessors, I found that:

1. These authors took a step of great importance for the science of man: they applied to that science the same method that is used in the other sciences of observation, that is, they based their reasoning on observed and examined facts instead of adopting the method used in the conjectural sciences, which derives all facts from reason.

2. All the questions of importance in this science were dealt with by one or other of these four authors.

I concluded from this examination that the next most important step to be taken by the science of man, the step which would follow on directly from those taken by Vicq-d'Azyr, Cabanis, Bichat, and Condorcet, was to deal with the whole of this science in one single work by completing the material provided by these four great men.

Such is the object I have set myself in the present memoir, which will be divided into two parts each consisting of two sections.

The first part will deal with man as an individual, and the second with man as a species.

The first section of the first part will be a physiological résumé, the second section will be psychological.

The first section of the second part will contain an outline history of the progress of the human mind from its point of departure to the present day.

In the second section I shall present a survey of the future course of the human mind following the present generation.

I shall entitle the first part *Examination of the Works of Vicq-d'Azyr,* and the second *Examination of Condorcet's Historical Picture of the Progress of the Human Mind.* In the first I shall discuss the ideas of Vicq-d'Azyr, and in the second those of Condorcet ...

Both Cabanis and Bichat have certainly dealt with questions of the greatest interest. However, as both of them, or rather each of them, has dealt with only one particular question relating to the science of man, I have not thought it necessary to devote a part of my memoir to the examination of their ideas. I have regarded them as appendices to those of Vicq-d'Azyr . . .

Three persons, more than any others, have contributed to my knowledge of the ideas which will be produced and developed in this work: MM. Burdin, Bougon, and Oelsner. I shall discuss each of them separately and specify how my debt to them is to be regarded.

M. Burdin[31]

It was Doctor Burdin who first taught me the importance of physiology. Here, more or less exactly, are the words he used:

'All the sciences were at first conjectural. The great natural order has destined them all to become positive. Astronomy began as astrology; chemistry was originally merely alchemy. Physiology, which for a long time weltered in charlatanism, is today being based on observed and examined facts. Psychology is beginning to be based on physiology and to rid itself of the religious prejudices on which it was founded.

'The sciences were at first conjectural because at the beginning of scientific study only a few observations had yet been made, because there had not been sufficient time to examine, discuss, and verify these few facts through long experience, and because they were only presumed facts, conjectures. They had to become, they will become positive because through its daily experience the human mind acquires knowledge of new facts and rectifies its knowledge of facts which it observed earlier, when man was not yet able to analyse them.

'Astronomy, being the science in which facts are viewed in their simplest and least numerous relations, had to be the first to assume a positive character. Chemistry inevitably followed after astronomy and before physiology because it considers the activity of matter in relations which are more complex than in astronomy but less detailed than in physiology . . .

'Physiology does not yet deserve to be classed among the positive sciences, but it has to take only one more step in order to rise completely above the conjectural sciences. The first man of genius to appear in that field will base the science's general theory on observed facts. Virtually all that is required in order to organise the general theory of physiology is to bring together the works of Vicq-d'Azyr, Cabanis, Bichat, and Condorcet; for these four authors have dealt with nearly all the important physiological questions, and have based all their reasoning on examined observations.

'I shall list the major consequences which will follow the positive organisation of physiological theory, a science whose summit is the science of man . . .

'1. The teaching of physiology will be introduced into public education. I base my conjecture in this respect on the observation that each of the physical sciences was introduced into public education as soon as it became positive.

'2. Morals will become a positive science. The physiologist is the only scientist able to prove that in every case it is the path of virtue which leads to happiness. The moralist who is not a physiologist has to show how virtue is rewarded in another life, because of his inability to treat moral questions with enough precision.

'3. Politics will become a positive science. When those who cultivate this important branch of human knowledge have learned physiology in the course of their education, they will no longer regard the problems they have to solve as anything but questions of hygiene.

'4. Philosophy will become a positive science. The weakness of human intelligence has forced man to divide the sciences into general science and the particular sciences. The elementary facts of general science or philosophy are the general facts of the particular sciences, or, if you like, the particular sciences are the elements of general science. That science, which could only be of the same nature as its elements, was conjectural as long as the particular sciences were conjectural. It became semi-conjectural and semi-positive when one part of the particular sciences became positive, the other still remaining conjectural.

'Such is the situation today. It will become positive when physiology is based entirely on observed facts, for there are no phenomena which cannot be observed from the viewpoint of the physics of inorganic bodies or the physics of organic bodies, which is physiology.

'5. The religious system will be perfected. Dupuis, in his work on the origin of cults,[32] has produced evidence which shows that all known religions were based on the scientific system, and that consequently every reorganisation of the scientific system leads to the reorganisation and improvement of the religious system.

'6. The clergy will be reorganised and reconstituted. The religious system is divided into two parts: one passive and theoretical, the other active and practical. The first involves the coordination of principles; the second involves the organisation of applications of these principles. These two parts are closely linked and interdependent, so that the improvement of principles leads to the improvement of the clergy's education, and a better clergy produces an improvement in the intrinsic value and coordination of principles. But it is always an improvement of the principles which starts and restarts the movement which, for a long or short period, then becomes alternate and reciprocal. Thus, the clergy will necessarily be reorganised when the system of ideas, the system of religious principles, is reorganised. But we have seen above that the passive religious system is (as Dupuis has demonstrated) nothing but the materialisation of the scientific system. Thus, the reorganisation of the clergy can be nothing but the reorganisation of the scientific corps, for the clergy must be the scientific corps. It can only be of use, it can only have power as long as it is composed of the most learned men, as long as the principles known to it are still unknown to the common people . . .'

Finally Doctor Burdin said to me: 'The combined labours of two persons are required in order to enable human intelligence to take this general step forward, and take it quickly. It demands the combination of the intellectual powers of a physiologist and a philosopher, the coordination of their efforts. Their joint work will consist of the organisation of the following four series:

'1. Series of comparisons between the structures of inorganic and organic bodies, which will prove that the effects produced by the phenomena of these two classes are proportionate to their organisation.[33]

'2. Series of comparisons between different organic bodies, which will prove that the effects produced by them during their phenomenal existence, and their level of intelligence, are proportionate to the degree of perfection of their organic structure.

'3. Series of comparisons between man and other animals, at different periods, which will prove that man is the only one whose intelligence has improved, while that of other animals has retrogressed; that the best organised animal is the only one, out of any group of animals, whose intelligence can be improved; that the intelligence of the others must necessarily retrogress as a result of the continuous action and reaction of animals on each other; that it is a philosophical prejudice to believe that man is the only animal able to improve itself; that he is not, in fact, the only one with this faculty of self-improvement; in short, that if man were to disappear from the globe the animal with the next best organisation would improve itself.

'4. Series of the progress of the human mind. This series should be divided into two parts, one dealing with the past and the other with the future. What is said about the future must be a clear consequence of what has been stated about the past. In charting the advance of the human mind as much prominence as possible should be given to the following observations: i) The superiority of man's intelligence over the intelligence of other animals was, to begin with, no more than the natural superiority resulting directly from his superior organisation, which was very small. ii) It took a long time, several generations in fact, for man to evolve a language; and the system of conventional symbols was only completed when general ideas, *causes* and *effects,* were clearly distinguished and related to different signs. Henceforth the intelligence of man was decidedly superior to the instinct which other animals possessed. The religious system began to take shape. At first this system was idolatry, that is, the belief that first causes, the great causes, are visible, and the worship of these causes by those who do not study the relation between causes and effects, or work to improve knowledge. iii) From the idea of visible causes man rose to the idea of several invisible and animate causes: polytheism. iv) From the idea of several invisible and animate causes man rose to the idea of a single invisible and animate cause: deism. v) From the idea of a single invisible and animate cause man rose to the conception of several laws ruling the various classes of phenomena. vi) Man will rise to a belief in a single and unique law ruling the universe (this lies in the future) . . .

'This work should be carried out in two parts: both the physiologist and the philosopher should make their contributions. When they have completed their outlines they will communicate with each other and start again on the basis of a common agreement, with the understanding that the views of the physiologist should be given precedence in the establishment of the first two sections, or rather fractions of the general series, while the philosopher's views should have the greatest influence on the organisation of the last two and the general coordination of the four.

'You shall be the philosopher in this work; I will be the physiologist.'

It is fifteen years since M. Burdin said this to me and made his proposal, which I accepted.

For fifteen years this work has occupied and absorbed me. At last I have completed my outline in all its parts. I was going to communicate it to Doctor Burdin when I learned that he had gone to work in the army hospitals, which makes communication absolutely impracticable. I do not know what stage his own work has reached. I am sending him this commencement of my work, and am also submitting it to some physiologists. Through this communication with him and his colleagues I appeal for a collaborator. I am in great need of one. I appeal for a person who is more capable than myself of fulfilling this task which is so important for the happiness of the human race, and which is, I recognise, infinitely beyond my powers . . .

M. Bougon[34]

I shall now speak of my debt to Doctor Bougon. I am not exaggerating in this respect.

Chance led me to meet Dr. Bougon, who was formerly provost to M. Dubois in Paris, and now practises medicine in the provinces. He is a man of extraordinary sagacity: to my mind he has a great future in physiology in front of him. After informing him of my work-plan I told him that I was having difficulty with two points in the series, where I needed a solution to a problem of factual continuity. He completely eliminated the first of these difficulties, and M. Oelsner removed the other. First let us discuss the service rendered to me by M. Bougon. I said to him: One of the important tasks of physiology and consequently of my work is to prove that the intelligence of each animal is proportionate to its organisation, that the former is accordingly a consequence of the latter, and that the scale of intelligence is the same as the organisational scale. Now, I see that physiologists have placed the ape immediately below him man on the organisational scale, whereas the beaver clearly deserves to be placed above the ape on the scale of intelligence.

After much thought and investigation Doctor Bougon said to me: 'Physiologists are wrong to place the ape immediately below man. It should not be in that position by virtue either of its level of organisational perfection or of its species' intellectual capacity and the results to which that capacity has led it. The truth is that the beaver's organisation is superior to that of the ape on account of the fact that the ape's hand can only grasp, whereas the beaver possesses the abducent thumb muscle, which gives it the sense of touch. The truth is, equally and constitutionally (since these two truths are organically linked), that the beaver's intelligence, as its work has proved, is very superior to that of the ape . . .'

Dr. Bougon rendered me a much more important service than the ones of which I have just spoken, by clearly understanding what is involved in the scientific enterprise to which I have dedicated myself.

No one is more able to execute the physiological part than he is . . .

M. Oelsner[35]

I was having great difficulty with my account of the progress of the human mind. Then I met M. Oelsner who solved my problem. Here are the facts:

D'Alembert in his preliminary discourse to the Encyclopaedia, Condorcet in his *Sketch of an Historical Picture of the Progress of the Human Mind,* and to an even greater extent the less important writers, have all depicted the Middle Ages as a period during which the human mind retrogressed. I did not see any way of refuting this idea of retrogression. I searched without success for a way of presenting the facts so as to establish a sequence of continuous progress. M. Oelsner, who won the Institute's prize for the best memoir dealing with the influence of the scientific works of the Arabs on the intelligence of Europeans, said to me: 'Europeans — the scientific vanguard of the human race — proceeded in the direction indicated by Socrates until the Arabs thought of looking for the laws which rule the universe, by making an abstraction of the idea that it is ruled by one animate cause. The Arabs guided the human mind in the realm of discoveries until the fifteenth century, a period when the Europeans chased the Arabs from Spain and overtook them in intelligence through their efforts to discover a single law to which the universe is subject.'

I have understood M. Oelsner's idea. My work will prove it . . .

SERIES OF THE DEVELOPMENT OF HUMAN INTELLIGENCE

. . . Without any further preamble let us establish the series of the various stages observed in the development of human intelligence.

First Stage

The superiority of the first men over other animals was no more than that which resulted directly from their superior organisation. Their memory was not much better than that of the beaver or the elephant. This may be included in the class of observed facts, because it was clearly observed in the savage of Aveyron.[36]

Second Stage

The human race in the condition discovered by Captain Cook in the Magellan Straits: living in caves, not knowing how to construct dwelling-places, without leaders, not knowing how to make fire.

Third Stage

The human race in the condition discovered by Captain Cook in the

northern parts of the north-west coast of America: with constructed
dwellings, the beginnings of political organisation (since they
recognised leaders), and the beginnings of a language, which was still
very limited since its numerals only went up to three.

Fourth Stage

The human race in the condition discovered by Captain Cook and
other navigators on the north-west coast of America towards the 50th
degree of northern latitude: with a fairly complete language,
completely subject to leaders, actively cannibalistic. This stage is
even more evident in New Zealand.

Fifth Stage

The inhabitants of the Friendly Islands and the islands of Société
and Sandwich. Civilisation is already very advanced in these countries:
the language spoken is not poor, and cannibalism is almost completely
abolished. The inhabitants are divided into two classes: the Eares and
the Toutous. There is a religious cult with an organised clergy which
is respected by all classes in society.

Sixth Stage

The Peruvians and Mexicans in the condition revealed by the Spaniards
when they discovered and conquered their countries. At this time they
formed two very large and quite distinct political societies. The arts
and crafts and the fine arts had already made striking progress, as these
peoples had discovered methods of mining metals, working them, and
using them for decorating buildings.

Seventh Stage

The Egyptians, whose progress in the arts and fine arts had been
greater than that of the Peruvians, and who were superior to the latter
in the moral sciences and the sciences of observation.
    The Egyptians took one of the most difficult steps which human
intelligence has ever had to take in the long course of its development:
they invented conventional written symbols.
    We may readily attribute to them the invention of writing. Whether
they actually invented it or merely re-invented it makes little difference,
for our object is to establish clearly the series of the development
of the progress of the human mind, and with tentative ideas it would
be impossible to attain this end.

I regard the age of the Egyptians as a second point of departure for human intelligence, and it seems to me that a more detailed examination of its subsequent progress is necessary, an examination involving a division between the views of the men engaged in the sciences, who were working to discover causes and to coordinate their ideas on causes with those on effects, and the beliefs of the mass of the people which, ever since, have always been abstract beliefs ...

Egypt's scientific community fulfilled the functions of the priesthood. It was the chief, the only political power in the country, and its power was absolute. The community had two doctrines: one which it taught to the people, and one which it reserved for itself and a small number of initiates to whom it was communicated.

The doctrine taught to the people was idolatry, materialism, the belief that visible causes are first causes. They were taught to worship the Nile, the God Apis (the ox), the crocodile, the onion, as well as the sun, the moon, the various constellations, etc.

The doctrine reserved for the scientists was of a much higher order, and was much more metaphysical. It regarded visible causes as no more than secondary causes, as nothing but the effects of higher causes, which were thought to be invisible.

The Egyptian scientists very carefully collected all the observations made by their predecessors on the movement of the stars, the rising of the Nile, and various other aspects of physics. They worked with great fervour to add to this precious knowledge.

No other historical age presents us with such a clear division between thinkers and believers. It is through a study of this people's history that one becomes convinced of the fact that the priestly power and the scientific capacity are essentially the same. By that I mean that the clergy of any religion must be the most educated body; that when it ceases to be the most educated body it successively loses respect and falls into debasement until it is finally destroyed and replaced by an association of the most learned men; and that this change occurs when there is an improvement in the general idea. We must not be too eager to develop this idea now: it will become perfectly clear when it is seen to be simply the result of an observation on the advancement of the human mind. For the moment let it suffice to say that it is with the Egyptians that this observation has its starting-point.

Eighth Stage

In this second part of the series of the progress of the human mind we shall never have to consider more than one people or at least one political society at a time, since in every major period there has always been one political society which has gained a decisive ascendancy over all others, an ascendancy in both the sciences and in war. Hence, it is solely to that society that we have to attribute the human mind's progress during the age when if flourished.

We began this second part of the series with a discussion of the Egyptians. We shall now go on to discuss the Greeks, then the Romans, the Saracens, and finally the modern peoples . . .

The vital intellectual force which united the Greeks and made them the scientific vanguard of the human race for several centuries was first revealed in the person of Homer. Homer, the earliest Greek of whom we have any historical record, and whose own writings have been preserved, was the founder of polytheism, in the sense that he was its organiser . . .

The whole of the Greek population adopted the belief in the existence of invisible causes. It was this view which served as the basis of the religion of polytheism, the religion shared by all Greeks.

It was with the Greeks that the human mind first began to concern itself seriously with social organisation. It was they who laid down the principles of politics. They applied themselves to this science in both its practical and its theoretical aspects. They gave birth to great legislators such as Lycurgus, Draco, and Solon. It was not just a small number of people who were engaged in this science: it was the subject of ordinary conversation among several thousand citizens; principles and their application were often discussed in the public assemblies . . .

Religion was the general link of Greek society. The Temple of Delphi was common to all the Greek peoples and independent of each of them, for it had been built on land which was regarded as sacred, on which neighbouring peoples had no right, and which was respected by their neighbours in even the fiercest wars. The priests of Delphi took care, in their oracles, to uphold the union of the Greek peoples, and to inspire them to oppose the Persian assaults on their liberty . . .

Under the Greeks the religious system and the political system shared exactly the same basis, or rather the religious system served as the basis of the political system, the latter being made in imitation of the former and copied from it. The Greek Olympus was in fact a republican assembly, and the national constitutions of all the Greek peoples, although different from each other, were also republican . . .

A conception of general science discovered in one period is always put into effect in the following period. It was the Egyptian priests who invented polytheism, but it was the Greeks who were polytheists, that is, who believed in the existence of several invisible causes and worshipped them. It was the same with theism: Socrates was its inventor, but it was the Romans who were theists, five hundred years after Socrates' death.

Socrates was the greatest man who has ever existed. No man will ever equal Socrates, because this pre-eminent genius produced the greatest conception which the human mind is capable of creating . . . It consisted of two general and elementary ideas: First, a system must be a whole, organised in such a way that secondary principles may be deduced from a single general principle, and may themselves serve as the starting-point for the deduction of tertiary principles. In this way one would be able to move along a moral scale, divided into equal gradations, from the single general principle to the most particular ideas. The other idea entering into the composition of his conception was that man, in order to organise his scientific system, that is, to coordinate his ideas on the organisation of the universe and to establish a firm basis for his knowledge of the composition and movement of phenomena, must proceed alternately *a priori* and *a posteriori* in the coordination of his ideas. Because his intellectual powers are extremely limited his attention always tends to see things from the same point of view, and his only means of hastening its progress is to change direction. Thus, if after making an effort to descend from the idea of a single cause ruling the universe to the most particular effects, his attention is so tired that he can no longer discover anything new, and his abstract and concrete ideas are so mixed up that he can no longer sort them out, the best thing he can do is to change direction: he should adopt the opposite, *a posteriori* approach and rise from the consideration of particular facts to more general facts, making his way by the most direct route possible to the most general fact. In short, Socrates invented *method*, and none of his successors apart from Bacon has been able to equal the loftiness of this idea. None of his disciples had a mind of such vast scope, so his school split up some time after the death of its leader and founder.

Plato and Aristotle were the two most distinguished members of the Socratic school, and they divided it into two quite distinct parts with different names and whose work proceeded in quite different directions. One was called the School of Academicians, the other was the School of Peripatetics. The names *prioricians* and *posterioricians* would have been preferable, since they indicate the doctrines which were taught by each of these philosophers.

I am not claiming that Plato reasoned exclusively *a priori*, or that Aristotle reasoned exclusively *a posteriori*, but only that the former believed and taught that *a priori* considerations took precedence over *a posteriori* considerations, while the latter taught the opposite . . .

Ninth Stage

... It was the Romans who organised theism and who founded public law, and who made the greatest progress in that science. These are the two contributions of this people to the development of general intelligence ...

These two advances were certainly important, for a large political society composed of peoples with different languages and customs, living in different climates, and with different agricultural products could not possibly be founded on polytheism, which is a religion with no unitary character ...

About a thousand years after the establishment of polytheism in Greece, the Romans, who had adopted it with some modifications, were plunged into the greatest political crisis recorded by history, on the occasion of the transition from the idea of several gods to that of a single god. This change in the general idea was the major cause of the terrible disorder into which the huge Roman Empire fell for several centuries, a state of disorder which has been attributed in the past to mere secondary causes ...

Tenth Stage

It was the Saracens, that is, the Arabs, who advanced the human mind through its tenth stage by inventing algebra and founding the sciences of observation.

The Saracens had this in common with the Egyptians, the Greeks, and the Romans: they assumed the role of vanguard in the development of human intelligence; and they lived in a country separated from its neighbours by natural barriers, the sea for a large part, and the desert for the rest. But in many respects they were different from the Egyptians, the Greeks, the Romans, in fact from all other known peoples (excluding the Arabs): Since only a very small part of their country was suitable for farming, the population remained chiefly nomadic. There was no development, no improvement in general government. The people lived in separate tribes, independent of each other. Such a social organisation did not lend itself to depotism, but once it was exported into cultivated lands with large towns and an established seat of government it was bound to degenerate quickly into despotism. This is what happened to those Arabs who settled outside the boundaries of Arabia, when the Arabs became conquerors ...

Eleventh Stage

Charlemagne was the founder of European society. It was he who firmly united the different European peoples by means of a religious link with Rome, and by securing that city's independence from all temporal power. Since Charlemagne Europe has remained the strongest society in material terms, but in terms of intelligence it has been in the first rank only since the expulsion of the Moors from Spain, and it has still to advance the human mind one general step. All the scientific progress made by this society has been partial progress, that is, it has only improved the particular sciences. Its works up to the present can thus be considered only as a preparation for the realisation of a general improvement in the system of ideas. An analysis of its works since the fifteenth century shows that the result has been the complete disorganisation of the scientific system organised two thousand years ago, and considerable progress towards the organisation of the scientific system founded by the Arabs under the caliphate of Al-Mamoun. But this result, I repeat, does not amount to a general advance: modern Europeans do not yet deserve to be ranked by the impartial historian, the man who does not seek to flatter his contemporaries, with the Egyptians, Greeks, Romans, and Saracens. The first established the division between ideas of *cause* and *effect*, and organised the system of religious ideas; the second organised polytheism; the third organised theism; and the last replaced the idea of one animate cause, which is theism, by the idea of a universe ruled by laws. Let us now look at what we have done. We have, I repeat, continued and improved the work of the Saracens; but we have not allowed the idea of several laws to develop into the idea of one single law, or at least we have not yet reorganised the scientific system and the system of application in accordance with the conception of a single law. As this operation has not yet been carried out it must belong to the future, which obliges us to establish a twelfth stage . . .

Twelfth Stage

The general system of our knowledge will be reorganised on the basis of the belief that the universe is ruled by a single immutable law. All the systems of application, such as the systems of religion, politics, morals, and civil law will be placed in harmony with the new system of knowledge. . .

[*O.c.*, vol.II, pp.8-9, 17-18, 20-25, 31-5, 37-9, 41, 52-3, 97-101, 103-5, 107-13, 118-19, 122-3, 129-33.]

6. STUDY ON UNIVERSAL GRAVITATION

(Extracts from *Travail sur la gravitation universelle,* 1813)

DEDICATION (TO HIS MAJESTY THE EMPEROR)

... I beg Your Majesty to deign to accept the dedication of this study.

I have called this first sketch of my plan for the reorganisation of European society *Study on Universal Gravitation* because the new philosophical theory must be based on the idea of universal gravitation, and because the new political system of Europe must be a consequence of the new philosophy ...

Sire, the progress of the human mind has reached the point where the most important reasoning on politics can and must be deduced directly from the knowledge acquired in the high sciences and the physical sciences. It is my aim to imprint a positive character on politics. If my enterprise is successful, my greatest satisfaction will be to have contributed to the glory of Your Majesty's reign ...

[BACON'S DISCOURSE]

... The great Bacon ... is still at present the philosophic head of the English and French Schools, for since this great man's death no scientist has risen to conceptions as general as his ...

Just suppose that this great man, returned to life, were present at a meeting of the Institute. What would be his astonishment at seeing that philosophy had no place in any section of the first class, indeed in any class of this general scientific body, so that if he, Bacon, who guides its daily work, wanted to enter the Institute, he could not be admitted under any pretext into the first class, the second would receive him only as a wit, and the third only as a scholar?[37]

Suppose that this philosopher were to leave the Institute and go to the University.[38] What would be his astonishment at seeing that science's *teaching* body was in no way linked organically to the body responsible for scientific *improvement?*

Suppose that after leaving the University he visited all the political cabinets of Europe. What would be his astonishment at seeing that they all realised clearly and acutely how unfortunate and troublesome their position was, but that in all of them only insignificant proposals were being made to remedy a great evil? What would be his astonishment at seeing that no one saw the need to re-establish a political institution common to all the European peoples in order to forge a political link between them and check their national ambitions? . . .

Here is what Bacon would have to say, first of all to the Institute:

'Gentlemen: you are one hundred and sixty in number; all of you are men of great merit, able and erudite. You have regular meetings. You are divided into classes and sections with different scientific interests. You have presidents and secretaries. Yet you do not form a scientific body; you are merely a gathering of scientists. And your studies have no unity; they are merely series of ideas which are joined together, because they are not related to any general conception, and because your association is not organised systematically. It is because of your lack of organisation that your replies to the Emperor's superb question *(What means must be employed to hasten the progress of the sciences?)* were only partial and therefore mediocre and inadequate.[39]

'Gentlemen, do you want to organise yourselves? Nothing could be easier. Select an idea to which you can relate all others and from which you can deduce all principles as consequences. Then you will have a philosophy. This philosophy will certainly be based on the idea of *Universal Gravitation,* and from that moment your studies will assume a systematic character. As for the means of organising your body, it is just as simple, it is the same. Give one of your classes responsibility for philosophy. Instruct the members you admit either to *deduce* or *relate* all known phenomena *from* or *to* the idea of universal gravitation, depending on whether they proceed *a priori* or *a posteriori.* You will then be systematically organised both *actively* and *passively,* that is, both in terms of *ideas* and as a *corporate body.* Your strength, in both respects, will become incalculable.'

Next, to the University:

'Your corporate body has only a spurious existence. It cannot possibly survive for long unless you take prompt action to consolidate it. The only means of achieving this goal are as follows:

'1. You must work as closely as possible with the Institute; you must form an intimate link with it, so intimate that you become a single corporate body, the greatest in French science. This body must then be divided into two parts, each with its own quite distinct task: the Institute will *improve* science, and you will *teach* it.

'2. You must never lose sight of the fact that in teaching you must always give preference to the *a priori* approach over the *a posteriori* approach.

'3. In the field of public education, which is your responsibility, you must arrange as quickly as possible a course in philosophy based on the idea of universal gravitation, a course whose object will be to deduce from this principle, as directly as possible, the explanation of all classes of phenomena.'

Finally, to the cabinet at Les Tuileries, addressing his words to the Emperor:

'*Sire,*

'Your armies have traversed the entire continent, from Cadiz to Moscow, from Hamburg to the farthest reaches of Italy. Thus, your military glory is at its height and any efforts you make to increase it can only diminish it. Your youthful years as Emperor have been the most brilliant in all history. You have now reached maturity, and your reign should assume the honourable character appropriate to that time of life: it should become calm and stable.

'Sire, you have modelled yourself on Charlemagne. In military terms you have greatly surpassed him. But Charlemagne was not only a soldier; he also distinguished himself in politics. Can your great soul tolerate the idea of being his inferior in this respect?

'Charlemagne was the true organiser of European society. He systematically united its peoples through a political link which remained intact and fulfilled its purpose perfectly from the 8th century to the 15th. Since the 15th century it has gradually fallen apart, and Your Majesty has finally destroyed it by restricting the Pope's sovereignty to Rome.

'Charlemagne knew that the huge population of one entire part of the world and its neighbouring islands, composed of several nations with well-established customs and radically different languages, separated by natural barriers, living in different climates, with different diets, could not live under the same government. He also knew that these different peoples living in adjacent territories would inevitably be in a state of continuous war unless they were linked through common general ideas, and unless a corporate body of the most learned men was made responsible for the application of general principles to objects of common interest and formed a tribunal of the law of nations. He knew that religion was a moral code which should be common to all the European peoples, and that the administrative body, consisting of the ministers of this religion, should also have the character of a general institution. Finally, he knew that it was necessary to give the religion and the heads of the clergy independence, and consequently to remove them from the direct influence of every national government. These are the reasons why he decided to give the sovereignty of Rome and its territory to the Pope.

'Sire, I shall divide the rest of what I have to say to you into three parts. In the first I shall quickly examine what happened from Charlemagne to the fifteenth century. In the second I shall show you, on the one hand, how the political link used by Charlemagne to unite the European peoples has been gradually broken up by the effect of the progress of enlightenment, and on the other hand how the sciences have provided the means of reorganising European society and improving its political system. In the third part I shall tell Your Majesty with frankness how you can use your all-powerful intellectual strength and your enormous political power for the happiness of Europe, the glory of the French nation, and your personal satisfaction: aims which posterity will require you to achieve simultaneously if you are to be granted pre-eminence over Charlemagne, whom you have taken as your model . . .'

THE SCIENCE OF MAN

We shall re-examine the science of man and base it on physiological observations.

The system of morals will be based on this principle: Experience has proved that every man who does not pursue happiness in a way which is useful to his fellow men is unhappy, no matter how prosperous he may appear to be.

Not everyone is able to work for the happiness of his fellow men in an equally general and important way. It is therefore necessary to divide moral theory into four adaptable parts:

The first for those whose intellectual activity can be useful to the progress of philosophy.

The second for those who are inspired by the sentiment of patriotism.

The third for those destined by nature to find happiness in the families of which they are the worthy heads.

The fourth for those who are capable of doing no more than fulfilling their duties, and whose inclination disposes them to assist more able men.

[*O.c.*, vol.II, pp.173-4, 184, 190-95, 240-41.]

PART II PROPOSALS FOR POST-WAR RECONSTRUCTION (1814-15)

There will undoubtedly come a time when all the peoples of Europe will feel that questions of common interest must be dealt with before coming down to national interests. Then evils will begin to lessen, troubles abate, wars die out. That is the goal towards which we are ceaselessly moving, towards which the advance of the human mind is carrying us! But which is more worthy of man's prudence: to be dragged there or to hasten towards it?

S.W., p.136.

7. THE REORGANISATION OF EUROPEAN SOCIETY

by Saint-Simon and Augustin Thierry

(Extracts from *De la réorganisation de la société européenne*, 1814)

TO THE PARLIAMENTS OF FRANCE AND ENGLAND

My Lords,
 Until the end of the fifteenth century all the nations of Europe formed a single body politic at peace within itself,* armed against the enemies of its constitution and independence.
 The Roman religion, practised from one end of Europe to the other, was the passive link of European society. The Roman clergy were its active link. Spread everywhere, everywhere independent, compatriots of all peoples, and with their own government and laws, the clergy were the centre from which emanated the will which gave life to this great body, and the impulse which set it in motion.
 The government of the clergy was a hierarchical aristocracy like the governments of all the European peoples.
 A territory independent of all temporal domination, too large to be conquered easily, too small to enable its owners to become conquerors, was the seat of the leaders of the clergy. Through their power, which opinion raised above the power of kings, they checked national ambitions. Through their policy they maintained that European balance which was beneficial then but which became disastrous when it was seized upon by one people.
 In this way the Court of Rome reigned over other courts, just as the latter reigned over the peoples, and Europe was one great aristocracy divided into several smaller aristocracies, all dependent on it, all subject to its influence and its checks.
 No institution based on an opinion should outlive that opinion. Luther, by undermining the ancient respect on which the power of the clergy rested, disorganised Europe. Half the Europeans freed themselves from the chains of papism, shattering the only political link which bound them to the larger society.
 The Treaty of Westphalia[40] established a new state of affairs through a political device called the balance of power. Europe was divided into two confederations which were supposed to remain equal. In this way war was established and made constitutional, for two

*When I say at peace, I mean in comparison with what one has seen since and what one sees today.

leagues of equal power are inevitably rivals, and rivalry means war.

Henceforth each power was concerned only with increasing its military forces. Instead of pitifully small armies, brought into service for a short time and quickly disbanded, there were now formidable standing armies everywhere; and they were nearly always in action, for since the Treaty of Westphalia Europe has been in a state of permanent war.

It was against this background of disorder, which was and still is called the basis of the political system, that England rose to greatness. Cleverer than the continental peoples, it understood the real nature of this balance of power; and through a dual calculation it saw how to turn it to its own advantage and the detriment of others.

Separated from the continent by the sea, it ceased to have anything in common with those who lived there by creating its own national religion and a government different from all other European governments. Its constitution was no longer founded on prejudice and custom, but on what is required at all times and in all places, on what should be the basis of every constitution: the liberty and happiness of the people.

Strengthened internally by a healthy and strong organisation, England sought to exert its great influence on the outside world. The aim of its foreign policy was universal domination.

In navigation, commerce, and industry it favoured itself and hindered others. It used its power to support the arbitrary governments which oppressed Europe, reserving liberty and its blessings for itself alone. Its wealth, its army, its politics were all used to maintain this supposed balance which, by destroying the continental powers of Europe one by one, left it free to do everything with impunity.

It was out of this dual political system that arose the colossus of English power which threatens to overrun the world. For a century it has enabled England – free and happy internally, harsh and despotic externally – to treat the whole of Europe as its plaything, to cause a disturbance whenever it feels like it.

Such a state of affairs is too monstrous to last. It is in Europe's interest to free itself from the tyranny which shackles it. It is in England's interest not to wait for an armed Europe to achieve liberation.

Let there be no mistake: these are not evils which can be cured by secret negotiations and minor cabinet manoeuvres. There cannot possibly be any rest or happiness for Europe until a political link rejoins England to the continent from which it is separated.

Europe was formerly a confederate society united through common institutions and subject to a common government which stood in the same relation to peoples as national governments stand in relation to individuals. Only such an arrangement can provide a complete solution.

I am certainly not claiming that one should raise from the dust that old organisation whose useless remains still tire Europe. The nineteenth century is too distant from the thirteenth. A constitution strong in itself, based on principles derived from the nature of things, independent of transitory beliefs and short-lived opinions: that is what Europe needs and what I am now proposing . . .

THE BEST POSSIBLE CONSTITUTION

I wish to discover if there is a form of government whose very nature is good, and which is founded on certain, absolute, universal principles, independent of time and place . . .

Understanding constitution to mean any system of social order directed towards the common good, the best constitution will be that according to which institutions are organised and power distributed so that every question of public interest is dealt with in as much detail and as comprehensively as possible.

Now, every question of public interest, precisely because it is a question, must be decided in the same way as any other question.

Logic offers us two methods of deciding any question, or rather a single method involving two operations: synthesis and analysis. In the first, one considers the matter under examination as a whole, that is, *a priori*. In the second, one divides it up in order to consider it in detail, that is, one examines it *a posteriori*.

The results obtained by synthesis should be verified by analysis, and conversely those obtained by analysis should be verified by synthesis; which is the same as saying that a question has been treated with certainty and comprehensiveness only when it has been successively examined *a priori* and *a posteriori*.

Now that has been established, I say that the best constitution is the one according to which every question of public interest is always examined both *a priori* and *a posteriori*.

Now, in society, to examine questions of public interest successively *a priori* and *a posteriori* simply means to examine them first in terms of the general interest, and then in terms of its members' particular interests.

It only remains to find a way of organising a constitution so that every question of public interest is always examined in the manner I have just described.

The first requirement is to establish two distinct powers constituted in such a way that one examines things from the viewpoint of the nation's general interest, and the other from the viewpoint of the particular interests of its individual members.

I shall call the first the *power for general interests,* and the second the *power for particular or local interests.*

Both powers should be given the right to conceive and propose any legislative measures they judge necessary.

So far we have simply provided for two powers which approach the same goal by different routes. But the fundamental provision which gives the constitution its strength is that no decision of either power may be executed without being examined and approved by the other.

In this way every legislative measure conceived in terms of the general interest will be examined in terms of particular interests, and conversely. Or, to return to the terminology of logic, every legislative measure conceived *a priori* will be examined *a posteriori,* and conversely.

Only good laws will be made, for none will be approved or executed without the agreement of the two powers to show that it is for the good of the people, both as a whole and as individuals; which is the same as saying that no public measure will be passed until its goodness and wisdom have been demonstrated by the most rigorous logical methods.

As the equality of the two powers, of which I have spoken above, is the basis of the constitution, the latter would break down as soon as one power predominated over the other, since questions would then be examined only from a single point of view and either the general interest would be sacrificed to particular interests, or particular interests would be sacrificed to the general interest. Hence, a third power, which may be called the *regulating* or *moderating power,* is necessary to maintain the balance between the two others and contain them within their proper limits.

The third power should have the right to re-examine questions of public interest already examined by the other two powers, correct their errors, reject laws which it regards as defective, and propose others which should be sent forthwith to the first two powers for examination . . .

The goodness of a constitution founded on the principles which I have just established is as certain, absolute, and universal as that of a good syllogism.

And it should not be thought that this constitution is one of those impracticable theories or fantastic speculations whose only use is to provide material for the pens of authors. It has existed and survived for more than a hundred years, and the experience of these hundred years confirms our reasoning. Through this constitution one people has achieved freedom and become the most powerful people in Europe.

THE ENGLISH CONSTITUTION

England is governed by a parliament, a supreme authority composed of three powers: the King, the House of Commons, and the House of Peers . . .

Interested in the nation's greatness and glory, which are also his own, free from the ties which bind every other citizen to a certain section of the State which he prefers to others, the King, in all he proposes, is bound to have only general views and general interests . . .

The House of Commons is composed of deputies from all the provinces, members of all the corporations in the State, who together represent every kind of local or particular interest . . .

A body of men, highly regarded by virtue of their birth, their services, and their wealth, is placed between the King and the Commons to re-examine the decisions that are taken, to balance and correct them, and make new proposals.

They exercise that intermediate power which I have called *regulating* or *moderating power.*

Considered from another point of view, the House of Peers checks the natural tendency of the King and the Commons towards absolute power, a tendency common to all individuals and corporations . . .

It is not enough to establish the constitution on its foundations. It is also necessary to ensure that these foundations cannot be shaken.

The King represents the interests of the whole State, just as the Commons represent the interests of every part of the State . . . But the Commons are elected and the Crown is hereditary; and heredity, which is a guarantee for the people that the succession will not be disturbed, does not guarantee that birth will place the most able man on the throne.

That part of the legislative power which the constitution gives to the King will be badly administered if he lacks the necessary ability. And if he is unjust the executive power which he holds will be employed for personal vengeance and acts of arbitrary authority.

In order to avoid these difficulties the monarchy has been divided into two naturally distinct parts. One embraces the pomp, magnificence, and honour — all the attributes of sovereignty; the other embraces the administration of affairs. The first is transmitted by heredity and placed in the hands of the ruling dynasty; the second, essentially elective, is given to the Prime Minister.

Ministerial responsibility protects the people against every abuse of power and bad administration . . .

Reason has led me to the conclusion that the best possible constitution is the parliamentary constitution; and experience has confirmed what reason has proved. It is nearly a hundred years since

England fully established this form of government by completing its revolution. Have not its prosperity and power continually increased since then? What people is freer and richer internally, greater externally, more skilled in the industrial arts, navigation, and commerce? And to what is this incomparable power to be attributed if not to English government, a government more liberal, more vigorous, more conducive to national happiness and glory than all the governments of Europe?

THE NEW ORGANISATION OF EUROPEAN SOCIETY

... Europe would have the best possible organisation if all its constituent nations were governed by parliaments, and if they recognised the supremacy of a common parliament set above all national governments and invested with the powers of settling their disputes...

The European Parliament will be established without difficulty as soon as all the peoples of Europe live under parliamentary regimes.

Hence, the European Parliament can begin to be established as soon as that part of the European population subject to representative government is superior to the part remaining under arbitrary governments.

Now, such a state of affairs actually exists at present in Europe: the English and the French are unquestionably superior in strength to the rest of Europe, and they have parliamentary forms of government.

It is therefore possible to begin the reorganisation of Europe immediately.

The English and French should associate to form a common parliament. The association's chief aim should be to grow by attracting other peoples to it. Consequently, the Anglo-French Government should assist all supporters of representative constitutions in other nations, and should do so with all its power so that parliaments will be established among all peoples subject to absolute monarchs. As soon as it adopts the representative form of government each nation should join the association and send its own members to the common parliament. Then the organisation of Europe will be achieved gradually, without wars, catastrophes, or political revolutions...

CONCLUSION

In this work I have sought to prove that peace and stability can be achieved in Europe only through the establishment of a political system appropriate to the level of enlightenment, and the creation of a common power invested with a force capable of curbing the ambitions of peoples and kings . . .

After great efforts and much work I have reached the viewpoint of the common interest of the European peoples. Only from this point can one perceive both the evils which threaten us and the means of avoiding those evils. If those who direct our affairs rise to the same heights they will all see what I have seen . . .

There will undoubtedly come a time when all the peoples of Europe will feel that questions of common interest must be dealt with before coming down to national interests. Then evils will begin to lessen, troubles abate, wars die out. That is the goal towards which we are ceaselessly moving, towards which the advance of the human mind is carrying us! But which is more worthy of man's prudence: to be dragged there or to hasten towards it?

The imagination of poets has placed the golden age in the infancy of the human race, amidst the ignorance and coarseness of ancient times. It would have been much better to consign the iron age there. The golden age of the human race is not behind us; it lies before us, in the perfection of the social order. Our fathers did not see it; our children will arrive there one day; it is up to us to clear the way.

[*Oeuvres,* vol. I, pt. 1, pp.161-5, 182-93, 195, 197, 207-8, 244, 246-8.]

8. ON THE ESTABLISHMENT OF AN OPPOSITION PARTY

(Extracts from *Lettre de M. le comte de Saint-Simon, sur l'établissement du parti de l'opposition, Le Censeur, vol. III,* 1815)

I have had a brochure published entitled *The Reorganisation of European Society*. The success of this work, which was favourably received by the public, despite the efforts of journalists, has encouraged me to undertake a new work on which I am now engaged. This work will take a long time to complete, and circumstances are pressing. I have therefore extracted some of the ideas which form the basis of this project — a project whose prompt execution is of obvious use. I warn that the link between the ideas I am presenting and the principles of political science will be methodically established only in the complete work.

THE MINISTRY AND THE OPPOSITION

One thing is necessary above all if a parliamentary government is to act firmly and regularly: the division of public opinion into two parties — the ministerial party and the opposition party.

These two parties must exercise a reciprocal action on each other, the equality of which is the basis of the constitution, the guarantee of public order, the firmest protection against revolutions. For a revolution occurs only when one part of the State, opposed to the rest by its principles or interests, becomes preponderant and crushes it. This is something which will never happen as long as the equal force of the two parties maintains an equilibrium between principles and therefore between interests, of which political principles are but an expression.

There are two types of action by the ministerial party on the opposition party, and by the opposition party on the ministerial. party: namely, through the principles that they adopt and which they tend to make dominant; and through the watch which each keeps on the other's constitutionality.

Thus, properly speaking, there cannot be either a ministerial party or an opposition party unless both are constitutional; or rather these names are only seditious and revolutionary if those who adopt them do not recognise the State constitution as the basis of these principles.

The Charter[41] is the basis and therefore the expression of the French constitution. An opinion is constitutional according to whether it conforms or does not conform to the Charter.

The most remarkable period since the establishment of the

parliamentary regime in France began when the declaration was made by the King to the members of the Chambers, and notified to the journals by His Majesty's Chancellor, that he accepted constitutional principles. Before then France still had a turbulent and revolutionary attitude. The so-called 'ministerials' announced proudly that they sought to overthrow the Charter, and that His Majesty himself had no intention of maintaining it. The sound part of the nation, thrown out of the bounds of moderation by the violence of these invectives, seemed prepared to defend its liberty with force. The King's declaration made everyone return to their limits. It curbed those who dared to be more royalist than he, and with the fury of one party it put an end to the fury of the other. Henceforth, there will only be opinions that one dare acknowledge — constitutional opinions. The only power that honest men can contemplate employing is the power of reason.

It is thus only since that time that the two parties of which I have spoken have been able really to organise themselves, and that members of the nation have been able to discuss civil and political matters without disturbing the State. Since then opinion has had a fixed base — the maintenance of the Charter — and therefore discussion has been kept within limits which it cannot go beyond, and has become legal, which it could never be if everyone were free to base their opinions on caprice, so that controversy increased all the time, and concentrated on first principles instead of only secondary points.

Thus, this impulse given by the King to public opinion has provided a way of organising the ministerial party and the opposition party without any danger. These two parties are, in other words, the pivots on which parliamentary government proceeds; so they will secure the basis of the constitution, and the secure constitution will maintain on the throne that august dynasty which has been given to us . . .

THE ORGANISATION OF THE MINISTRY AND THE OPPOSITION

A party is organised when all its members, united through common principles, recognise a leader who concerts all its movements and directs all its operations, in such a way that there is both unity of action and unity of views, and that consequently the party's force is as great as possible.

This principle may be applied without difficulty to the opposition party; for in that party, where favour does not play a role, where men, accustomed to bringing their forces together, know themselves and each other, the man whose superior talent is generally recognised will naturally become the unopposed leader.

If we apply this principle to the ministry, we shall see the Prime Minister at the head, then the rest of the ministers, and then finally those who are members of this party either through their conviction or hope of favour.

Now, the ministerial party cannot be organised by itself, for it would be remarkable if the ministers, chosen by the King from totally unrelated classes, had precisely the same way of thinking, the same political principles, and recognised with one accord the superiority of one individual to whom they would give the direction of the party. It is only through the opposition that the ministry can be organised. It is in opposition that the ministry is formed. It is thus the opposition that ought to be formed first, and we have seen that it could be organised by itself and through its own powers.

In national politics we are merely the imitators of England; and in England the ministry is always formed from the opposition and nearly always renewed in its entirety. At each new election the King admits to the ministry men of the same party, men of the same political doctrine, men whose superior talents are recognised by everyone, such as Mr. Pitt and his friends, Mr. Fox and his friends. In short, without opposition there will be ministers but never a ministry.

THE OPPOSITION AND THE MINISTRY IN FRANCE

... It follows from what I have said above that it is the opposition party which ought to be organised first.

The organisation of the opposition party can be achieved only through the power of public opinion.

ON PUBLIC OPINION

... It is thus necessary to find a way of creating immediately in France a public spirit sufficiently powerful to organise an opposition party.

Public opinion is nothing but the habit of recognising the link between one's private interest and the public interest. Thus, if there are men whose personal interest in the present circumstances is attached to the maintenance of the Charter and the affirmation of the constitution in as evidently invariable a manner as can be, these men have no need of habit in this respect, and should be disposed to make sacrifices for the stability of the Government, which is nothing but the protection of their interests. Now, there is today in France a numerous class of property owners whose possessions can have no guarantee but the Charter.[42] Not only that, these possessions must decrease or increase in value depending on whether constitutional opinion becomes less or more influential.

THE OWNERS OF NATIONAL LANDS

Only when the whole of France is intimately convinced that the King's successors, whatever their will, are constrained to submit to the Constitutional Charter, will the value of national properties rise to the same level as other properties.

The national lands have fallen to their paltriest price. Several of them have even been uselessly put up for sale, which is clearly a result of the uncertainty which there has been, and which unfortunately a large number of persons still feel, concerning the maintenance of the Charter.

Now, only the formation of an opposition party, capable of putting a stop to all kinds of enterprise in this respect, can re-establish general confidence; and only a re-establishment of confidence can restore the credit of national properties.

It is thus in the interest of the owners of national lands to work with all their power for the organisation of the opposition party, since, as far as they are concerned, to organise this party is only to re-establish and secure their wealth which has been diminished by public distrust.

It follows that the owners of national lands, inspired both by patriotic interest and personal interest, must form an association.

This association will aim to organise as quickly and as completely as possible the opposition party, and to encourage and issue writings tending to convince people of the Charter's inviolability . . .

If an opposition party is not formed, who will watch over the ministry when Parliament is not assembled? The ministers will be in a fine position when the representative body is no longer assembled, and the French are therefore a sparse multititude, and consequently incapable of resistance. Who can say that once they see our weakness they will not act arbitrarily, will not dare to infringe the Charter, perhaps even attempt to destroy it? And what resources will those men have who want to be free, except to oppose force with force, that is, with violence and insurrection? . . .

[*Cens.* III, pp.334-8, 342-50.]

9. LETTER TO THE MINISTER OF THE INTERIOR[43]

(1815, during the 'Hundred Days', 20 March — 22 June)

My Lord,
   It is the wish of Your Excellency, the wish of all well-informed and well-intentioned men that France should enjoy as liberal a social order as the present state of enlightenment will allow.
   But there is one fact to which people do not pay enough attention: liberty in France will always be endangered as long as France is the only continental state to be free. France cannot possibly be reorganised soundly and permanently unless the majority of European nations are reorganised in the same way.
   Thus, it is not by limiting one's view to France that one can most usefully work for the liberty of France. It is by promoting simultaneously in all the enlightened nations of Europe the progress of knowledge and the course of events to which that progress leads.
   The latest political movements in Spain, Italy, northern Germany, etc. offer incontestable proof that the whole of Europe is now moving towards the social order which we are seeking to establish in France and of which England provided the first example. Thus, to any person of sound judgement, such as Your Excellency, the present era marks not only the end of the French Revolution, but also the beginning of the European Revolution without which the French Revolution would never end.
   We can thus render a great and important service to the French nation by directing our attention to the possible means of promoting the European Revolution and destroying the obstacles that stand in its way. It is this subject which I want briefly to discuss with Your Excellency.
   We are on the brink of one of those great epochs that may be called revolutions of the human mind, when the changes that have occurred over a number of centuries in every sphere of human science impose a new character and direction on social organisation, or, more precisely, on morality and philosophy, which are its foundations.
   I understand morality to include the science of public law, which is morality applied to nations.
   The last revolution of this kind was the one which abolished slavery in Europe, or rather which allowed only civil slavery to survive while abolishing domestic slavery. This was the establishment of the Christian religion.
   This resulted, for the first time, in a general moral code on which the relations between individuals, between individuals and society, and

between societies were based: the evangelical moral code.

The great political principle of the Christian code was that power derived from God, that princes were accountable for their conduct to God alone, and that the people were accountable both to God and to princes.

Since the time when such maxims were the best that political science could offer and the basis of the social order, our enlightenment has increased, our institutions have changed and been prepared for changes, and we have reached a point at which we find these principles and their consequences ridiculous. Yet the old moral code from which they are deduced is the only one taught in the schools of Europe. Everywhere people are concerned with new institutions, yet everywhere the spirit of the old institutions is propagated and sanctioned, with the result that education, the foundation and support of the social order, is in total opposition to the social order which is now being established, or which is emerging through the progress of knowledge. What people are taught to think is the opposite of what they do or want to do.

This is a result of the fact that all the recently discovered political ideas do not form a body of doctrine, but are still scattered and incoherent in the minds of thinkers. There are partial observations but no theory. There is general agreement about principles, but no certainty. There is disagreement concerning the consequences of principles and the links are missing.

Is it surprising then that the establishment and progress of liberal institutions in Europe is so slow and uncertain, when the social theory of which these institutions are only the application is too incomplete to be taught universally, and when a quite contrary theory is taught; when education, far from urging minds along the route followed by human intelligence, far from helping them to remain there, actually diverts them from it and leads them astray?

Kings are made by the people and for the people; they must be accountable for their conduct to the people, while both must contrive to be accountable to God. This is the principle on which every social order in Europe is now being based; on which England has based its government, on which France is establishing its own, and on which the peoples of one part of Italy and of almost all northern Germany are seeking to establish theirs. It is the principle on which a European code of political law must be based. It must also be taken as the basis of social education if civil slavery is to be destroyed in Europe, if France is to be free and is to know how to be free.

We have codes of civil law superior to anything ever established in that field. We owe them to His Majesty; it is his finest title to glory, the one achievement which even his greatest enemies have respected.

The code of political law to which I have referred is, so to speak, only the completion of the great work that His Majesty began when he gave us our civil codes. It is up to him to complete this work. It is a new glory which awaits him, one which is worthy of his great soul. In order to achieve what he has done, he had only to summon the most famous lawyers. To achieve the rest he will need only to summon the most famous publicists in Europe. Great genius and great power make all that easy.

If His Majesty gathered round him all those persons in Europe who have achieved success in the field of social organisation, and initiated discussions under his presidency on this subject, it would be astonishingly easy to clear up all the points of controversy, and to resolve all the problems which need to be solved if a theory of modern politics is to be formulated. For in the present situation first principles are the same or very nearly the same for everyone engaged in these studies; the whole task would thus be reduced to the deduction of secondary principles, and from the same general idea minds of the same probity and wisdom can hardly infer contrary or even very different particular ideas.

Thus a task would be accomplished which has already been attempted more than once but which was never practicable until today. For political science is like all other sciences: it takes a long time to reduce them to clear, simple theories based on observed facts. If physics and chemistry achieved this only yesterday, is it surprising that the moral sciences, whose researches are concerned with much more complex and more difficult relationships, are still not positive?

In France, where the most astute minds are still irresolute and uncertain on questions of social organisation because of the lack of positive education, and where this uncertainty could lead to new revolutions, it would be very useful to establish public chairs of politics. The principles of all governments, ancient and modern, could then be discussed, and it could be proved by reasoning and experience that of all possible governments the one most suitable for Europe at the present level of enlightenment, the only one towards which all our desires and efforts ought to be directed, is the kind of limited democracy which exists in England and which His Majesty is seeking to establish in France. Such courses would inspire people with a love of law and the public good; and the young would learn to cherish our institutions, not only because they are those of the fatherland, but because they are also the best.

The studies which such an education demands have been my life's work; and I shall continue to devote myself to them without respite.

There is one further consideration: the political unity which Europe needs, which has been sought hitherto in religious unity, but which can only be found in the unity of moral doctrines and public law. Religious unity as it has been conceived, as it has existed up to a certain point in Europe, would today be as fruitless as it is impossible. For, first of all, it is not a question of getting the peoples of Europe to agree on just any ideas; they must be ideas in harmony with their enlightenment, derived from the knowledge they have acquired, without which the effort would be both absurd and useless. Now, we know what religions were born in our time, which religious ideas are those of today, and whether what was good and wise a thousand years ago is good and wise today.

Secondly, as far as the relations between peoples are concerned, unity of moral doctrine is everything, unity of worship nothing. This unity of doctrine can be achieved through existing religions; no reforms are necessary. For religions are essentially no more than different ways of representing the philosophical and moral principles useful to society, of popularising them, of authorising them in accordance with manners and enlightenment. Now, if one can ensure that the same principles are taught, then the manner in which they are propagated, that is, the difference between religions, is unimportant.

The civilisations and manners of the enlightened nations of Europe are so similar that the same moral doctrine, once established and codified, is bound to be taught in all schools and introduced into all European religions.

If that were done, not only would a better educated Europe advance more quickly towards liberty, but there would also be established first, through the community of moral and political principles, a kind of union of European nations, pending the day when they could join in a closer and more indissoluble union based on common institutions.

As a man, My Lord, you are devoted to the good of humanity; as a minister to the glory of the nation and the Emperor. It is this twofold capacity which makes you so dear to the public and respected by them, and which has encouraged me to address this outline to you, and ask if it would be proper for you to submit it to His Majesty.

As for myself, my life has been employed in the search for what is useful to my fellow men. I should be happy to see the realisation of hopes which I no longer dared conceive, and which have been revived by the return of His Majesty to us.

I have the honour to be, My Lord, with respect
Your most humble servant,
Saint-Simon.
rue des Fossés-Saint-Germain-des-Prés, no.16.

[*Revue d'histoire économique et sociale,* vol. XIII, no. 2 (1925), pp.129-32. Textual errors corrected by Jean Dautry in *T.c.,* pp.160-61.]

10. TO ALL ENGLISHMEN AND FRENCHMEN WHO ARE ZEALOUS FOR THE PUBLIC GOOD

(Aux Anglais et aux Français qui sont zélés pour le bien public, 1815)

We propose that all Englishmen and Frenchmen who are zealous for the public good should found an Anglo-French society to establish and propagate the political doctrine most advantageous to those men whose work is most useful to society in general.

This association, which will consist chiefly of the most important industrials,[44] the most distinguished positive scientists, and the most commendable artists, will put metaphysics entirely aside and base all its work, all its reasoning, every part of its doctrine, in short, all its published ideas on observed facts.

This society will concentrate on producing a perfectly exact account of the advance of civilisation up to the present, and in particular since the fifteenth century. With the greatest care it will establish the following facts:

The first important crisis of the revolution which is now disturbing the entire human race, the crisis which gave this revolution its positive character, was made manifest in the fifteenth century. Historians have preserved for us a detailed record of this crisis which they have called the *Renaissance* of the fine arts, sciences, and industry. This crisis was caused by the rapid development of the two capacities introduced into Europe by the Arabs: the positive scientific capacity in the spiritual sphere, and the industrial capacity in the temporal sphere. Before the fifteenth century society was divided into two spiritual classes: the clergy who formed the beliefs, and the laity who submitted to those beliefs. The positive scientists are introducing a new arrangement: they belong neither to the class of believers, nor to the class which forms beliefs; they acknowledge and propose only demonstration.

In the temporal sphere every people was divided into just two classes: one composed of those who commanded, and the other of those who obeyed. The industrials are introducing a new arrangement: they do not command; they do not obey; they conduct all their affairs by mutual agreement, whether with the rulers or the ruled; and all their relations are based on a combination of the particular interests of the various contracting parties.

This society will show that since the fifteenth century positive scientists have demonstrated their intellectual superiority over theologians. In fact, the opinion which served as the basis of the entire theological edifice was that God had made man in his own image, that he had given him the earth to live on, that he had placed the earth at the centre of the world, that he had created the whole universe for man, the sun to give him light during the day, the moon and stars to guide him at night. Now, Copernicus proved that this system of belief was absurd by showing that it is the sun which is the centre of the system; that the earth — which is infinitely smaller than the sun — several planets, and all the stars move round the sun, on which the earth is dependent; and that therefore man and the earth he inhabits can consequently be considered only as creations of a very subordinate order in the universe.

This society will also show that since the fifteenth century the political superiority of the industrial capacity over military talents has been proved. In fact, under the Medicis, who were all manufacturers and merchants, the Government of Florence contributed more to the progress of civilisation in Europe than the Governments of Charles the Fifth and all other princes, before and since that period, who have belonged to the feudal class.

This society will give an account of the progress made by the positive sciences and industry, as well as of the political importance acquired by the industrials and the scientists since the fifteenth century.

The society's work will be divided into three parts. The first will aim to give an account of the progress of civilisation since its origin. Our intention in the previous pages was to give an idea of the way in which historical facts should be conceived, connected, and presented.

At the end of this study the society will observe that the present situation is monstrous, because all particular interests are directed by the scientific and industrial capacities, while general interests are still subject to theological and feudal principles. It will show that the only way to establish calm is to give the capacities which now direct particular interests responsibility for administering general interests.

In the second part of its work the society will present, with the necessary elaboration, the plan of social organisation most advantageous to the industrials and positive scientists of England and France.

This plan will serve to unite closely the English and French nations, while at the same time preserving their national independence.

We shall indicate the four main series to be included in this second part of the society's work.

FIRST SERIES: GENERAL CONSIDERATIONS

The English above all, and the French after them, are the richest and most powerful of the major peoples. It is in these nations that men enjoy the greatest moral and physical well-being.

More work of positive utility is done in England and France than in any other country.

The wealth, power, and well-being of the English and the French have increased in direct relation to the development of their scientific and industrial work.

Thus, in order to add to their well-being, the English and French should take the most appropriate measures to develop their scientific and industrial work as far as possible.

Now, the best way to give the greatest encouragement to scientific and industrial work in England and France is to allow the most distinguished scientists and the most important industrials to organise the English and French nations, and then to give them the power to administer the interests of these two nations, for the class which makes the law is always the class which is best treated by the law.

SECOND SERIES: PLAN FOR AN ANGLO-FRENCH UNION

English and French public affairs will be administered by two distinct powers: a spiritual power and a temporal power. The two nations will share a common spiritual power, but each will have its own temporal power. The spiritual power and the temporal powers will be directed by their own legislative and executive councils.

The Spiritual Power

The spiritual power will be given the task of establishing a new social doctrine and a new system of public education. It will be given the task of making the general laws which, by their nature, must be common to the two nations. It will also be given the task of settling any disputes which might arise between the two nations. The executive council will arbitrate in the first instance, and the legislative council will give a final ruling on appeal.

Each year the legislative council will reward all the world's scientists whose discoveries have contributed to the progress of the physical and mathematical sciences. These rewards will be of an importance which will make them worthy of Anglo-French munificence.

Every five years the legislative council will publish a work giving an account of the progress made by the sciences during the previous five years, and indicating the research which the council thinks scientists should concentrate on.

The Social Doctrine

The legislative council will establish a social doctrine essentially different from the Christian doctrine. The latter imposed the fundamental obligation to pray and give alms. The new doctrine will prescribe work and the acquisition of positive knowledge.

In this doctrine every kind of work in which man can engage, and every action he can produce will be analysed and categorised in three classes: useful, harmful, and indifferent to society. This doctrine will show that the men whose work is most useful to society are the ones who will obtain the greatest personal satisfaction under the new regime.

This doctrine will be taught to all children without exception in France and England.

Every Sunday, in all the towns of England and France, sermons will be delivered in which the preachers will show that the only way men can increase their moral and physical well-being is to perfect both the positive sciences and industry, and to practise morality more strictly. In each place the preachers will indicate how the conduct of the inhabitants of that locality can best further the progress of the sciences and industry. They will draw attention to any moral laxity in their conduct.

Public Education

All children in England and France will be taught to read, write, and count. They will all be given a more or less extensive grounding in astronomy, physics, chemistry, physiology, drawing, and music. The teaching of the social doctrine will serve as the basis of the instruction given in the schools at all grades.

There will be four grades of school. A school of the lowest grade will be established in every town without exception. Then, according to the importance of the town, schools of the second, third, and fourth grades will be established.

In addition, a training college will be established, forming a fifth grade of education. This college will be common to the English and the French, and will be directed by the spiritual legislative council. The members of this council will teach the sciences in the college.

Composition and Organisation of the Teaching Body

The scientific capacity is the true spiritual capacity. Thus, the spiritual power is nothing more than the scientific power. Thus, the organisation of the teaching body is at the same time the organisation of the spiritual power.

The legislative council of the spiritual power will be composed of the twenty-four most distinguished scientists in England and France. Twelve of these scientists will be chosen from physicists working on inorganic physics, the other twelve from the ranks of those working on organic physics.

All professional English and French physicists will assemble at the council's inauguration to nominate its members.

Any vacancies which arise will be filled by competition. The council will judge this competition.

The executive council of the spiritual power will be composed of thirteen members.

The president of this council will be nominated and may be dismissed at will by the legislative council.

The twelve members of the executive council will be nominated by the president of this council, and may be dismissed by him.

The president of the executive council and two councillors of his choice will have the right to attend the deliberations of the legislative council; they will have a consultative vote.

All members of the executive council will be selected from the rich class. They will receive no salary for their appointment and no gratuity. The public treasury will pay only for the cost of their accommodation.

The legislative council will meet for only one month per year. The executive council will always be in operation.

Each grade of school will be dependent on the grade immediately above it. Schools of the highest grade will be directly subordinate to the executive council.

All teaching posts will be filled by competition. Competitions for vacancies in the lower schools will be judged by teachers in the schools ranked immediately above.

Competitions for vacancies in the higher schools will be judged by members of the legislative council.

Seat of the Spiritual Power

The spiritual power will have its seat in England until the major continental powers recognise the Anglo-French constitution. It will then sit alternately in England and France.

The Old Spiritual Power

The old spiritual power will be invited by the new power to continue its functions until the latter is organised. The legislative council will give rewards to any members of the old spiritual power who help to establish the new one.

When the new spiritual power is operational, the teaching and the cult of all religions will become entirely free, but no minister of any religion will receive a salary from the public treasury.

The Temporal Power

The English and French temporal powers will be linked organically by the Anglo-French spiritual power, but in relation to one another they will be quite distinct, completely separate and entirely independent. Thus, each must be dealt with separately.

The English Temporal Power

The new English temporal power will be invested with all the powers presently attributed to the three branches of Parliament, except for authority over spiritual power. The new power will be directed by a legislative council and an executive council.

Composition and Organisation of the Legislative Council. The legislative council will be composed of the sixteen farmers, sixteen manufacturers, sixteen merchants, and eight bankers who are the most important in England. Total: 56 members.

At the first election for this council the leading farmers, manufacturers, merchants, and bankers will vote. They will nominate only those men whose businesses are the most important in the four great classes of industrials.

The council will then put forward nominations for any posts which become vacant, always according to the same principle that the choice must be made from the most important businessmen in the four major classes of industry.

Every councillor who retires from industrial affairs will cease to take part in this council.

The council will choose four retired industrials to be commissioners, responsible for maintaining good relations with the legislative council of the spiritual power. The commissioners will have the right to attend meetings, where they will have a consultative vote.

The council will organise itself as it thinks fit.

Powers of the Legislative Council. Each year the legislative council will draw up the financial law and the secondary laws needed by the nation.* The aim of all laws made by the council will be to establish

---

*The financial law must serve as the basis of the temporal reorganisation of society, just as the new general doctrine will be the foundation of its spiritual reorganisation. The two devices are similar in these two respects: they are of equal importance, and they are equally difficult to establish well. But they are entirely different in another respect: the general doctrine must be conceived and produced at the start of the movement towards the regime which is most favourable to the men who do the most useful work; while the financial law must be improved only through successive modifications.

The cause of this difference is easy to grasp. The general doctrine must be taught principally to children, who have not contracted any habits. The financial law must govern the social relations of mature men, whose bad political habits are second nature to them.

the regime most favourable to production.*

Each year the council will examine the conduct of the executive council, especially the use it has made of the funds granted to it by the financial law. After this examination it will publish its opinion on the conduct of the executive council, and will replace the council if it has committed any serious errors.

Each year the council will give national rewards to all men whose discoveries or important improvements have made noteworthy contributions to the amelioration of society's moral and physical well-being.

The council will function for at least fifteen days and at the most one month per year, except in the first year when its session will last as long as business demands.

Executive Council. The executive council will consist of a president and six councillors. The councillors will be nominated by the president and may be dismissed by him. The president will be chosen by the legislative council, which may replace him if it is not happy with the way he fulfils his duties.

The president and two councillors of his choice will have the right to attend meetings of the legislative council, and will have a consultative vote there.

The president will nominate one commissioner who will be responsible for maintaining good relations with the French temporal power.

The members of the executive council will be chosen from the wealthiest class, and will receive no state salary. The public treasury will pay only for the cost of their accommodation.

The executive council will use all its influence over the nation to diminish the latter's respect for *rentiers*. It will make every effort to stimulate all those who do not invest their capital in industrial enterprises to spend their money in a way which contributes to the improvement of society's moral and physical well-being.

Under the industrial regime, which will be essentially a regime of equality, it is not desirable that the same families should keep wealth for several generations. All men must work to enrich their children loyally or to impoverish them honourably. All capital must be continually employed. It would be monstrous for those who possess the instrument, but do not make use of it, to enjoy more respect than those who show themselves to be capable of putting it to good use.

The French Temporal Power

The French temporal power will be organised (in its chief arrangements)

*One of the secondary laws which will contribute most to the new progress of civilisation will be the law mobilising landed property, the aim of which will be to increase productive activity by increasing the volume of disposable capital.[45]

in the same way as the English temporal power, and like the latter it will work to establish the social organisation most favourable to production. But each temporal power will employ different methods of execution, because of differences between the French and English climates, and between the characters of the English and French nations.

Whether the English or French industrials ought to be the first to constitute the temporal social organisation most advantageous to them is a question we shall not answer here. We shall simply summarise the arguments for and against each of them.

French industrials have a more ardent character. They suffer more harassment from their Government and more insolence from the nobles. Thus, they have a greater incentive to change the established order. It is necessary to add that they are more spirited in terms of producing new political ideas, since their insurrectional tendency to improve their condition is a hundred years more recent than that of the English industrials. But, on the other hand, the French industrials are less wealthy, less educated, and less accustomed to combining their efforts to attain an aim of common interest; and besides that, they have the opposition of the German feudality, supported by the ignorance and barbarity of the Russian Government and nation, to fear.

The English industrials are richer, more educated, and more used to uniting to achieve an aim of common interest. They have no foreign opposition to fear, but on the other hand they have less of an incentive to change the established order, because they do not suffer as much harassment from their Government or as much insolence from the nobles; because the kind of commercial monopoly they enjoy over the rest of the human race is a kind of compensation for the inconveniences they suffer; and finally, because their land army is much smaller than the French, so that the arbitrary authority exercised over them is inevitably much more moderate. And to this we must add that their character is such that they are much more willing than the French to tolerate their class's subordination to the rich idlers and the lawyer-metaphysicians.

In any case, what is certain is that the scientists' efforts to constitute the Anglo-French spiritual power will precede the efforts of English and French industrials to establish new temporal powers.

THIRD SERIES: METHOD OF EXECUTION

In order to establish the social organisation which we have just outlined, the industrials and scientists must use two chief methods: they must use demonstration, and strength in support of demonstration.

The scientists must demonstrate to all classes of society, especially to the first and the last, that is to say the princes and the peoples, that the constitution whose foundations we have just presented is the one which would increase the moral and physical well-being of the human race as quickly as possible.

The scientists must preach this doctrine in every part of England and France with the same zeal as the apostles preached Christianity.

There will be one major obstacle to the execution of this measure: The scientists who (especially in France) have only the salaries they receive from the Government to live on will find themselves deprived of those salaries. But the Anglo-French society will remedy this difficulty by compensating them for any losses they incur.

The industrials must support the demonstrations of the scientists with strength.

The chiefs of industrial works in England and France must declare to the English and French Governments that if these Governments have not agreed to the establishment of the scientific and industrial constitution for the two nations by a certain fixed time, they and their workers will stop paying taxes. They should tell them that if they do agree to the change of social organisation demanded by the progress of civilisation, they will be treated well and compensated as much as possible for any losses they might incur. Otherwise they will receive no compensation.

There will be one major obstacle to this measure: the dangers which will threaten those who come forward to make this declaration. But the Anglo-French society will remedy this difficulty by arranging for the declaration to be made simultaneously by all industrials, who constitute more than nineteen-twentieths of the population of the two countries.

FOURTH SERIES: OBSTACLES TO BE OVERCOME

In England and France the class of industrials is so superior in strength to all other classes put together that it can easily establish the social organisation most advantageous to it. Its superiority is such that any timidity on its part would be dishonourable — one could even say shameful if it agreed to tolerate any longer the yoke of the phrasemongers, swashbucklers, and idle rich. In the present state of enlightenment it is monstrous that the idle should enjoy more power and respect than the workers, and that men of doubtful capacity should direct those who each day prove their capacity to be of positive use.

The English and French industrials will find it just as easy to overcome external difficulties as internal obstacles, for all those who have observed the respective strengths of nations have long been convinced that together the English and French could resist all other peoples united against them.

As the English and French industrials are strong enough to establish in England and France the social order most advantageous to them, which is at the same time the order most conducive to the public good, the laws of morality, of honour, and of common sense all require them to effect this change as soon as possible.

Once this change is effected, all the industrials of the globe will have a solid centre of support in the Anglo-French association, and under the protection of the Anglo-French they will be able to bring about the same changes in their own countries according to whether they have acquired sufficient enlightenment and strength to establish the industrial regime.

Eventually, all the peoples of the earth will attain the great goal of civilisation, and they will all adopt the same doctrine and organise themselves according to this doctrine, so as to unite all men in the work which is most suitable for increasing the moral and physical well-being of the entire race.

In the third part of its work the Society will show that its constitutional proposal fulfils the following six conditions which are the most important for the happiness of the human race:

1. This constitution gives responsibility to the men who have shown the greatest capacity in work of positive utility. It thus satisfies as far as possible the passionate desire felt by all men to increase their moral and physical well-being.
2. This constitution places the most distinguished scientists and industrials in the first rank, and therefore satisfies as far as possible the passion for equality, since experience has shown that the majority of the most distinguished scientists and industrials usually come from the lowest classes of society.
3. It gives all posts requiring great display exclusively to the rich, and it thus satisfies their passion for outward esteem.

This constitution fulfils three other very important conditions:

1. It is the best possible guarantee of public tranquillity, since it entrusts the supreme direction of all powers to the men with the greatest interest in maintaining order, namely the industrials, the scientists, and the rich.
2. The provisions it contains will enable nations to be governed as cheaply as possible, since the only functionaries who are in a position to put on a great display are chosen from the wealthy class, and are not payed in money, but only in respect.
3. Finally, this constitution gives preponderance to the doers, and subordinates the talkers. It places positive knowledge in the first rank, and makes metaphysical knowledge descend to the second, which amounts to the social organisation of positive good.

RULES OF THE SOCIETY

The Society will be called the *Anglo-French* or *Baconian* Society.

All Englishmen and Frenchmen who so desire may gain admittance to the Society by signing the following declaration:

I accept the general principles set out in the Society's prospectus.

All members of the Society will make an annual subscription proportionate to their means.

The Society's funds will be used to pay for the studies which its administrative council judges useful for the formation and propagation of the social doctrine it wishes to establish.

The Society's administrative council will consist of the twenty-five subscribers of the largest sums. Its president will always be the donor of the largest subscription.

The Society's council will nominate its secretary, treasurer, and all the agents it considers necessary to employ, and it will organise itself as it thinks fit.

The Society's council will be established in London. Every member of this council will have the right to be replaced in the council if he is absent; but his replacement will have only a consultative vote.

All persons whose works are rewarded by the Society will have the right to a consultative vote in the administrative council.

Subscriptions may be made to all English and French bankers, merchants, and manufacturers who are zealous for the public good. The first year's subscriptions should be accompanied by the aforementioned declaration.

The present plan for a society will certainly succeed if the following two conditions are fulfilled:

The first of these conditions is that as soon as the Society is formed it should include a large number of important industrials, distinguished scientists, and esteemed artists. In order to achieve this aim, the persons to whom this prospectus-plan is sent are invited to show it to all their friends who are zealous for the public good.

The second of these conditions is that the Society should be able, as soon as it is formed, to publish works which will develop the principles set out in this prospectus-plan. In order to achieve this aim, and so that the works may be commenced as quickly as possible, the persons to whom this prospectus is shown will be invited to subscribe in advance to the manufacturers, merchants, and bankers of London and Paris who are most zealous for the public good.

Note: At this moment we are preparing to have the first volume of the Society's memoirs printed.

[Original manuscript, Bibliothèque Nationale, Paris, ref. N.A.F. 24607, pp.49-59.]

PART III FROM THE GOVERNMENT OF MEN TO THE ADMINISTRATION OF THINGS (1817–20)

Hitherto men have, so to speak, exercised on nature only purely individual and isolated efforts. Furthermore, their forces have always in large measure destroyed each other, since the human race has hitherto been divided into two unequal parts, and the smaller has constantly employed all its power, and often even some of the power of the larger part, in order to dominate the latter, while the larger part has used up a great deal of its power in order to withstand domination. Nevertheless, it is certain that in spite of this enormous loss of power, the human race has, in the most civilised countries, achieved a quite remarkable degree of comfort and prosperity.
From this one may judge the level it would reach if almost no power were lost, if men, instead of commanding one another, organised themselves to exercise their combined efforts on nature, and if nations adopted the same system!

S.W., p.208.

11. DECLARATION OF PRINCIPLES

(Déclaration de principes, L'Industrie, vol. II, 1817)

We regard society as the ensemble and union of men engaged in useful work. We can conceive of no other kind of society.

Society has two enemies which it fears and detests equally: anarchy and despotism.

The constitution is the only restriction which the thought of the political writer has to respect. Against and outside the constitution there can be no useful work; within the limits it prescribes the most complete liberty can do no harm. This liberty is the property of the writer, just as the constitution itself is the property of the nation and the Government.

Men engaged in industry, whose association forms the true society, have only one need: liberty. Liberty for them is to be unrestricted in productive work, to be allowed free enjoyment of what they produce.

Man is lazy by nature. The man who works overcomes his laziness only because his needs have to be fulfilled, or through his desire for pleasure. He only works, therefore, according to his needs and desires. But in the state of society the pleasures which attract him are increased and are much more numerous than his productive powers. He is therefore forced to give up a part of what he produces in exchange for certain products which he cannot obtain directly through his own work. This necessity (which is transformed for him into a source of wealth) is the only one he recognises, the only one to which he willingly submits; that is to say, the industrious man, such as he is, is really subject to only one law: that of his self-interest.

But there is surrounding society, there circulates in its bosom a throng of parasites who, although they have the same needs and desires as the others, have not been able to overcome the natural laziness common to all men, and who, although they produce nothing, consume or seek to consume as though they did produce. These men use force to live off the work of the rest, either off what they are given or what they can take. In short, they are idlers, that is, thieves.

The workers are thus liable to see themselves deprived of the pleasure which is the aim of their labour. As a result of this danger they develop a particular kind of need, which in turn gives rise to a quite distinctive type of labour. The aim of this labour is to prevent the violence with which idleness threatens industry.

In the eyes of industry a government is simply an enterprise for carrying out this task. Government is concerned with idleness. As soon as its activities go beyond that, it becomes an arbitrary usurper and consequently the tyrannical enemy of industry. It commits the evil which it is supposed to be preventing. In working for himself man desires to work in his own way. Whenever a superior and alien activity interferes in industry and claims to govern it, it hinders and discourages industry. Industrial activity declines at a rate which is an exact function of the restrictions to which it is subject.* If industrials are to be governed, it is not in their capacity as industrials.

Since governmental activity may be deemed a service which is useful to society, society should consent to pay for this service.

While the seaman is crossing the seas, he cannot farm the fields. While the ruler is looking after the safety of the producers, he cannot produce. But the seaman and the ruler both do their share of useful work. Both earn their share of what is produced. The seaman's share is easily determined through competition. But what should the Government's share be?

Industry's chief concern is to solve this problem. For if it does not make the necessary sacrifices, the service will deteriorate and the safety required by industry will not be complete.

If, on the other hand, it lacks sufficient information to estimate the value of the service, and pays more than it should for it, industry suffers a double disadvantage. First, it deprives its productive occupations of some of the capital they need in order to prosper. And also, it grants to the Government an excess of force and activity which is bound to be felt by industry and exercised to its detriment.

Industry needs to be governed as little as possible, and this can only be done if it is governed as cheaply as possible.

Suppose one could find the least intelligent man in industrial society, a man whose ideas extend no further than his domestic affairs. After informing him that most of the tax he pays is used as a salary for work which secures his security and the unhindered enjoyment of his property, one might ask him this question:

If it were possible to enjoy these same advantages for less money than you pay today, would you not prefer it?

And if it were obvious to you that by paying less for your sècurity, the latter would be more completely and better assured, would you not be even more inclined to favour cheapness?

There can be no doubt about this man's reply. Very well, we shall say to him, that is what we want to achieve for you, what the whole of society desires as naturally as you, and what we are seeking as well. That is the aim of our enterprise.

It was in America, while I was fighting for the cause of industrial liberty, that I first felt the desire to see this plant from another world

*If, since the enfranchisement of the commons, industry has made continual progress, it is because it has been subject to less and less government control.

flower in my own country.[46] This desire has since dominated all my thinking. Without respite I studied the course of advancement and further assured myself that the progress of civilisation could have no other end. And I invoked this aim of true liberty, true public happiness, with my most fervent hopes. For me every event that seemed to point in that direction was a new joy, a new hope. The French Revolution broke out, and at first it seemed to be thoroughly industrial. But it soon lost that character, and the many noble efforts which ought to have produced liberty resulted only in the tyranny of the Jacobins and military despotism. A happier age has now started to dawn for us: at last a government has been established which declares its own power to be based on the power of opinion. *Ever since then France has yielded to common sense, that is, to the free discussion of its common interests.*

If this discussion was to be as complete as possible, if it was to lead to certain and important results, one precondition seemed to me to be necessary, and that condition I now believe to be fulfilled.

We have identified two kinds of workers in society: those who produce, and those who safeguard the producers. There is also a third: those men whose job it is to think about the general interests of society, political writers. Now, since it is the Government which actually administers the general interests of society, it is with the Government that this class of workers is naturally allied.

This state of affairs would cause no problem if the Government always regarded writers as a council of enlightened men who can clarify and facilitate its work. But that is not the case: the interests of governments do not always coincide with the general interest. Indeed, in one sense the two are naturally opposed.* Also, governments are much less inclined to seek advice on what is expedient, on what it is best to do, than to regard as good what they have actually done or what they intend to do. They strive with all their influence to form public opinion rather than to encourage its expression. And rather than look for men who will debate, they prefer those who will approve and demonstrate, in short, advocates rather than advisers.

It may be argued that writers stick to their convictions and serve only the truth, and that they only approve and support governmental conduct when they judge it to be in the interests of the governed. We accept that. We know that even those writers working under the eyes and under the influence of the Government always work, or at least claim to work only for society as a whole, and would be offended if it were thought otherwise. Nevertheless, we are convinced that the

*Industry wants to be governed as little as possible, while the rulers inevitably want to govern as much as possible. Industry wants to pay as little as possible, while the rulers want to obtain as much money as possible from industry.

governed know better than anyone what they want and what is in their interest. We believe that government is at least an unnecessary intermediary between those who think about the public interest and those who feel it, between political writers and industry.

Accordingly, I consider it necessary to find a means of abolishing this useless and often dangerous intermediary. Direct relations should be established between industry and men of letters. Liberals, who think that governments exist only for those who are governed, and not vice versa, should expect something more for their good heart than abandonment and poverty. In short, there should be established, besides the favour and protection of power, a national protection and power.

That is industry's aim in launching the present enterprise.* That is the spirit in which industry presents itself and which it takes as *its personal stake* in the proposed association: *the union of commercial and manufacturing industry with literary and scientific industry.*

[*Oeuvres,* vol. I, pt. 2, pp.128-37.]

---

*When we say 'industry', everyone else will realise that we are referring only to some of the most important firms, which, inspired by a feeling for the common interest, are making personal sacrifices which they consider to be useful for the good of all. Common utility has always been served in this way, and it is still the only means of serving it today.

Industry is but one single, vast body, all of whose limbs respond to each other and are thus in solidarity. The good and evil of each part affect all the others. Always it has just one interest, one need, one life. But if the whole possesses feeling, it is the head alone which does the thinking for the body. It is there that revolutions take shape, needs are felt, and desires expressed.

12. LETTERS TO AN AMERICAN

(Extracts from *Lettres de Henri Saint-Simon à un Américain, L'Industrie,* vol. II, 1817)

SECOND LETTER

During my stay in America, sir, I occupied myself much more with political science than with military tactics. The war in itself did not interest me, but its aim interested me greatly, and that interest led me willingly to support its cause. I desire the end, I often used to say to myself, I must certainly desire the means.

When I saw peace approaching I was completely overcome with disgust for the military profession. I perceived clearly what career I had to take up, the career towards which my tastes and natural inclinations called me. It was not my vocation to be a soldier; I was destined for a quite different, and I might say quite contrary kind of activity. To study the advance of the human mind in order subsequently to work for the improvement of civilisation: that was the aim I set myself. From that moment I devoted myself to it totally; I consecrated my entire life to it, and this new task began to absorb all my powers. I employed the rest of my time in America to reflect on the great events I had witnessed. I sought to discover their causes, to predict their consequences. Above all, I applied myself to studying the likely consequences for my own country.

I now saw that the American Revolution marked the beginning of a new political era; that this Revolution must inevitably result in major progress for civilisation in general; and that it would soon bring about great changes in the European social order. I studied carefully the circumstances of the inhabitants of America, and compared them with those prevailing in the Old World. I realised that they were essentially different, and I concluded from this that civilisation would not follow the same course in the two hemispheres.

The observations I made then still seem to be of interest at the present time. Indeed, I venture to say that they are the very points on which it is most desirable to fix public opinion today. I shall therefore reproduce some of them.

I observed then:
1. In that country toleration was taken to the highest degree. It was absolutely unlimited, since there was no dominant religion, no specially favoured religion, no religious dogma regarded as the dogma of the State. There were many different religions, all of which were permitted, and everyone was free to invent new ones

and seek converts. Within each religion, whatever its character, every kind of controversy was permitted.
2. There was no privileged group, no nobility, no vestige of feudalism, since feudalism had never existed there. In short, the nation was not divided into castes, but formed a body politic composed of homogeneous parts.
3. No family in the country had enjoyed a monopoly, for several generations, of the principal public offices. Consequently, no one considered the business of governing to be his patrimony. Finally, opinion was openly hostile towards every citizen, whoever he was, who dared claim an exclusive right to exercise State power.
4. The character of one of the first founders of the English colonies in the New World, the famous Penn, was also the dominant character in the American nation: this nation generally showed itself to be essentially peace-loving, industrious, and economical.

I concluded from these observations that the Americans would establish for themselves a regime infinitely more liberal and more democratic than the one under which the peoples of Europe lived; that their national spirit would not be the military spirit; that in their constitution and all their laws and regulations they would dedicate themselves to promoting agriculture, commerce, and every kind of industry; that the constant aim of their legislation would be to guarantee the individual liberty and full property rights of all citizens without distinction, including foreigners; that public opinion, as well as the laws, would treat military service simply as a temporary, casual occupation which all citizens are obliged to assume when circumstances demand it, but which ought not to become the one special profession of any major part of the population, and which, even more importantly, should not be regarded as giving soldiers a right to the highest offices.

I further concluded that in other equally important respects the Americans would follow a course of development quite different from the Europeans.

In Europe the greatest statesman, or at any rate the one who is regarded as the most able, held in the greatest esteem, promoted, and praised most highly, is always the man who can find a means of increasing the revenue from taxation without arousing the wrath of the taxpayers. In America I saw that the greatest statesman would be the one who could achieve the greatest reduction in the people's burden without causing the public services to suffer. In the Old World the people — the governed — accepted the view that for the common good functionaries must be highly paid; large salaries were judged necessary for the sake of dignity. I could see that the Americans would view things quite differently, and that functionaries would be more highly esteemed the less luxury they displayed, the more accessible they were, and the simpler their manners.

Finally, I thought that the old and new continents would base their social organisation on different fundamental principles: in America public office would be regarded as an enormous burden, accepted out of duty and submission to the general will; whereas in Europe, by contrast, to have a share in government was to exercise a right, a right transmitted through inheritance, a kind of patrimony because it was based on wealth.

How far the French people were in 1789 from being able to found such a social order! . . .

SIXTH LETTER

If I look for the passion which brought about the French Revolution, and the class of society which experienced it most strongly, I see that it was equality, and that men of the lowest class were the ones most inclined, through their ignorance and their interest, to embrace its cause with violence. The effect of the passion for equality was to destroy the social organisation which existed at the moment of its eruption. I now ask whether, now that everything is destroyed, another passion is not needed to stimulate reconstruction; in other words, whether it is passion or moderation that can bring a revolution to an end.

The habits contracted under old institutions are great obstacles to the establishment of a really new regime. This establishment demands great philosophical efforts and great financial sacrifices. Only passion has the force to inspire men to make great efforts.

Moderation is not an active force; it is essentially timid, and far from making us change our habits it inclines us to retain them.

Moderation recommends that we strike a balance between the habits contracted under arbitrary and theological institutions, and liberal-industrial ideas and institutions. But the latter are naturally exclusive, and nothing can be achieved until they have become dominant, until they are completely rid of those alien elements of that flaw which cramps their strength.

It is an exaggeration to say that the French Revolution completed the ruin of the theological and feudal powers. It did not destroy them; it merely reduced people's confidence in the principles on which they were based, so that today these powers do not have sufficient force or credit to serve as a link in society. In what ideas, then, shall we find this necessary organic link? In industrial ideas: there and only there should we seek our salvation and the end of revolution.

Yes, sir, in my view the sole aim to which all our thoughts and efforts ought to be directed *is the organisation most favourable to industry,* to industry understood in the most general sense, including all kinds of useful work, theory as well as application, mental labour as well as manual. Such organisation calls for a government under which the activity and force of the political power are no more than is necessary to prevent useful work being hindered; a government under which everything is arranged so that the workers, whose association forms the true society, can exchange with each other directly and with complete freedom the products of their various labours; a government, finally, that allows society — which alone knows what its requirements are, what it wants and what it prefers — to be the sole judge of the merit and utility of work, and that consequently allows the producer to depend solely on the consumer for his salary, the reward for his service . . .

In my view, the moment has come for the general revolution, the revolution common to all civilised peoples, whatever part of the earth they inhabit.

Governments will no longer command men; their functions will be limited to ensuring that useful work is not hindered. They will no longer have at their disposal more than a small amount of power or money, for their aim will require no more. The funds required by useful undertakings, whatever their scale, will be provided by voluntary subscriptions, and the subscribers themselves will supervise the use and administration of their money.

EIGHTH LETTER

So it is a question, sir, of finding a new system of political organisation.

To what extent has this task been achieved?

It it were simply a matter of assembling a large amount of material, we could say that everything has been accomplished. Numerous ideas have been acquired, ideas which even have a sort of link between them. But has the most important condition been fulfilled? Is there an agreed fundamental principle to which one is led through discovered truths and from which one can deduce those same truths? That is what is lacking, what has to be attained.

Of all those who have undertaken the task, the writers on political economy seem to me to have done the most useful work, and M. Say's treatise on political economy[47] seems to me to be the book which provides the greatest number of positive, coordinated ideas.

In my opinion this author, so justly renowned, has come nearest to the goal without ever actually achieving it.

Here are the first two pages of his preliminary discourse. They contain the author's whole conception: it is the most general idea and, if I may use such an expression, the philosophy of his work.

'A science only makes real progress when the scope and aims of its researches have been clearly determined. Otherwise, one grasps a few isolated truths without understanding the link between them, and many errors without being able to discover their falsity.

'For a long time *politics* properly understood — the science of the organisation of societies — has been confused with *political economy,* which teaches how wealth is formed, distributed, and consumed. However, wealth is essentially independent of political organisation. Under all forms of government a state can prosper if it is well administered. Nations have been seen to grow rich under absolute monarchs, and ruin themselves under popular councils. If political liberty is more favourable to the development of wealth, it follows indirectly that it is more favourable to education.

'Since, in the same research, the principles which constitute a good government have been confused with those on which the increase of wealth is based, whether public or private, it is not surprising that ideas have been muddled rather than clarified. It is this criticism which may be directed at Steuart, who entitled his first chapter 'The Government of the Human Race';[48] at the group of 'economists' in nearly all their writings;[49] and at J.-J. Rousseau in the Enyclopaedia.[50]

'It seems to me that since Adam Smith[51] these two doctrines have always been distinguished, the name *political economy* being reserved for the science which deals with wealth, and the name *politics* only being used to signify the relations between the government and the people, and between governments.'

It can be seen clearly that M. Say here views politics and political economy as two distinct and separate things. On the other hand, those who have read his work or heard his public lectures will know what importance he attaches to the science which he deals with, and how often he repeats that it alone has given to morals and politics any certainty and positiveness they might have.

This contradiction proves that the author has sensed vaguely, almost in spite of himself, that political economy is the true and sole foundation of politics, but that he has not seen it in a precise enough manner, since he in fact makes it known only in the details of his work and not in his general considerations.

Nevertheless, his work has rendered the greatest service. It comprises all that political economy has yet discovered and demonstrated. It is at present the *ne plus ultra* of that science in Europe.

Here, it seems to me, are the most general and consequently the most important truths which it will one day reveal:

1. The production of useful things is the only reasonable and positive

aim that political societies can set themselves. Consequently, the principle *respect for production and producers* is infinitely more fruitful than *respect for property and property owners.*
2. Government always damages industry when it meddles in its affairs, even when it tries to encourage it; from which it follows that governments should restrict themselves to protecting industry against every kind of trouble and impediment.
3. As the producers of useful things are the only useful men in society, they alone should come together to regulate its development. And as they are the only men who really pay taxes, they alone should have the right to vote taxation.
4. Men can never direct their powers against each other without damaging production. Wars, whatever their object, are thus injurious to the whole of the human race, even to the peoples who emerge as victors.
5. The desire of one people to exercise a monopoly over other peoples is badly conceived, because a monopoly can be acquired and maintained only through force, and is therefore bound to diminish the total production of the very people who enjoy that monopoly.
6. Morals certainly improve as industry develops. This observation is true whether one is concerned with the relations between peoples or between individuals. Consequently, education should aim to strengthen in all minds, to render universally dominant, those ideas which will increase each individual's productivity and his respect for the production of others.
7. The entire human race shares one aim and has common interests. Therefore, in his social relations every man should consider himself to be engaged in a company of workers.*

I believe, sir, that we have there a summary of every observed fact in political science. But what general idea results from these facts? To what common point do they lead us? Only there can we find, will we inevitably find the principles of the whole of politics.

There is an order of interests common to all men, interests which concern the maintenance of life and well-being. This order of interests is the only one on which all men agree and on which they need to agree; the only one on which they have to deliberate and act in common; the only one, therefore, with which politics can be concerned, and

---

*Before Smith, political economy, still in its infancy, was cleverly presented as an aid to governments, and was confused with politics. Strengthened by the power of truth and the authority of common sense, it finally assumed a purer and more definitive character, and declared itself independent of politics.

With just a little more courage and a little more philosophy, political economy will soon rise to its true position. At first it was dependent on politics; in future politics will depend on it, or rather it will itself comprise the whole of politics. This moment is not far off.

which must be taken as the standard when criticising all institutions and social affairs.

In short, therefore, politics is *the science of production,* that is, the science whose object is the order most favourable to every kind of production . . .

[*Oeuvres,* vol. I, pt. 2, pp.148-53, 163-6, 168, 182-8.]

13. LETTER TO THE PUBLICISTS

(Prospectus for *L'Industrie,* vol. III, 1817)

OPINION WHICH WILL BE PUT FORWARD IN THE THIRD VOLUME OF *L'Industrie*

The philosophical enterprise which Bayle started to execute[52] was, by its nature, a twofold enterprise, that is, it comprised two parts, or, if one likes, two tasks which were equally difficult to fulfil, which required the same amount of time to complete, which called for the same care and the same kind of efforts, and which had to be accomplished in succession.

An examination of the way in which the first of these tasks was fulfilled must therefore serve as a guide for those who desire to undertake the second.

The first enterprise involved overturning the edifice that the clergy had taken centuries to construct.

The clergy had forged nearly all the ideas then in circulation, and had linked them together so as to form a general theological system; or rather they had reduced the system of our ideas to no more than a system of theology. To break a chain which had taken so much trouble, time, and care to form was certainly a great enterprise. It demanded an entire revision of ideas, and consequently the separate examination of each of them.

A detailed account of the way in which this task was undertaken would certainly be very useful, and it will inevitably be the subject of a very interesting work. But for the moment I want to confine myself to giving an indication of the principal conditions which were fulfilled:

1. Every kind of literature contributed to this philosophical aim, so that theology saw itself attacked at the same time from all sides, from all heights, among all classes and all minds. If one surveys the works written in the eighteenth century, from the treatises of Condillac to the collections of songs, one will see that everywhere the *anti-theological* spirit was dominant.
2. The philosophical writers did not have to rely solely on their own forces: they were supported by the King of Prussia, the Empress of Russia, the King of Poland, and (in many respects) Ganganelli himself, even though he was Pope. In short, one can say that during the eighteenth century men of all ranks who had some ability and energy contributed to the *philosophical work.*

3. After each individual had completed his own task, the writers of the eighteenth century assembled in a single workshop and together they produced a general work, an encyclopaedia which could have been called: general *anti-theology*.

There you have a summary of the way in which the first task was fulfilled, a task whose aim was to disorganise the theological system. Let us now turn to the question of how one should proceed with the execution of the second task, whose aim is to organise a system of terrestrial morality.* It is easy to see that this second task calls for exactly the same work as the first. In both, every idea must be considered and discussed separately: in the first it was a question of effacing the theological imprint which each had been given; in the second it is a question of imprinting on each the seal of common sense.

Thus, the following facts can, indeed must, be regarded as certain:

1. Every kind of writer, from philosophers proper to the composers of songs, will share the common nineteenth-century aim of rendering all ideas positive.
2. Those who exert the greatest influence on public opinion, through the respect and wealth they enjoy, will contribute to the *philosophical work* of the nineteenth century.
3. A time will come when the writers of the nineteenth century will unite their efforts in one general work, the *encyclopaedia of positive ideas*.

Finally, I believe that the philosophical studies required for the execution of this second task will take up the whole of the nineteenth century, and that it will not be until the end of the century that the establishment of a truly positive, industrial, and liberal regime will be practicable. However, the more actively these studies are pursued, the more the present ministries of Europe will be forced to act in the interests of peoples and kings.

Now, if I am asked when the philosophical studies of the nineteenth century will begin, I reply: They will begin as soon as industry wants them to begin and provides the means. And if I am then asked when industry will express itself in this way, I reply: It will be soon after the time when either some very wealthy or very talented energetic men are able to make industry realise what is really in its interest.

[*Oeuvres*, vol. I, pt. 2, pp. 215-20.]

*The philosophers of the eighteenth century convinced people in general to accept the right of the individual to practise his own religion and to decide which religion his children should be taught.

The philosophers of the nineteenth century will convince people that all children should study the same code of terrestrial morality, since the similarity of positive moral ideas is the only link which can unite men in society, and since ultimately an improvement in the social condition is nothing more than an improvement in the system of positive morality.

14. [VIEWS ON PROPERTY AND LEGISLATION] [53]

(Extracts from *L'Industrie*, vol. IV, pt.2, 1818)

... We attach too much importance to the form of governments. It would seem that the whole of politics is concentrated there, and that once a good division of powers is established, everything is organised in the best possible way.

There are in Europe two peoples living under the absolute power of a single man: the Danes and the Turks. If there is any difference between them it is that despotism is more severe in Denmark than in Turkey because it is legal and constitutional. And yet, under the same form of government, what a difference in the condition of the governed! No people is more unhappy, more plagued, more worn, in short more unjustly and more dearly administered than the Turkish people. While nowhere is more liberty actually enjoyed than in Denmark; nowhere, except in England, is power less arbitrary or administration less expensive. What is the cause of this difference? It is certainly not the form of government, since this form is the same in both cases. Thus, tyranny must have another cause. And it is this: Relatively speaking, the King of Denmark is the poorest prince in Europe, while the Sultan is the richest, since he is the only property owner in Turkey as well as the only ruler.

This example is proof that the law which constitutes the powers and form of government is not as important, and does not have as much influence on the well-being of nations, as that which constitutes property and regulates its exercise. However, it should not be supposed that we thereby conclude that the law establishing the division of powers is not essential. We are far from professing such a heresy. Certainly, the parliamentary form of government is most preferable to all others. But it is only a form, and the constitution of property is its foundation. Hence it is this constitution which is the true basis of the social edifice.

Thus, the most important question to be resolved, in our view, is that of knowing how property should be constituted for the greatest good of society as a whole, in terms of both liberty and wealth.

Now, it is to this general question that the particular question we are about to consider is related.

As long as consumers form the majority in the deliberations they take part in, they will always be in a very strong position, as strong as they wish to make it; so that in spite of your parliamentary forms you will be governed arbitrarily. On the other hand, as soon as the industrials, that is, those persons interested in liberty and public economy, are granted the exclusive right to vote taxation, then they will give only what they really want to give, and they will be truly free to exercise their rights fully. Again, what must be done in order to achieve this? The nature of the right to property must be fully understood, and this right must be founded in the way most favourable to the increase in the wealth and liberties of industry. Now, this is the condition we intend to fulfil through the legislative measure explained in this work and submitted for examination by public, that is, industrial opinion . . .

What is necessary is a law which establishes the right to property itself, and not one which establishes it in any particular manner. The existence of society depends on the preservation of the right to property, but not on the preservation of the law which first granted that right. This law is itself dependent on a higher and more general law, that law of nature according to which the human mind makes continual progress, and which gives all political societies the right to modify and improve their institutions . . .

The individual right to property can only be based on the common and general utility of the exercise of that right, a utility which can vary from one age to the next.

Thus, a law placing agricultural workers on the same footing in relation to their lessors as merchants and manufacturers stand in relation to theirs, which consequently permits them to invest their capital in the same way as the latter: this law, we say, can and should be passed if it is judged useful.[54]

The electoral law was a result of the progress of enlightenment.[55] The law of which we speak and which we want to see introduced has become just as necessary as that one. Society cannot emerge from its state of suffering except through this legislative provision . . .

In commercial and manufacturing industry it is the workers who pay the taxes levied on that branch of national production. The measure which we are proposing would involve treating agricultural industrials in the same way as commercial industrials, and would consequently provide that they should manage their enterprises in their own names and should therefore pay the direct taxes levied on agriculture themselves, instead of them being paid by the landowners as is the case today.

As a result of this measure industry would thus pay by far the largest part of direct taxation, for there is only a very small part of taxation which is not levied on land or on commercial and manufacturing industry.

Now, industry would thereby have an electoral majority and would soon achieve a majority in the House of Commons. Since this House possesses great political power . . . industry would soon be in the dominant position of being able to give the nation the social organisation of its choice. This organisation would inevitably be the one most favourable to industry, in other words to the industrial regime. Thus, as a result of the measure we are proposing, the industrial regime would naturally be established, and idlers would at last be ranked below workers.

We would then have completely achieved the aim of all our desires, the goal of all our efforts, and our epigraph *'All by industry, all for industry'* would have been both a prediction and a signal for this fortunate revolution . . .

Agricultural industry is, by itself, infinitely more important than all the other branches of industry put together. If one were to establish in a general fashion (that is, by considering all the work of the human race) the relations between agricultural products and all manufactured and commercial products, one would certainly find that the former are at least a hundred times more important.

In England, where commercial and manufacturing activity has advanced further than in any other country, agriculture is still three or four times as wealthy as all the rest of industry.

In France all the products of commerce and manufacturing together account for no more than one-seventh or even one-eighth of agricultural production.

Thus, in France every agricultural advance would achieve for the nation an increase in production and consequently in wealth seven or eight times greater than a similar advance in the other branches of industry.

Public attention must thus be fixed above all on agriculture . . .

The measure we are proposing would place a sum of 30,000 millions at the disposal of French farmers. It would turn the soil of France, which today is almost dead, into thoroughly productive capital. Hence, as a result of this measure the landed wealth of France would be doubled in a few years . . .

[*Oeuvres,* vol. II, pt. 1, pp. 81-4, 89-91, 95-6, 107-8, 110.]

15. ON THE POLITICAL HISTORY OF INDUSTRY

(Extracts from *Coup d'oeil sur l'histoire politique de l'industrie, L'Industrie,* vol.IV, pt.2, 1818)

I PRELIMINARY OBSERVATIONS

Every political arrangement, every institution, in order to be truly good, must satisfy two conditions:
1. It must be useful to society, that is to say it must result in positive advantages for society.
2. It must be in harmony with the present state of society, in conformity with existing ideas and circumstances, and its establishment must be suitably prepared. In short, it must come just at the right time.

This second condition, although much less appreciated than the first, is nevertheless also absolutely indispensable. It alone makes institutions acceptable, for if they are to be possible or at least durable they must be neither more nor less than society's present requirements: they must not be untimely. This is the chief reason why historical considerations are useful, for only through the philosophical observation of the past can one acquire an exact knowledge of the real elements of the present . . .

The considerations expounded in previous chapters, as well as those that will follow in the continuation of this work, aim to show that the measure we are proposing[56] is bound to result in a large increase in national income and a large decrease in expenditure; which shows that the measure is useful.

The considerations which we are now going to present are of a different order.

They aim to show the industrial class, that is, the nation, that the position it has gradually achieved makes its adoption of the proposed measure quite natural; that its past progress and present needs both demand such adoption; in other words, that the adoption of this measure is a step naturally reserved for industry in the nineteenth century, the last step which industry must take in order to assume the direction of society — a constant goal towards which all the progress made by the industrial class since its origin has been leading.

II POLITICAL PROGRESS OF INDUSTRY

. . . If one traces the history of industry back to the era of the Greeks and the Romans, one finds that among these peoples the industrial class was completely enslaved by the military class.

The slavery of industry continued under the northern warriors who destroyed the Roman Empire and established themselves in western Europe in place of the old masters or conquerors.

This revolution, which at first appeared to involve industry in no more than a simple change of masters, was in fact of the greatest importance for industry because of the fortunate consequences resulting from this change of rulers.

The slavery of the industrial class changed its nature; it became slavery to the soil, which was a great improvement. Besides, because the conquerors had moved into the country, the industrials – who were settled in the towns – were no longer subject to direct and continual supervision by the masters, which was again very much in their favour.

So, for these two reasons the conquest of the Roman Empire by the peoples of northern Europe brought about the first notable improvement in industry's condition.

The second stage in the progress of the industrial class was its enfranchisement . . . This important step forward is usually called the enfranchisement of the commons; and this expression is certainly justified, for the commons and industry are one and the same thing, the commons originally consisting entirely of artisans and merchants who had settled in the towns. This is a very important fact which ought to be noted, and of which one should not lose sight if one is to have a clear understanding of what the commons are today.

When the industrials bought their liberty, their condition improved inasmuch as each of them was freed from the direct arbitrary authority of the lord on whom he was previously dependent. This was certainly a great alleviation for them. But as a whole these men who had bought their freedom were no less dependent on the priests, nobles, and the military; they were no less obliged to give them a large part of the product of their labours, and to suffer the frequent outrages to which their position exposed them. This is how industry freed itself from this second kind of arbitrary authority:

The privileged men who composed the entire Parliament and who had no intention of sharing their power conceived the idea of summoning deputies from the commons, from industry, to give a statement of their possessions, so that they could collect more from them in revenue than they could hope to get by force. This is the true origin of the parliamentary commons . . .

The establishment of this practice must be seen as extremely favourable for the industrial class, since it formed the basis of all its subsequent political successes. However, at first the commons – industry (we repeat) – thought it very disagreeable to have to send deputies to Parliament, because these deputies had no rights and their mission was limited to giving an account of their constituents' wealth. But things did not and could not continue in this way. Industry, in spite of the fact that it was burdened by the military and feudal class with every kind of outrage and provocation, eventually grew wealthy through work, patience, and economy. It acquired importance and respect, because it grew in size and because marriages between the industrials and the military linked the interests of many individuals from the military class with the interests of many members of the commons. For these and many other reasons, above all because industry was able to show the military that much more money could be taken from it if it was allowed to pay less — in other words because of industry's financial capacity, which it convinced the military was of use to them — the latter allowed the commons to have a voice in Parliament.

This great step taken by industry deserves careful attention, for in some ways it marks the beginning of a new era for the human race. Henceforth, the law of the strongest ceased to be the only law; or rather, force and ruse ceased to be the only elements involved in the making of law: the general interest also began to play a part.

The next step taken by industry, and the most recent in purely political terms, followed the English Revolution. It involved the introduction of the practice whereby the House of Commons was granted the sole and exclusive right to vote the budget. The great European Revolution could have been ended at this point, the industrial and pacific regime could have been established if, on the one hand, the commons of England had been represented only by members from industry, and if, on the other hand, English industry had seen that it was naturally more closely linked in interest with the industrials of other countries than with the English members of the military or feudal class.

But at this period feudalism still exercised great power, and industry had little appreciation of its interests and the course it should follow. Hence, it allowed itself to be dominated by the feudal spirit, which is essentially a spirit of conquest.

The natural order of things and the advance of civilisation have reserved for French industry the glory of ending the great European Revolution; for French industry took the step of which we are speaking later than English industry, and was thus able to act more completely and more decisively, achieving success at a time when feudalism has no more power and when industry can easily appreciate its interests and follow a well-determined course.

We shall here end our summary of industry's political past. Let us now look at the civil successes it has achieved since the House of

Commons was granted the exclusive right to vote taxation.

The importance acquired by industry since this period is incalculable. It has invaded every sphere; it has taken possession of everything. By improving its products it has accustomed men to pleasures which they have come to regard as needs. But above all it is government which has become a tributary of industry, has become dependent on it. Can the Government wage war? Its chief problem is not to recruit men who can kill: it has to look to industry, first of all for money, and then for all the things it needs and which it buys from industry with that same money. It is industry which provides it with canon, guns, powder, uniforms, etc., etc., etc. Industry has taken possession of everything, even war.

Through a fortunate and inevitable effect of improvements in the military art, war has become more and more dependent on industry, so that today real military power has passed into the hands of the industrials. A country's military force is no longer to be seen in its armies, but in its industry. The armies of today (by army we mean the collection of warriors, from the ordinary soldier to the most eminent leader) fulfil only subordinate functions, for their merit consists only in employing the products of industry . . .

Industry has also taken possession of finance. In France and England today it is industry which advances the funds needed by the public service, and it is industry which receives the proceeds from taxation . . .

III WHAT HAS HITHERTO RETARDED INDUSTRY'S ADVANCE

If industry's advance has hitherto been very slow, if even today industry, in spite of its many important successes, finds itself in fact in only a subordinate position, and if society is still governed mainly by the feudal class, or at least by the feudal spirit (which amounts to almost the same thing), the reason is that up till now the commons have lacked the right principles; they have made progress and achieved success only by a sort of practical instinct and routine.

By industrial principles we mean the knowledge of the way in which industry could use power. Hitherto, industry has lacked this knowledge, which is nothing but a political plan conceived from industry's point of view and formulated in its interests. Now, it is quite clear that this knowledge is indispensable to industry if general power is to pass into its hands, and that as long as it has lacked principles industry has been able to play only a subordinate role.

The military or feudal class has its own principles, and it is for this reason that it has retained the general power. But industry, with no principles, has hitherto engaged and still engages only in critical action towards feudalism. It has not been able in its turn to take the initiative and provide the impetus.

All its principles may be reduced to the vague desire to be well governed, that is, to be governed in conformity with its interests. But it is clear that without knowledge of the means of governing in the interests of industry, this desire can only lead to critical action.

The principles which the commons have lacked for so long have at last been produced by the immortal Smith, for these principles are nothing but the general truths which result from the science of political economy . . .

Smith, after observing the processes employed in various industrial enterprises, brings together observations. He shapes them into a whole; he generalises his ideas; he establishes principles and creates a science based on the art of acquiring wealth, just as Aristotle produced poetics out of his observations on the works of the poets who had preceded him . . .

Smith's book was the most vigorous, most direct, and most complete critique ever made of the feudal regime. Each of its pages demonstrated that the commons or industry were devoured by this regime, a regime of absolutely no use to them; that such governments as were established tended continually to ruin the peoples, since they only ever consumed, whereas the only means of growing rich was to produce.

His work may be considered as a collection of detailed refutations of all the operations of governments, and it may consequently be seen, in sum, as a proof of the need for peoples to change the principles and the nature of their governments if they want to stop living in poverty and to enjoy peace and the fruits of their labour.

At the same time this work contained the proof that a nation, in order to acquire the comforts of life, must proceed in the same way as manufacturers, merchants, and all persons engaged in any kind of industry, and that consequently a nation wishing to become free and rich should frame its budget according to the same principles as the budget of any industrial firm. The only sensible aim for a nation, therefore, was to produce as much as possible with the least possible administrative expenditure.

M. Say revises Smith's ideas. He classifies them more methodically; he gives his work much more of a doctrinal character than the inventor did; he adds new considerations to those produced by Smith, and he entitles his work *Treatise on Political Economy.*

In M. Say the critique of the present conduct of governments assumes a clearer character. The comparison between the principles of military administration and those of industrial administration is established more directly.

Smith brought the science he created into the world in a very modest manner. He presented it as a means whereby governments could grow rich. He announced it only as a secondary science, auxiliary to and dependent on politics.

In philosophical terms M. Say goes one step further than Smith. At the beginning of his work he establishes that political economy is distinct from and independent of politics. He says that this science has its own basis, quite different from the basis of the science which aims to organise nations . . .

IV THE STEP WHICH INDUSTRY MUST TAKE TODAY

Following what we have just established, industry today possesses real strength, and furthermore it possesses the principles which it used to lack, or at least it can very easily acquire them now that they exist.

If this is, as we believe, the true point reached by industry today in its political career, why is it that the direction of society has still not passed into its hands? Why is it that the industrial regime has not been established, and the feudal and military regime still exists? It is a result, first, of the fact that industrial principles are still not generally known, and have thus not been able to acquire the credit which brings confidence and strength. Secondly, real strength and principles are not sufficient, as one might suppose, to place industry at the head of society: a means is necessary, and a legal means whereby power can pass into its hands. It was out of ignorance of this means that industry, when it did seek to seize power, employed and could only employ insurrection. Now, insurrection is first of all the most inadequate of all means. It is also absolutely contrary to industry's interests, since for the latter all use of force is an evil. Whenever there are popular disorders it is industry which bears the greatest burden, because industrial property, of all property, is the easiest to destroy . . .

It requires neither great intellectual powers nor much effort to devise an insurrection; but to find a legal means is much more difficult. We are striving to settle this question, convinced that a solution to it is the only thing which industry now lacks, the last remaining step to be taken before the industrial regime can be established . . .

We firmly believe that we have found this solution, and we think that the proposed measure can certainly achieve the aim; for in time, as an inevitable result of this measure, all, or at least the vast majority of members of the House of Commons will come from the commons, from industry. And on the other hand, since the House of Commons possesses great political power, through its exclusive right to vote the budget, it follows that the proposed measure must bring that power into the hands of industry, and do so in a thoroughly legal manner entirely in conformity with the existing constitution, with (furthermore) no sudden change, because the effect of this measure, by its very nature, can only be gradual[57] ...

[*Oeuvres,* vol. II, pt. 1, pp.139-56, 158-61.]

16. THE POLITICAL INTERESTS OF INDUSTRY

(Extracts from *Des intérêts politiques de l'industrie*, 1818?)

... What is still the basis of education among the most civilised peoples of Europe? Is it not the idea that man's life on earth is only a passage to a future life in which we shall be rewarded or punished by an all-powerful Being, according to whether we have or have not followed the wishes of this Being as taught to us through the medium of the priests, his direct interpreters?

Thus, it cannot be doubted that revelation is still regarded as the basis of politics. Now, it follows from this that politics has not yet been able to become a positive science. We must emphasise that we are certainly not denying that God exists, or that he created us and destined us to a happy or unhappy eternal life depending on whether our earthly conduct towards our neighbours is helpful or injurious. This belief is not in opposition to any observed fact; but the existence of God is not itself an observed fact, and this is sufficient reason for us not to include the science based on that idea among the positive sciences ...

One would be seriously mistaking our intentions if one thought that we seek to destroy in man all idea of a future life, to tear from the human heart the hope of divine rewards and the terror of heavenly punishments. It is certainly not our intention to destroy beliefs which have been useful for such a long time, and which can still be very useful. That is by no means necessary in order to transform politics and morals (the science from which politics is derived) into positive sciences. All that is necessary is to take the ideas that have been established in inverse order, and present supernatural beliefs as the crown of the social edifice instead of the base. Theism has prevented social science from becoming positive only inasmuch as supernatural power has been seen as the source of all rights and duties, and revelation has been the science of good and evil. Henceforth, the science of societies should be treated in the same way as all other sciences, by employing no other means but reasoning and observation. On the basis of purely human principles man should establish what he ought to do, what he should avoid, what is proper for society, what is harmful to it; and theism should intervene only at the end of the calculation, presenting grounds for conduct of another order, but which are no less forceful than principles which have been demonstrated. Establish in an earthly manner the ideas of good and evil, of virtue and vice, etc. Seek the conduct which can bring man the greatest happiness on earth, and then add that God will reward this conduct in another life; there can only be advantages in this, no disadvantages. By presenting the life to come not as the principle, but as the reward of the present life, you allow supernatural ideas to intervene only in a useful way. But as long as you make these ideas the universal criterion of all morality, as long as you look to the supernatural power for knowledge of the rules which must govern your actions, you will remain completely dependent on the men who undertake to explain the heavenly will. It will not be *God* whom you obey, but the priest, and this dependence will be all the more terrible as you will have no means of refusing the priesthood's orders, which come from a sacred fountain-head, a fountain-head to which the priesthood will have been given sole right of access by you . . .

[*T.c.*, pp.170-72.]

17. ON M. BARTHÉLEMY'S PROPOSAL TO THE HOUSE OF PEERS

(*Sur la proposition faite à la Chambre des pairs par M. Barthélemy, Le Politique*, pt. VI, 1819)

M. Barthélemy has introduced a motion in the House of Peers intended to deprive industrials of the right, by virtue of their moveable property, to vote in elections to the House of Commons, as do owners of landed property.[58]

The explicit purpose of this proposal is to have the commons represented by the nobility and those property owners whose interests are directly opposed to those of the industrials. It seeks to bring the labouring, productive, and thrifty part of the nation back under the yoke of extravagant, despotic, and idle men. It is thus the most anti-liberal or anti-industrial (which is the same thing) proposal there could be.

M. Barthélemy's proposal will give rise to a debate between the industrials and the non-industrials, a debate which will inevitably prove that the interests of the industrials are also the interests of the nation and the King, while the interests of the nobility stand in opposition to the latter.

Thus, a great benefit for the liberal-industrial party can result from the blunder made by the reactionaries; but it depends on one indispensable condition: that the industrials sustain the debate in a suitable manner and treat the question with the degree of generality urgently required by present circumstances.

The industrials must be aware, fully aware, that at this moment it is the terms of the Charter which are being discussed, and that consequently any measures taken, any laws passed, are constitutional not ordinary laws.[59] Finally, they must bear in mind, for their own good as well as for that of the King and the nation, that they should be aiming to have the House of Commons composed exclusively of members from industry, because only then will economy in public expenditure be securely established.

One thing which severely hinders the good cause, particularly in these circumstances, is that the industrials are accustomed to allowing themselves to be governed; consequently, they hardly realise that it is they alone who are capable of directing the nation's affairs, of framing its budget. They are not in the right state of mind to profit from the advantages presented to them by the present debate.

In order to cure (as far as it is in my power) the dangerous habits that the industrials have contracted under the yoke of despotism, a yoke which they bore as much under the *ancien régime* as under the

183

rule of the mob and then the military, I shall provide them with a brief history of their political past, present, and future.

It is my fervent hope that this exact, although miniature picture will inspire in their souls an awareness of their rights; for the obstacles we are facing in the attempt to establish liberty and economy in France arise less from the resistance of the nobles and other supporters of despotism, than the indifference, I venture to say the apathy of the industrials.

POLITICAL PAST OF THE INDUSTRIALS

The industrials remained in slavery until about the twelfth century, when they were allowed by the nobles, then their masters, to buy their freedom.

From their emancipation to the promulgation of the law allowing them to vote in elections to the House of Commons by virtue of their moveable property, they did not participate at all in the making of laws. In their capacity as free men they had political rights, but they did not exercise any legislative power by virtue of the wealth they acquired through their work, work which benefited the State as well as themselves.

Only since the promulgation of the electoral law have the industrials had any share in sovereignty.

POLITICAL PRESENT OF THE INDUSTRIALS

The majority of peers, supported by the clergy and the nobility, are demanding that the industrials cease to have any share in sovereignty.

At any time now the House of Peers will beseech the *King* to deprive the industrials of the political powers which *His Majesty* obtained for them from Parliament.

In order to make *His Majesty* once again dependent on Chambers inspired by the political spirit that governed the nobles representing the commons in 1815, the anti-liberal, anti-royal, anti-national, anti-social party is begging the King to rid himself of the support of the industrials who have just loaned him 2,000 millions which were indispensable to him.

Thus, the political present of the industrials consists of a struggle between, on the one hand, the labouring, productive, and rich part of the nation, linked in interest and intention with the King and, on the other hand, the nobility, clergy, and supporters of arbitrary rule, linked with the majority of the House of Peers.

POLITICAL FUTURE OF THE INDUSTRIALS

As the nation has become more enlightened, the political importance of the nobles has declined, while that of the industrials has increased.

The nobles began by enjoying exclusive sovereign rights; the King was then their chief, whereas today he has become the first French citizen.

Next, the nobles became no more than the privileged servants of the King, who concentrated the whole of sovereignty in his hands.

Finally (peers excepted) the nobles are today no more than ordinary citizens. Their only political rights are those of property owners, if they have any property.

The industrials, who were originally slaves, became citizens, and next they obtained a share of sovereignty by virtue of their moveable property.

Now, since what will happen is inevitably a consequence of what has happened, I am entitled to say, on the basis of what has happened, that in time sovereignty will be exercised exclusively by the industrials, and that the nobles as well as the other non-producers must successively lose all the political advantages which the Government, to its great detriment, still allows them to enjoy at present.

The law of the strongest was the first law to rule societies.

The law of the common interest has increasingly modified the law of the strongest, and must in the end become the one from which all others are derived.

The nobles are born supporters of the law of the strongest, and they are its true upholders in their capacity as military chiefs.

The industrials, because of the nature of their occupations, are bound to march under the banner of the common interest, and they are its defenders in their capacity as National Guardsmen.

In the present situation sovereignty is divided between supporters of the law of the strongest and defenders of the law of the common interest.

This situation gives rise to a struggle between the industrials and the nobles.

This struggle will inevitably last until one of the two parties is annihilated politically; and the nobles as well as other supporters of arbitrary power will inevitably give way in the end, since the King and the nation have a clear interest in joining the ranks of the industrials.

CONCLUSION

Every man always fights more bravely when he feels himself to be the strongest, and when he is certain of achieving victory.

The industrials cannot fail to develop great energy in the coming struggle since they can rely on the support of the nation and the King.

M. Barthélemy's proposal to the House of Peers is a most memorable political event, since it marks the beginning of a struggle between the industrials and the nobles, giving to each of them a share of sovereignty.

M. Barthélemy's proposal is a very fortunate political event, since it is exactly what is needed to stir the industrials out of their indifference to public affairs.

The day when the industrials are properly aware of their strength and their rights will be the eve of the day when liberty and economy are firmly established in France. To hasten the arrival of that happy day is the object of the labours we have undertaken in this work.

The authors of *Le Politique* and their successors will not have achieved their aim until the law of the strongest has lost all its credit, and the law of the common interest is the only one to which nature is willing to submit.

[*Pol.*, pp.183-90.]

18. COMPARISON BETWEEN THE NATIONAL (INDUSTRIAL) PARTY AND THE ANTI-NATIONAL PARTY

(*Le parti national ou industriel comparé au parti anti-national, Le Politique*, pt. X, 1819)

I COMPOSITION OF THE TWO PARTIES

The national party consists of:
1. Those whose work is of direct use to society.
2. Those who direct this work or whose capital is invested in industrial enterprises.
3. Those who contribute to production through work which is useful to the producers.

The anti-national party consists of:
1. Those who consume but do not produce.
2. Those whose work is neither useful to society nor of assistance to the producers.
3. All those who profess political principles whose application hinders production and tends to deprive the industrials of the highest degree of social importance.

It is of the greatest importance to note that since citizens have become equal in the eyes of the law it is not accident of birth which places them in one or other of these parties. Their occupations and opinions alone determine which of the two they belong to.

Thus, M. de Lafayette, who is a farmer, M. de Larochefoucault-Liancourt (manufacturer), M. Le Voyer d'Argenson (iron-master) clearly belong, by virtue of their occupations and the liberality of their opinions, to the industrial class; whereas MM. Barthélemy, Bellard, and Pastoret, although born commoners, are included in the anti-national party because of their views.

II THE MORALITY OF ONE PARTY – THE IMMORALITY OF THE OTHER

Who is moral? Who is immoral? This question must be resolved before we can compare the morality of the industrials and the anti-industrials.

In politics as in religion upright men, whether or not they are devout, recognise that all morality derives from the great principle proclaimed by Jesus Christ:

Love your neighbour as yourself. Do unto others as you would have others do unto you.

The question thus comes down to knowing which of the two,

industrials or non-industrials, conform most to the basic principle of morality. Now, it is clear that the industrials employ the whole of their lives in a way which is useful to their neighbours, since they devote their time and resources to the production of those things which satisfy society's primary needs and bring it pleasure.

It is also clear that the conduct of those who do not belong to the industrial party is immoral, since they consume but do not produce; since they do, in reality, live at other people's expense; since they enjoy all the advantages procured for them by the work of the industrials without giving them anything in exchange which is either useful or pleasing; and since, finally, they do not do unto their neighbours as their neighbours do unto them.

The reader must thus agree with my own firm conclusion: that the conduct of the industrial party is moral, while that of the anti-industrial party is completely immoral.

The moral superiority of the industrials can be viewed from another point of view.

It is a fact that owners of landed property are held in low esteem, while merchants, manufacturers, and other industrials are highly respected.

What is the reason for this difference? It is that industrial property owners have long been regarded as more reliable in fulfilling their obligations than non-industrial property owners.

Now, one has a moral duty to pay one's debts, since one must treat one's neighbour as one would want to be treated by him. In this respect the industrials' conduct is more moral than that of the non-industrials, since the former pay their debts more promptly.

III THE WEALTH OF THE TWO PARTIES

He who spends all his income, however wealthy he is, ought not to be considered rich. It is the man who is economical who possesses the real wealth, for each man's wealth depends essentially on what he has left, on the amount he has to dispose of.

In 1815 the House of Commons was composed almost exclusively of landowners. The State needed money. The rich were hard up and could not come to its assistance, because they had no savings to dispose of. Moreover, as their income was insufficient to meet the expenditure they regarded as necessary in order to maintain themselves properly as nobles, they were simple-minded enough to ask the nation for capital at a time when it was shattered by the burdens it had to bear.

The King wisely decided to chase off the drones and summon the bees. He appealed to industry for the resources he needed.

What happened?

The producers, even though they have much less capital than the landowners, eagerly provided the State with all the money it required.

This leads me to conclude that the real wealth is in the hands of the industrials, even though the non-industrials possess most of the capital.

IV THE POLITICAL CAPACITY OF THE TWO PARTIES

Before comparing the political capacity of the two parties, I must give a clear answer to this question:

What is the highest political capacity today?

My reply is natural and easy:

Since men have become equal in the eyes of the law, political rights are no longer based on the possession of money or of things which can be bought with money. The greatest, most important power entrusted to the Government is the power to tax the citizens. All its other powers spring from this right. Today, therefore, political science is essentially a matter of framing a good budget.

Now, the capacity needed to frame a good budget is administrative capacity. Hence, it is administrative capacity which is the highest capacity in politics.

Let us now see whether it is industrial property owners or individuals whose capital is not invested in industrial enterprises who need the greatest administrative capacity to manage their affairs.

It is clear that without administrative capacity the industrials can neither grow rich nor even conserve their wealth; whereas landowners can conserve theirs simply by not spending in excess of their income, and can grow rich simply by saving their income.

It remains for us to examine whether industrial property owners or landowners have best administered their private affairs.

We have proof, as I have already said in the previous section, that it is the industrial property owners, since it is they who came to the aid of the King and provided him with the funds he needed, whereas the landowners left him in trouble.

The reader will surely conclude with me that industrial property owners are superior in their political capacity to landowners, since they are superior in administrative capacity. Thus, the question I set out to investigate in this section is resolved.

V THE STRENGTH OF THE TWO PARTIES

The national or industrial party includes:

1. All those who cultivate the land, as well as those who direct agricultural work.
2. Wheelwrights, blacksmiths, masons, locksmiths, carpenters, weavers, shoemakers, tailors — in short, all artisans, manufacturers, merchants, entrepreneurs of land and sea transport, as well as all those whose work is of direct or indirect service to production or the utilisation of the things produced.

Consequently, all positive scientists belong to the industrial party, because their discoveries contribute greatly to improving the processes employed by artisans, and often result in new productive methods.

Artists must also be considered industrials, because they are in many respects producers, not least through the designs and patterns they provide for artisans, which contribute greatly to the prosperity of our manufacturing.

Lawyers of liberal outlook who apply their talents to the defence of industrials against the claims of the aristocracy and the arbitrary action of functionaries.

The small number of priests who preach sound morality, that is, the obligation to employ one's time and means in useful work.

Finally, all citizens (whatever position they are placed in by accident of birth or circumstance) who sincerely employ their talents and their means to free producers from the unjust supremacy exercised over them by idle consumers belong to the great corporation of industrials.

The anti-industrial party comprises the nobles who are working for the re-establishment of the *ancien régime;* those priests who see morality in terms of blind belief in the decisions of the Pope and the clergy; landowners who live like nobles, that is, who do nothing.

Judges who uphold arbitrary rule, the military who support it — in short, all who are opposed to the establishment of the regime most favourable to economy and liberty.

Thus, we have a rough sketch of the basic forces and the way in which they are grouped together in the form of two distinct, opposing parties.

I cannot give an exact estimate of each party's strength, but I am certainly not exaggerating when I say that the industrials outnumber by at least fifty to one the supporters of that system in which the bees are ruled by the drones.

VI SUMMARY

The conduct of the industrials is moral; that of the supporters of arbitrary rule is immoral. The industrial party thus has moral strength, which is the most important of all. It also has physical strength, since it is at least fifty times as large as the party of idlers.

This party also possesses the strength of reason, since the positive scientists (who are the best reasoners) are on its side.

It has strength of imagination, since the artists are industrials.

The industrials are also superior in political capacity to their adversaries.

Finally, the industrials have financial strength, since they have at their disposal more money than the non-industrial landowners.

I move on to a summary of the strength and means of the anti-industrial party, that is, the party whose object is to maintain the domination of the producers by those who are immoral enough to regard the nation as a collection of men destined by God to provide them with pleasure.

All the strength of this party derives from the habits acquired by the people under the *ancien régime,* from superstition, the venality of judges, the corruption of functionaries, and the military's lack of patriotism when they place themselves at the service of power without examining how that power is exercised.

I shall not comment on the result of this comparison. For the time being I shall just say that a struggle between two parties as unequal in strength and means is quite extraordinary.

[*Oeuvres,* vol.II, pt. 1, pp. 195-206.]

19. PROSPECTUS FOR *L'ORGANISATEUR*

(Dated 1 August 1819)

The nineteenth century has not yet assumed its proper character. Our philosophical literature is still dominated by the character of the eighteenth century; it has remained essentially critical.

It is because the philosophical spirit maintains this approach that we are still in revolution, and that we are menaced by new social crises; for no system (and consequently no political system) can be replaced by the criticism which overthrows it. One system can only be replaced by another system.

The philosophers of the eighteenth century had to be critics, since the first thing to be done was to show the disadvantages of a system formed in an age of superstition and barbarity. But now that this system has been completely eradicated by them, it is clear that the task of their successors (that is, of today's philosophers) is to produce and discuss the political system appropriate to the present level of enlightenment; and it is equally clear that the old system will not completely die out until our ideas concerning the means of replacing the institutions (derived from that system) which still exist have been sufficiently clarified, linked, and coordinated, and have been sanctioned by public opinion.

This is the view arrived at by the author of this work after a great deal of thought on the subject.

He has submitted this view for examination by those most capable of judging it, and has obtained their approval.

But one man by himself cannot organise the new political system needed by the human race. The author of this work must therefore seek a means of bringing together the most able men in the various branches of our positive knowledge.

The project he has conceived (and which will be expounded in this work) involves forming a scientific society divided into four classes, and sharing all the work to be done between these four classes in such a way that each one can act independently of all the others, while at the same time they can still unite with the same effectiveness for the organisation of the system.

And this project, which has been submitted for the criticism of several esteemed scientists, has been approved — one could even say adopted — by them.

There you have the antecedents of *L'Organisateur*. The special object of *L'Organisateur* will be — 1) to establish the principles on which the new political system must be based; 2) to present the plan of organisation to a scientific workshop capable of establishing a social doctrine proportionate to the level of enlightenment; 3) to prove that it is in the interest of all classes of society to have this work carried out as quickly as possible; 4) to indicate the means of maintaining public order during the organisation of the new system.

Its general aim will be to examine all questions whose solution will affect the happiness of the majority in society.

The first part of *L'Organisateur* will appear next month, and will give details of the publication arrangements and subscription rates.

[Original manuscript in the University of London Goldsmiths' Library, ref. A.L. 212(ii). Bound with a volume of Saint-Simon's *Lettres au Bureau des Longitudes* (Paris, 1808).]

20. [A POLITICAL PARABLE][60]

(Premier extrait de L'Organisateur, 1819)

Let us suppose that all of a sudden France loses fifty each of its best physicists, chemists, physiologists, mathematicians, poets, painters, sculptors, musicians, authors, mechanics, civil and military engineers, artillerymen, architects, doctors, surgeons, pharmicists, sailors, clockmakers, bankers; its two hundred best merchants and six hundred best farmers; fifty each of its best iron-masters, arms manufacturers, tanners, dyers, miners, manufacturers of cloth, cotton, silk, linen, ironmongery, earthenware and porcelain, crystal- and glass-ware; shipowners, carriers, printers, engravers, goldsmiths, and other metalworkers; masons, carpenters, joiners, blacksmiths, locksmiths, cutlers, foundrymen, and one hundred other persons in various unspecified posts, eminent in the sciences, fine arts, and arts and crafts, making in all the three thousand best scientists, artists, and artisans in France.*

As these Frenchmen are the most essential producers, those who provide the most important products, who direct the work which is most useful to the nation, and who are responsible for its productivity in the sciences, fine arts, and arts and crafts, they are really the flower of French society. Of all Frenchmen they are the most useful to their country, bringing it the most glory and doing most to promote civilisation and its prosperity. The nation would become a lifeless corpse as soon as it lost them. It would immediately fall into a state of inferiority *vis-à-vis* its present rivals, and it would remain their subordinate as long as this loss was left unretrieved, as long as it was waiting for a new head to emerge. It would take France at least one whole generation to make up for this disaster, as the men who distinguish themselves in work of positive utility are really the exception, and nature is not prodigious in producing the exceptional, especially in this species.

Let us proceed to another supposition. Let us say that France retains all its men of genius in the sciences, fine arts, and arts and crafts, but has the misfortune to lose on the same day Monsieur the King's brother, Monseigneur the duc d'Angoulême, Monseigneur the duc de Berry, Monseigneur the duc d'Orléans, Monseigneur the duc de

---

*Usually the term 'artisan' is only used to refer to ordinary workmen. In order to avoid circumlocution, we shall take this expression to mean everyone involved in material production, i.e. farmers, manufacturers, merchants, bankers, and all the clerks or workmen employed by them.

Bourbon, Madame the duchesse d'Angoulême, Madame the duchesse de Berry, Madame the duchesse d'Orléans, Madame the duchesse de Bourbon, and Mademoiselle de Condé.

Let us suppose that at the same time it loses all the great officers of the Crown, all Ministers of State (with or without portfolio), all Councillors of State, all chief magistrates, all its marshals, all its cardinals, archbishops, bishops, vicars-general, and canons, all prefects and sub-prefects, all ministerial employees, all judges, and, on top of all that, the ten thousand richest property owners who live in the style of nobles.

This accident would certainly distress the French, because they are good, and could not regard with indifference the sudden disappearance of such a large number of their fellow countrymen. But this loss of the thirty thousand individuals who are deemed the most important in the State would grieve them only from a purely sentimental point of view, for it would not result in any political harm to the State.

This is because, first of all, it would be very easy to fill the vacancies. There are many Frenchmen who could perform the functions of the King's brother as well as Monsieur can. There are many who could fill the princely positions just as well as Monseigneur the duc d'Angoulême, Monseigneur the duc de Berry, Monseigneur the duc d'Orléans, Monseigneur the duc de Bourbon. Many Frenchwomen would make just as good princesses as Madame the duchesse d'Angoulême, Madame the duchesse de Berry, Mesdames d'Orléans, de Bourbon, and de Condé.

The antechambers of the palace are full of courtiers ready to replace the great officers of the Crown. The army has many soldiers who would make just as good captains as our present marshals. How many clerks there are who are just as good as our Ministers of State; how many administrators who could manage departmental affairs better than the prefects and sub-prefects; how many advocates who would make just as good lawyers as our judges; how many clergymen who are just as capable as our cardinals, archbishops, bishops, vicars-general, and canons. As for the ten thousand property owners living like nobles, their heirs will need no apprenticeship to do the honours of their drawing-rooms as well as they.

The prosperity of France can only be achieved through the progress of the sciences, fine arts, and arts and crafts. Now, the princes, the great officers of the Crown, the bishops, the marshals of France, the prefects, and the idle property owners do not work directly for the progress of the sciences, fine arts, and arts and crafts. Far from contributing to this progress, they can only hinder it, since they endeavour to prolong the supremacy hitherto exercised by conjectural theories over positive knowledge. They inevitably hinder the nation's prosperity by depriving, as they do, the scientists, artists, and artisans of the highest degree of respect to which they are legitimately entitled; by employing their financial resources in a way which is not directly useful to the sciences, fine arts, and arts and crafts; and by costing the nation's taxpayers an annual sum of three to four hundred millions under the headings of appointments, pensions, gratuities, indemnities, etc. as payment for their work which is of no use to the nation.

These suppositions demonstrate the most important fact about contemporary politics. They provide a viewpoint from which we can see this fact in all its scope, and at a single glance. They prove clearly, although indirectly, that social organisation has not advanced very far; that men still allow themselves to be governed by violence and ruse; and that the human race (politically speaking) is still sunk in immorality.

This is so because the scientists, artists, and artisans, who are the only men whose work is of positive utility to society, and who cost society almost nothing, are subordinated by the princes and other rulers, who are merely incapable routine officials;

Because those who dispense respect and other national rewards generally owe their superiority to accident of birth, flattery, intrigue, or other doubtful methods;

Because those who are in charge of administering public affairs share between them every year half the taxes, and do not employ as much as a third of the remainder in a way which is useful to the citizens.

These suppositions show that society today is really a world upside down:

Because the nation has accepted the fundamental principle that the poor should be generous to the rich, and that consequently the less fortunate should deprive themselves each day of a part of their necessities in order to increase the needless wealth of the great property owners;

Because the most guilty men, the worst thieves, those who oppress the whole citizen body, and who take from them three to four hundred millions each year, are entrusted with the punishment of minor offences against society;

Because ignorance, superstition, idleness, and extravagant pleasure are the prerogative of society's leaders, while those who are able, thrifty, and hard-working are employed only as subordinates and instruments;

Because, in short, in every kind of occupation incapable men are in charge of capable men. From the standpoint of morality it is the most immoral men who are called upon to make citizens virtuous. And in terms of distributive justice it is the guiltiest men who are appointed to punish the faults of minor offenders.

Although this extract is very brief, we think we have given sufficient proof that the body politic is sick, that its illness is grave and dangerous, that it could not possibly be worse, since it afflicts both the whole body and all its individual parts. This proof had to come first, for those who are well (or who think they are well) are never disposed to listen to the doctors who prescribe medicines or a diet in order to cure them.

In the second extract we shall consider what medicine ought to be given to the patient.

[*Oeuvres,* vol. II, pt. 2, pp. 17-26.]

21. SKETCH OF THE NEW POLITICAL SYSTEM

(Extracts from *Esquisse du nouveau système politique, L'Organisateur,* pt. I, letters 3-6, 1819)

THIRD LETTER

I shall answer the following two questions:
   What should we have done?
   What have we done?
   I hope that my answers to these two questions will completely reassure all good men of my intentions, and that my aim will be sufficiently understood by them for me to be able in subsequent books to develop my principles and deduce consequences from them without causing anyone any anxiety, and without experiencing any anxiety myself.
   I shall divide my examination of what we should have done into four letters, because there are four things that we should have done, but which we have not done, and each of them deserves separate consideration.
   We should have started by clarifying our ideas concerning the political system we want to get rid of and also the social system required by the level of our enlightenment. Before taking any action we should have formulated a very clear idea of both of these. That would not have been difficult, for each of these two conceptions may be expressed in a few words, as I shall now show.
   The old political system (I refer to the one which is still in force and which we want to get rid of) originated in the Middle Ages. Two elements, quite different in nature, contributed to its formation: since its origin it has always been a compound of the theocratic and feudal systems. The combination of physical force (possessed to a high degree by armed men) and the guile and cunning invented by the priests invested the leaders of the clergy and the nobility with sovereign powers, and brought the rest of the population under their subjection.
   A better system could not be established at this time, for, on the one hand, all the knowledge we then possessed was still superficial and vague: general metaphysics contained the only principles which could serve as a guide for our ancestors of the Middle Ages, and consequently general metaphysics had to direct society's scientific affairs.
   On the other hand, since the only way a large people could make itself rich in this age of barbarity was through conquest, the military had to be given the task of directing the national affairs of each

particular state.

Thus, the fundamental basis of the old political system was, on the one hand, a state of ignorance, which meant that reasoning on the means of securing the welfare of society did not rely on observation, but rested only on simple guesswork.

And, on the other hand, a state of incompetence in the arts and crafts which made people incapable of producing wealth by improving raw materials through their labour, and left them with no means of enriching themselves apart from seizing the raw materials belonging to other peoples.

Through the effect of the progress of industry, the peoples acquired the means of achieving prosperity together, by enriching themselves through peaceful labour.

On the other hand, positive knowledge was acquired, phenomena of all kinds were observed, and philosophy, based on experience, today contains principles which can guide the peoples towards morality and well-being much more surely than metaphysics.

This situation makes the founding of a new political system possible and consequently necessary.

The fundamental bases of a new system are thus, on the one hand, a state of civilisation which provides men with the means of employing their powers in a way which is useful to others and profitable for themselves.

And, on the other hand, a state of enlightenment which enables society, knowing the means it must employ in order to improve its condition, to guide itself according to principles, and which no longer makes it necessary to give arbitrary powers to those it entrusts with the administration of its affairs.

It is not the difference in the division of power which constitutes the difference between the systems; it is the difference in the nature and quantity of the powers exercised by the rulers over the ruled.

All forms of government are applicable to all political systems.*

As long as the rulers are considered the most important, most capable, and most useful men in society; as long as their leaders are given enormous salaries to increase their importance and their power; as long as the nation allows them to choose the means they judge appropriate to improve its morals and secure both its peace and its prosperity; as long as they are drawn, on the one hand, from the class of metaphysicians (that is, persons who still submit to blind belief and possess only superficial knowledge, and who therefore seek to reason on general facts), and, on the other hand, from the military (men whose most

---

*By this I do not want to imply that forms of government and the type of division of power are unimportant. I just mean that these things are only of secondary importance.

exalted occupation is to improve the means of conflict between men), it will remain entangled in the old system. It will remain subject to this system whatever form of government it adopts, whether it be republican, aristocratic, pure monarchy, or constitutional monarchy. It will remain subject to it whether it chooses its military leaders from the heirs of feudal families or from the descendants of serfs; whether its leaders on the scientific side are chosen from theologians or from the metaphysicians who have established their seminary in the schools of law.

The nation will not reach the point of departure for the new political existence it must attain until it sees clearly all the immorality and monstrosity of the social regime to which it has remained subject hitherto; until it opens its eyes to the combination of force and guile employed by the nobility and the clergy in order to exploit it for their own advantage, and decides to dismantle this old machine completely and replace it with a new one, conceived and organised according to principles drawn from sound morality and true philosophy; until it recognises that its government will inevitably be arbitrary as long as its leaders are chosen from the military and the metaphysicians, and that its rulers will inevitably be despots as long as society deems them to be the most important persons in the State, the ones who are most useful to it and who consequently deserve most esteem; until, finally, having accepted the idea that it can only achieve prosperity through the progress of the sciences, the fine arts, and the arts and crafts, it regards scientists, artists, and artisans as the men who are most useful to it and who consequently deserve to be granted the highest degree of esteem. This will be a happy age for the human race, when the functions of rulers will be reduced until they are no more than supervisors in colleges. Supervisors are given only one task: to maintain order. It is the teachers who are responsible for directing the pupils' work. It should be the same in the State: the scientists, artists, and artisans should direct the nation's work; the rulers should be concerned only with ensuring that the work is not hindered ...

FOURTH LETTER

After rising to a clear conception of the system which can satisfy the political desires of the great majority of the nation at the present level of enlightenment, we should have reasoned as follows.

We should have said: Considering that it is impossible for us to establish the new system immediately, and that this system needs to be prepared, to be organised before it can be put into practice, we must endeavour to live as tolerably as possible without departing from the old system until we are able to abolish it entirely.

Thus, the second thing we should have aimed to do in 1789 was to answer the following question:

What is the least troublesome method of organising the old system?

The answer would not have been difficult to find, for experience has proved that the English constitution, that is, the parliamentary regime, is the least defective form of social organisation under the old system.

Experience has proved it, because the English nation has prospered with infinitely more speed than all others since it adopted this form of government.

Thus, the second thing we should have done was to adopt the parliamentary regime.

FIFTH LETTER

The second thing we should have done, then, was to adopt the English constitution as a provisional regime, as a transitional constitution, a kind of scaffolding which had to be put up in order to carry out with ease the construction of the new social edifice.

The third thing we should have aimed to do was to discover the means of improving this constitution; and we would certainly have found important improvements to make, since more than a century had passed since this political arrangement was put into practice, a century during which people were more concerned with politics than ever before.

What is the most important improvement that can be made in the English constitution? is thus the third question we should have tried to answer.

The English constitution is tarnished by one basic flaw which we would very easily have noticed, and which we could readily have remedied if we had bothered to analyse it. This flaw is the bad composition of the House of Commons.

The House of Commons votes taxation. Thus, it is in the nation's interest that this chamber should be composed of men personally interested in reducing taxation as much as possible; but the vast majority of members of the English House of Commons are interested in increasing rather than reducing taxation.

Many of these representatives are functionaries, and functionaries are obliged to support the Government's wishes under threat of losing their jobs or at least being deprived of promotion. Apart from being directly dependent on the ministry, they are inclined through their common interest to have a great deal of money placed at the

Government's disposal, since that part of their income consisting of salaries is inevitably proportionate to the level of taxation.

The members of the House of Commons who are not functionaries are mostly idle property owners who hope to obtain Government posts in order to increase their incomes and their esteem. Thus, they are, apart from some minor differences, in the same position as functionaries.

After recognising that the English House of Commons was badly composed, we should have looked for a way of improving the composition of our own House; and we would easily have discovered this means had we looked for it, since it occurs quite naturally to the mind: the expression House of *Commons* clearly indicates this.

The House of Commons should be composed of the principal members of the commons, that is, the chiefs of the various kinds of industrial operations, for these chiefs are the citizens most interested in economy in public expenditure and most opposed to arbitrariness, because taxation cannot be to their advantage and arbitrary power cannot be exercised by them: the task of conserving and increasing their wealth through the success of their operations takes up all their time and makes it impossible for them to accept posts in the Government.

Thus, in third place, we should have improved the parliamentary regime by ensuring that the Chamber of Deputies was composed entirely of the chiefs of all branches of industry.

SIXTH LETTER

Having done these three things we would have been ready to proceed to the establishment of the new political system, because the new composition of the House of Commons would have enabled it to establish the social organisation required by the present level of enlightenment, and the House of Commons is invested with supreme political power, since it votes taxation.

I shall show what course the House of Commons (composed, as I said in the previous letter, of the industrial chiefs) should have followed. In order to explain myself more resolutely and more quickly, I shall allow the House itself to speak:

'A first Chamber will be formed and called the Chamber of *Invention*.

'This Chamber will consist of three hundred members, and will be divided into three sections which may meet separately but whose work will only be official when they deliberate together.

'Each section will be able to call a joint meeting of the three sections.

'The first section will consist of two hundred civil engineers; the second of fifty poets and other literary inventors; and the third of twenty-five painters, fifteen sculptors and architects, and ten musicians.

'This Chamber will apply itself to the following tasks:

'At the end of the first year of its formation it will present a project for public works to be undertaken in order to increase France's wealth and improve the condition of its inhabitants in every useful and pleasing respect. Then, each year it will give its advice on additions to be made to its original project and on ways in which it thinks it might be improved.

'Drainage, land clearance, road building, the opening up of canals will be considered the most important part of this project. The roads and canals to be built should not be conceived only as a means of facilitating transport; their construction should be planned so as to make them as pleasant as possible for travellers.*

'This Chamber will present another report providing a project for public festivals.

'These festivals will be of two kinds: festivals of *hope* and festivals of *remembrance*.

'These festivals will be celebrated successively in the capital and chief towns of the departments and cantons, so that capable orators (who will never be very numerous) may spread the benefits of their eloquence.

*Fifty thousand acres of land (more, if it is thought right) will be chosen from the most picturesque sites crossed by roads or canals. This ground will be authorised for use as resting-places for travellers and holiday resorts for the inhabitants of the neighbourhood.

Each of these gardens will contain a museum of both natural and industrial products of the surrounding districts. They will also include dwellings for artists who want to stop there, and a certain number of musicians will always be maintained there to inspire the inhabitants of the canton with that passion whose development is necessary for the greatest good of the nation.

The whole of French soil should be turned into a superb English park, adorned with all that the fine arts can add to the beauties of nature. For a long time luxury has been concentrated in the palaces of kings, the residences of princes, the mansions and châteaux of a few powerful men. This concentration is most detrimental to the general interests of society, because it tends to establish two different grades of civilisation, one for persons whose intelligence is developed through habitual viewing of productions of the fine arts, and one for men whose imaginative faculties undergo no development, since the material work in which they are exclusively engaged does not stimulate their intelligence.

Present circumstances favour making luxury national. Luxury will become useful and moral when it is enjoyed by the whole nation. The honour and advantage of employing directly, in political arrangements, the progress of the exact sciences and of the fine arts since the brilliant age of their regeneration, have been reserved for our century.

'In the festivals of *hope* the orators will explain to the people the plans for public works approved by Parliament, and they will encourage the citizens to work with energy, by showing them how their condition will improve once the plans are executed.

'In the festivals dedicated to *remembrance* it will be the task of the orators to show the people how their present position is better than that of their ancestors.

'The nucleus of the Chamber of Invention will consist of:

'The eighty-six chief engineers for bridges and roads in the departments;[61]

'The forty members of the French Academy;[62]

'The painters, sculptors, and musicians in the Institute.

'Each member of this Chamber will enjoy an annual salary of 10,000 francs.

'Every year a sum of twelve millions will be placed at the disposal of this Chamber to be employed to promote the inventions it considers useful. The first section will dispose of eight millions, and the other two sections will have two millions each.

'The nucleus will itself arrange for the rest of the seats in the Chamber to be filled.

'The Chamber will constitute itself, that is, it will determine who may vote and who may stand for election. Its members may not be elected for more than five years, but they will be eligible for re-election indefinitely, and the Chamber may adopt whatever method of substitution it chooses.

'This Chamber may have one hundred national and fifty foreign associate members. The associates will have the right to sit in the Chamber, and will have a consultative vote.

'A second chamber will be formed with the name Chamber of *Examination*.

'This Chamber will consist of three hundred members: one hundred physicists working on the physics of organic bodies, one hundred working on the physics of inorganic bodies, and one hundred mathematicians.

'This Chamber will be given three tasks:

'It will examine all the projects presented by the first Chamber, and will give its detailed and reasoned opinion on each of them.

'It will draw up a project for general public education, which will be divided into three grades of teaching, for citizens of three different levels of wealth. Its aim will be to ensure that young people are as capable as possible of conceiving, directing, and carrying out useful work.

'As every citizen is at perfect liberty to practise whatever religion he chooses, and may consequently bring up his children in the one he prefers, on no account should there be any question of religion in the Chamber's education project. When the project has been approved by the other two Chambers, the Chamber of Examination will be responsible for its execution and will continue to supervise public education.

'The third task involving this Chamber should be a project for public festivals of the following kind: men's festivals, women's festivals, boys' festivals, girls' festivals, fathers' and mothers' festivals, children's festivals, managers' festivals, workers' festivals. In each of these festivals orators nominated by the Chamber of Examination will make speeches on the social duties of those in whose honour the festival is being celebrated.

'Each member of this Chamber will enjoy an annual salary of 10,000 francs.

'Every year a sum of twenty-five millions will be placed at the disposal of this Chamber, to be employed on the expenditure required by public schools and on ways of hastening the progress of the physical and mathematical sciences.

'The Chamber of *Examination* will be constituted according to the same conditions as the Chamber of *Invention.*

'The Class of Physical and Mathematical Sciences at the Institute will provide the nucleus of this Chamber.

'The Chamber of Examination may have one hundred national and fifty foreign associate members, who will have consultative votes.

'The House of Commons will be reconstituted once the first two Chambers have been formed. It will then assume the name Chamber of *Execution.*

'This Chamber will take care that in its new composition every branch of industry is represented, and that each branch has a number of deputies proportionate to its importance.

'The members of the Chamber of Execution will not have any salary, since they should all be rich, being chosen from the most important heads of industrial houses.

'The Chamber of Execution will supervise the execution of all approved projects. It alone will be responsible for the imposition and collection of taxes.

'The three Chambers will together form the new Parliament, which will be invested with sovereign power, constitutional as well as legislative.

'Each of the three Chambers will have the right to summon Parliament.

'The Chamber of Execution will be able to direct the attention of the other two Chambers to those subjects it considers suitable.

'Thus, every project will be presented by the first Chamber, examined by the second, and will only be definitely adopted by the third.

'If a project presented by the first Chamber is ever rejected by the second, in order to save time it will be sent back to the first without being considered by the third.'

Now, my dear fellow countrymen, I shall tell you the first three things the new Parliament should have done. I shall speak in its name, in the same way that I have just expressed myself in the name of the House of Commons.

'All Frenchmen (and jurists in particular) will be invited to propose a new system of civil laws and a new system of criminal laws in conformity with the new political system. Property should be reconstituted and founded on a basis which will render it most favourable to production.

'All projects presented to Parliament will be published at the nation's expense.* Parliament will choose the best projects for civil and criminal codes. It will give an important reward to their authors, and will admit them to the Chambers when their codes are discussed, giving them a consultative vote in this discussion.

'All Frenchmen (and military engineers in particular) will be invited to present a project for the general defence of the territory. This project should be conceived so as to require the smallest possible number of standing troops. The authors of these works should not lose sight of the fact that all means employed for the defence of our territory will become useless and will have to be abandoned as soon as neighbouring peoples adopt the same political system as the French nation.

'A national reward will be given to the author of the plan which is preferred.

'A loan of two thousand millions will be contracted with a sinking fund, to indemnify those persons with financial interests damaged by the establishment of the new political system.

'A national reward will be given to the author of the work which best fulfils the following three conditions:

'1. It must prove the superiority of the new political system over the old.
'2. It must establish the best method of allocating the indemnity of two thousand millions granted to those whose interests are damaged by the establishment of the new system.
'3. It must show that the sum of two thousand millions granted as indemnity to persons interested in opposing the establishment of the new system is extremely insignificant compared with the advantages that the peaceful establishment of the liberal regime will secure for the nation.'

There, my dear fellow countrymen, is the first survey of what I think we should have done, what we must do.

[*Oeuvres,* vol. II, pt. 2, pp. 36-61.]

* The proposals will not be printed in full. Only extracts will be published, and these extracts may not comprise more than one printed sheet.

22. [ON THE REPLACEMENT OF GOVERNMENT BY ADMINISTRATION]

(Extracts from *Deuxième extrait de mon ouvrage sur l'organisation sociale, L'Organisateur*, pt. II, 1820)

Hitherto rulers have regarded nations as patrimonies. The essential aim of all their political arrangements has been to exploit or expand these domains. Even those arrangements which have benefited the governed were really conceived by the rulers only as means of rendering their property either more productive or more secure. The resulting advantages have been regarded even by the people as favours, not as duties binding the rulers.

Undoubtedly, this situation has undergone successive modifications, but only modifications; that is, the progress of enlightenment has always reduced governmental action more and more, but it has not yet changed its nature. Today this action is exercised less freely and in a smaller sphere, but it retains the same character. The old principle that kings are, by divine right, the born owners of their peoples is still accepted, at least in theory, as the fundamental principle. This is proved by the fact that every attempt to refute it is treated by the law as a crime against the social order.

Nevertheless, on the other hand, a new general principle of politics has been put forward by the governed. It has been recognised that the rulers are only the administrators of society, that they must direct it in conformity with the interests and will of the ruled, and that, in short, the happiness of nations is the sole and exclusive purpose of social organisation. This principle has been adopted by the rulers, or at least it has already been accepted by them together with the old principle; that is, the rulers have recognised that they should administrate in this sense, although they still regard themselves as born administrators. One may consider the new principle to be established, since it is the constitutional function of one of the three parliamentary powers (the House of Commons) to defend it and turn it to account.

The establishment of this principle is undoubtedly a thoroughly capital step towards the organisation of a new political system; but nevertheless this principle cannot, in its present state, have any really important consequence. One cannot hide the fact that hitherto it has been only a modifying principle, not a guiding principle. This is because it is much too vague actually to become the basis and point of departure of a new social order. It will not definitely assume this character until it is stated precisely, or rather completed. This is what we shall now endeavour to develop and prove.

In the present situation it is acknowledged that the permanent and sole duty of governments is to work for the happiness of society. But how is society's happiness to be achieved? This is a subject on which public opinion has not yet pronounced at all, on which, perhaps, there is not even one definite and generally accepted idea. And what has been the result? The general direction of society is inevitably left entirely to the arbitrary decision of the rulers . . .

Without entering into more detailed considerations, every person who thinks about it for a moment will be convinced that as long as society merely orders its rulers in a vague fashion to make it happy, without having decided how, in general, its prosperity is to be achieved, rule will inevitably be arbitrary in the most general and most essential respect, since the rulers will find themselves having to add to their natural function of guiding society in a given direction, the function — also very important — of choosing the direction. It follows, therefore, that the main object of the work of publicists today should be to establish ideas on the route to be taken by society towards prosperity, and to persuade society to take that route . . .

In the new political order, the sole and permanent object of social organisation should be to apply as well as possible the knowledge acquired in the sciences, fine arts, and arts and crafts to the satisfaction of man's needs; to disseminate that knowledge, improve it and increase it as much as possible; in short, to combine in as useful a way as possible all the particular works of the sciences, fine arts, and arts and crafts.

This is not the place to show in detail what astonishing prosperity society could achieve through such an organisation. It can in any case easily be imagined. We shall simply give a general indication, as follows.

Hitherto men have, so to speak, exercised on nature only purely individual and isolated efforts. Furthermore, their forces have always in large measure destroyed each other, since the human race has hitherto been divided into two unequal parts, and the smaller has constantly employed all its power, and often even some of the power of the larger part, in order to dominate the latter, while the larger part has used up a great deal of its power in order to withstand domination. Nevertheless, it is certain that in spite of this enormous loss of power, the human race has, in the most civilised countries, achieved a quite remarkable degree of comfort and prosperity. From this one may judge the level it would reach if almost no power were lost, if men, instead of commanding one another, organised themselves to exercise their combined efforts on nature, and if nations adopted the same system! . . .

In a society organised for the positive aim of working for its
prosperity through the sciences, fine arts, and arts and crafts, the
most important political act, the act which involves determining
the direction in which society is to advance, no longer belongs
to men invested with social functions; it is exercised by the social
body itself, in such a way that society, taken collectively, can
really exercise sovereignty, a sovereignty which then consists not in
an arbitrary opinion established in law by the mass, but in a
principle derived from the very nature of things, whose justice men
have only to recognise and whose necessity they have only to
proclaim. In such a situation the citizens charged with the various
social functions, even the highest, only perform, from a certain
point of view, subordinate roles, since their functions, however
important they are, involve no more than following a course which
they themselves have not chosen. Furthermore, the aim and object
of such an organisation is so clear, so settled, that there is no
longer any room for the arbitrariness of men, or even of laws,
because both can be exercised only in the realm of uncertainty
which is, so to speak, their natural element. The act of governing,
in the sense of commanding, then plays no or almost no part.
All the questions which have to be debated in such a political
system — What are the enterprises through which society can
increase its present prosperity with the help of the knowledge
it possesses in the sciences, fine arts, and arts and crafts? What
measures must be taken to disseminate knowledge and improve
it as much as possible? Finally, by what means can these various
enterprises be undertaken with the least possible expense and in the
least possible time? — These questions, we say, and all those to
which they may give rise are eminently positive and answerable;
decisions can only be the result of scientific demonstrations,
absolutely independent of all human will, which may be discussed
by all those educated enough to understand them. Besides,
precisely because in such a system all social functions have a
positive character and a clearly determined object, the capacity
required in order to fulfil them is so clear, so easy to ascertain
that there could never be any indecision on the subject, and every
citizen must naturally tend to confine himself to the role for which
he is most suited. And just as every question of social interest
will then inevitably be decided as well as it can be with acquired
knowledge, so will all social functions inevitably be entrusted to
the men most capable of performing them in conformity with the
association's general aim. Thus, in this situation the three principal
disadvantages of the present political system — arbitrariness, incapacity,
and intrigue — will be seen to disappear all at once.

If, in our summary statement of the aim which social organisation should henceforth assume, we have not included the maintenance of order, it is because the maintenance of order is certainly a fundamental condition if society is to apply itself to any kind of enterprise, but cannot be regarded as the aim of society . . .

The functions which are particularly concerned with the maintenance of order will be classed, moreover, in the new social organisation only according to their natural rank, that is, as subordinate police functions.

. . . This part of social action is the only one in the new system requiring a certain degree of command in relations between men, since all the rest, as we have explained, involve the action of principles. It follows that the action of governing, properly speaking, will then be limited as much as possible. In this order men will consequently enjoy the highest degree of liberty compatible with the state of society. It must also be noted that this function of maintaining order can then easily become, almost entirely, a task shared by all citizens, whether it be to contain trouble-makers or to settle disputes . . .

[*Oeuvres,* vol. II, pt. 2, pp. 186-91, 193-5, 197-202.]

23. CONSIDERATIONS ON MEASURES TO BE TAKEN TO END THE REVOLUTION

(Extracts from *Considérations sur les mesures à prendre pour terminer la révolution*, 1820. Reprinted in *Du système industriel*, pt. I, 1821)

FIRST LETTER: TO THE INDUSTRIAL MEMBERS OF THE CHAMBER OF DEPUTIES

Gentlemen,

In the most essential respects it is the lawyers and metaphysicians who today direct public affairs. They occupy the most important government posts; their opinion is predominant in the Council of State; they have a majority in the Chamber of Deputies; they may even be regarded as absolute masters of this Chamber, for it is they who have provided the leaders of the two parties which compose it. In short, the lawyers and metaphysicians now dominate society in all its aspects and all its political relations. It is they who direct the rulers; it is also they who direct the ruled; it is they who make the plans for the Ultras; it is they who frame the Ministerial policies. Finally, it is they who devise, for the Liberals, the means of resisting the return of the *ancien régime*.[63]

Gentlemen, the lawyers and metaphysicians are much more concerned with form than with content, with words than with things, with principles than with facts. They are not used to directing their attention and their efforts towards a single, fixed, determined goal. Now, from all this it must follow, it does in fact follow, that their minds often lose their ways in the labyrinth of abstract ideas; and I therefore come to this conclusion:

As long as the lawyers and metaphysicians direct public affairs, the revolution will not come to an end; the King and the nation will not escape from the precarious position in which they have lived for thirty years; a stable situation will not be established . . .

Examine the precedents, that is, observe the course which civilisation has followed up to the present, and you will recognise that as a result of our political past the French Revolution will come to an end only when the administration of national affairs is organised so as to ensure the prosperity of agriculture, commerce, and manufacturing.

You will also recognise that this general evidence gives rise to further secondary evidence, in particular the following:

1. It is clear that the party whose direct object is to establish that organisation of government most favourable to industry will

triumph over all parties and end the revolution.
2. It is also clear that the nucleus of the party which will end the revolution will consist chiefly of farmers, merchants, artists, and manufacturers.
3. There can be no doubt that if the revolution, which has already lasted thirty years, has not made any further advance, it is because none of the established parties has been formed in the proper way, and because the industrials have hitherto played only a passive role in politics.
4. Finally, it is clear that your position as members of the Chamber of Deputies calls you to form the nucleus of the industrial party . . .

SECOND LETTER: TO THE INDUSTRIAL MEMBERS OF THE CHAMBER OF DEPUTIES

Gentlemen,
 . . . The work in which the industrials are engaged is of varying degrees of generality, and this fundamental arrangement results in a kind of hierarchy between the different classes which compose this enormous mass of citizens who are active in production.

Thus, the industrials can and should be considered as having an organisation and forming a corporation:

And in fact all the farmers and other manufacturers are linked together by the class of merchants; and all the merchants have their own common agents in the bankers; so that the bankers can and should be considered as the general agents of industry.

In this situation it is easy for the industrials to combine and act together in their political interests.

In this situation the chief banking houses of Paris are called upon to direct the political action of the industrials.

In this situation morality imposes on the heads of these houses the obligation to work for the formation of the industrial party.

Finally, in this situation, the most powerful and most active of all stimulants inspires the heads of the chief banking houses of Paris to raise the industrial standard; for the career which is open to them as general agents of industry's political interests can bring them the greatest esteem, respect, happiness, and wealth.

Gentlemen,

In the present state of civilisation the foremost political capacity is the capacity for administration; the most important ministry is the Ministry of Finance; and the ruler who acquires the greatest reputation is the one who produces the best budget, that is, the budget which best conforms to the interests of the farmers, merchants, and manufacturers.

Now, of all Frenchmen it is the industrials who have studied administration the most, because their capital is always employed, and because as a result of their credit the capital they have on account is three times the capital they actually possess. Thus, any administrative mistakes they make are sixty times more inconvenient than those made by other citizens who, in the public and private spheres, usually have only their own incomes to manage.

It clearly follows from the fact that the industrials are the most able administrators that:
1. An industrial should be given the task of framing the budget.
2. The most knowledgeable industrials should be given the task of discussing this project before it is submitted to the Chambers for examination.*
3. Every citizen employed in public administration must have served his apprenticeship in industrial administration . . .

SIXTH LETTER: TO THE KING AND THE INDUSTRIAL MEMBERS OF THE CHAMBER OF DEPUTIES

Sire and Gentlemen,

There is only one way to end the revolution: this is, to establish the administration of public affairs most favourable to agriculture, commerce, and manufacturing.

Now, clearly, the most certain way to render the administration of public affairs most favourable to agriculture, commerce, and manufacturing is to place the direction of general affairs in the hands of the most able farmers, merchants, and manufacturers.

Thus, the most appropriate measures to end the revolution are those which invest the industrials with the greatest political powers.

The measures which I am going to submit to Your Majesty, as well as to you, gentlemen, seem to me the most suitable for investing industrials with the general direction of public administration. For this reason I believe they are the best to employ in order to end the revolution.

*In my work on the electoral law[64] I examined the question of the capacity of the *industrials,* and this examination elucidated a fact of the very greatest positive importance.

The fact is that among the *industrials,* wealth is generally proof of capacity, even in the cases where the wealth has been inherited; whereas in the other classes of citizens it is always probable that the richest people are inferior in capacity to those who are just as well educated, but who only have a small amount of money.

This truth, I repeat, will play a very important role in positive politics.

Measures to be taken to end the revolution

The following will be decreed by the competent authorities:

Article I. The Ministry of Finance may only be occupied by a citizen who has been an industrial by profession for ten consecutive years.

Article II. A council of industrials will be established (to be called the Chamber of Industry). This council will be attached to the Ministry of Finance, and will consist of twenty-five persons.

The Minister of Finance will be a member of this Chamber and will preside over it.

To start with, this Chamber will consist of the four farmers with the most important farms, the two merchants who do the most business, the two manufacturers who employ the most workers, and the four bankers who enjoy the greatest credit.

This first half of the Chamber will proceed to nominate twelve other members, chosen from among the industrials, in the following proportion: six farmers, two merchants, two manufacturers, and two bankers.

Article III. The Chamber of Industry will meet once a year at the invitation of the Minister of Finance.

The Minister of Finance will submit his budget proposals to this Chamber.

This Chamber will discuss the budget submitted by the Minister for its examination, and will approve it after making those changes it considers appropriate.

All ministers will have the right to attend meetings of this Chamber, and will be able to take part in the discussions; but they will not have a deliberative vote.

Article IV. The object of the budget's first article, on the expenditure side, will be to secure the existence of the proletariat by providing work for all fit men, and relief for the sick.

Article V. The Ministry of the Interior may only be occupied by a citizen who has been an industrial by profession for six consecutive years.

Article VI. A council, attached to the Ministry of the Interior, will be established. The Minister will be a member and president of this council.

This council will consist of twenty-five members: first of all, seven farmers, three merchants, and three manufacturers; secondly, two physicists, three chemists, and three physiologists (all members of the Academy of Sciences), plus three engineers of the Bridge and Roads Service.

Apart from the Minister, the council members will be nominated by the Chamber of Industry.

Article VII. The council attached to the Ministry of the Interior will meet twice a year at the Minister's invitation.

This council will assemble once to discuss and approve the budget for the Ministry of the Interior.

It will assemble a second time to allocate the funds granted to the Ministry of the Interior by the general budget.

Article VIII. The Naval Ministry may only be occupied by a citizen who has lived in a seaport for twenty years, and who has been head of a firm of armament manufacturers for at least ten years.

Article IX. A maritime council will be established.

This council will be composed of thirteen members: one deputy from Dunkerque, two from Le Havre, one from Saint-Malo, two from Nantes, one from La Rochelle, two from Bordeaux, one from Bayonne, two from Marseille,* plus the Minister, who will be the council's president.

The shipowners of each of these places will nominate deputies to represent their interests.

The maritime council will meet twice a year at the invitation of the Minister for the Navy.

As its first meeting it will approve the navy's budget. At the second it will allocate the funds granted to the Navy Department by the general budget . . .

Sire and Gentlemen,

These measures can be regarded as constitutional provisions, and as such they could only be introduced by an authority invested with *ad hoc* powers.

But these measures can also be seen as the subject of regulatory laws. The agreement of the three directing powers would then suffice to put them into force.

Finally, these measures may be classed as administrative orders; and in that case an ordinance would suffice to put them into effect . . .

By whom should these measures be introduced?

I ask first *if they should be adopted by an assembly expressly chosen for that purpose?*

I do not think so, and for a number of reasons which it would be useless to discuss, considering that this method of adoption would take a long time, and would consequently be very inconvenient, since it would prolong both the dangers to the House of Bourbon and the suffering of the industrials.

Will these measures be put into effect by an Act of Parliament?

This method is quite impracticable in the present situation, for the majorities in the Chambers consist of men who are not industrials,

---

*This list of ports which should have the right to nominate members of the maritime council must be regarded only as a guide.

who are very much inferior to the industrials in administrative capacity, and who nevertheless maintain that they should administer public affairs. Accordingly, any bill introduced in the Chambers by the King would inevitably be rejected.

The project must be realised through an ordinance.

The King's will alone suffices to introduce this ordinance. The King could introduce it immediately. On the other hand, if he is badly advised by his colleagues, and hesitates to follow this course, the industrials could take legal steps to help His Majesty rid himself of the burden imposed on him by the clergy, the two nobilities, the judicial order, and his courtiers.

The important point is that the monarchy and industry should contact each other immediately. It does not matter which of the two powers takes the initiative . . .

[*Oeuvres*, vol. III, pt. 1, pp.35-6, 39-40, 46-9, 105-13.]

24. THIRD LETTER TO THE FARMERS, MANUFACTURERS, MERCHANTS, BANKERS, AND OTHER INDUSTRIALS

(Extracts from *IIIe lettre à messieurs les cultivateurs, fabricants, négociants, banquiers et autres industriels,* 1820. Reprinted in *Du système industriel,* pt. I, 1821)

Gentlemen,

I am honoured to send you a third fragment from my first discussion in defence of *my opinion on measures to be taken to end the revolution.*[65]

Observer. You give preference to the material over the spiritual. You subordinate theory to practice. You place the farmers, manufacturers, merchants, and bankers in the first rank: an organic provision which means that the physicists, chemists, physiologists, and mathematicians would be ranked only second. This is monstrous, because it is the scientists who improve all the general processes employed in agriculture and in all kinds of manufacturing, commerce, and banking; and it is much more difficult to improve general processes than it is to improve the details of their execution.

Reply. Sir, you are not adopting the same viewpoint as I am. That is why we do not agree. I am looking at things in general terms, while you are seeing them only on the secondary level.

The object of my enterprise is to free those men who are engaged in work of the most positive and most direct utility from the domination exercised over them hitherto by the clergy, the nobility, and the judicial order, as well as by the property owners who are not industrials. For the moment, I am regarding scientists who study the positive sciences as belonging to the same class as the farmers, manufacturers, merchants, and bankers. But just because I view all those who contribute to production as forming a single whole, it does not follow that the division between theoretical and practical work must disappear. It follows even less from my opinion that theoreticians must enjoy an inferior standing to practitioners. The truth is that this division cannot concern me at the moment. If I did allow it to concern me, it would hinder my enterprise, because it would add useless complications to my work.

This division will establish itself when the positive men have freed themselves from the domination of the soldiers and the phrasemongers. And there can be no doubt that under the industrial regime discoveries made in the physical and mathematical sciences will earn the highest esteem, since they are of the most general utility for the prosperity of agriculture, manufacturing, and commerce.

Two reasons persuaded me to address myself to the farmers, manufacturers, and merchants rather than the scientists in order to induce them actively to apply themselves to the administration of the nation's general interests.

My first reason was that practitioners have means of subsistence at their disposal which give them independence; whereas nearly all theorists live off incomes from posts sponsored by the Government, posts which depend, at the present time, on the clergy, nobility, judiciary, and idle property owners . . .

My second reason was that since administrative power should always remain in the hands of the practitioners, who are to be responsible for allocating national rewards, the theorists will always be dependent, in the temporal sphere, on the farmers, manufacturers, merchants, and bankers, even though they deserve to enjoy a higher standing than the men who grant them their rewards. The reputations of Corneille and Molière were made by their actors and their audiences, who did not themselves attempt to vie for glory with those founders of our dramatic literature, that important but secondary branch of industry.

If the unfortunate situation were to arise in which the scientists controlled the administration of temporal affairs, the scientific corps would soon become corrupt and succumb to the same vices as the clergy. It would become metaphysical, contriving, and despotic . . .

[*Oeuvres,* vol. III, pt. 1, pp.157-61.]

25. LETTERS ON THE BOURBONS

(Extracts from *Lettres sur les Bourbons*, 1820. Reprinted with revisions in *Du système industriel*, pt. I, 1821)

FIRST LETTER: TO THE KING

Sire,

In my analysis of the present political situation, in my last brochure, I demonstrated that the industrials are today the only firm supporters of the monarchy, and that consequently the aim of your dynasty's unalterable political plan must be a close union with them, put into effect as soon as possible. But, however invincible, however urgent the necessity of boldly and exclusively following this course, one cannot conceal the fact that its adoption will at first encounter great difficulties. It is these difficulties that I shall now venture to bring to Your Majesty's attention . . .

Sire, the chief obstacle to the establishment of a coalition between the monarchy and the industrials is, on the latter's part, a prejudice against your dynasty which the Bonapartist feudality first implanted among the majority of industrials with any political opinion, and which has caused them not so much to undertake or even support attempts to place the monarchy in other hands (which is contrary to their habits), but to refrain from opposing such attempts, and perhaps even to approve them. The direct object of this work is to combat this deadly prejudice by examining all the motives behind it. The special object of this first letter is to present Your Majesty with some reflections on this unfortunately incontestable fact.

Sensible people have long observed that any protracted discord signifies that both sides are at fault. It is a shameful and false policy which has represented the active and productive part of the French population — the industrials — to Your Majesty as a crowd of madmen who love disorder, blind dupes of a handful of intriguers aiming to overthrow your dynasty; a policy according to which, on the other hand, the monarchy has never been in error, is never in error, and could not possibly ever be in error. No, Sire, things are not like that. Undoubtedly, the prejudice which exists against the Bourbon dynasty is without any real foundation. Undoubtedly, the Napoleonic feudality exercises too great an influence on the opinion of the industrials. But to what is this influence due? What is the source of this prejudice? Is not all this obviously due to the retrograde course followed by the royal power since the Restoration? If one can justifiably reproach the industrials for allowing themselves to be influenced by the

Bonapartist nobility, cannot one with just as much reason reproach the monarchy for allowing itself to be dominated by the old nobility? . . . Yes, Sire, I have the courage to say it, and Your Majesty should have the even greater firmness to admit it: the wrongs have been and still are on both sides . . .

THIRD LETTER : TO THE INDUSTRIALS

Gentlemen,
 . . . For those who consider things from a philosophical point of view, the extreme political importance attached at the present time to a change of dynasty is clear proof, the most complete proof possible, that you have little appreciation of the great social reform reserved for the civilised Europeans of the nineteenth century, and have no clear, sound idea of the means which must be adopted to achieve that reform. Accustomed hitherto always to remaining passive in politics, unable to rouse yourselves to action, ignorant, or rather thinking yourselves ignorant of the simple step which is required to establish the regime most favourable to the general interests of agriculture, manufacturing, and commerce, you impose the burden on the monarchy. In your minds you give it the task of inventing and organising the industrial regime for you, reserving for yourselves, no doubt, the right to enjoy the finished product. If the reigning dynasty is not coming near to fulfilling these conditions that you impose on it in such a tacit, although in your eyes very obligatory manner, your desires call for another dynasty; and there is always someone ready to respond to such calls. That is, I presume, the line of thinking behind your desires for a change of dynasty. It is basically natural, although it must assuredly be regarded as very strange. Not understanding the means of dealing with things, or not yet having sufficient energy and confidence for it, you rest your hopes on persons. That is how minds usually work. But I do not hesitate, gentlemen, to give you a hazardous prediction, by announcing that if you continue to proceed this way in politics you will experiment with every possible dynasty without taking a single essential step towards the establishment of the regime which is the object of all your desires. The reason for this is very simple: the chief effort necessary to attain this end must come from you, can reside only in you; while the monarchy, in whatever hands it is placed, can only offer in this sense simple cooperation — powerful, no doubt, perhaps even indispensable, but nevertheless secondary in character. It is you and your collaborators, the scientists, who must prepare, elaborate, and finally organise the industrial regime through a continuous series of combined theoretical and practical works. The help of the monarchy

is necessary to clear the way for you, to give an impulse to your work; and it is for this reason that it is so important for you to form an alliance with it . . .

FOURTH LETTER: TO THE INDUSTRIALS

Gentlemen,

The example of the English having to rid themselves of the Stuarts in order firmly to establish the parliamentary regime presents the anti-Bourbon faction with a powerful argument which, with its usual skill, it uses to great advantage. But all the strength of this argument rests only on a supposed analogy of circumstances which is only apparent, and which disappears as soon as things are examined in any depth. You will, I hope, be convinced of this, gentlemen, once you have weighed the following considerations, which I need only expound in summary form.

The change which the monarchy must undergo today in France is quite different in nature from the change it underwent in England during the establishment of the parliamentary regime.

Monarchy was at first a purely feudal institution. But since the enfranchisement of the commons it has been constantly changing and has become partly industrial. The industrial character of monarchy has increased steadily in extent and importance. Its feudal character, on the other hand, has declined as the progress of civilisation has elevated industry and relegated feudality; so that the final destination of monarchy is naturally to lose every vestige of feudalism, to reconstitute itself and to flourish for ever as a purely industrial institution. In France, because of the present state of civilisation, the monarchy is today called to take this great step. But England, at the time of its revolution, was a long way behind such a goal. The only improvement then permitted by the progress of enlightenment amounted to limiting the feudal part of the royal power as much as possible. The establishment of the parliamentary regime did in fact take this modification as far as it could be taken.

Thus, between the two situations we are comparing there is the essential difference between a simple change and a total reorganisation on new foundations. Now, this difference means that the reasons which made a change of dynasty necessary for the English are in no way applicable to us . . .

* * * * *

FIFTH LETTER: TO THE INDUSTRIALS
Gentlemen,

In the preceding letters I have discussed the argument for a change of dynasty solely from the national point of view. In order to complete the examination it remains for me to present it to your minds from a more exalted point of view, the European point of view.

Gentlemen, the great movement of civilisation in which the French people have been caught up since 1789 should not be considered as simply national. It has a more general character. All the nations of western Europe participate in it in a way which is relatively easy to discern. The clearest proof of this has just been provided by the three recent examples of Spain, Naples, and Portugal ...

England was the first country to move towards the industrial regime. But in view of the imperfect state of civilisation when it undertook its political reform, it could attain only a modification of the feudal regime. In reality it is the French nation which is summoned, by the nature of things, to commence the organisation of the industrial regime. Although it has not yet clearly conceived the true aim of its mission, it has certainly felt the importance of it, and the signal which it gave in 1789 has impressed on all of western Europe the movement which must finally result in the establishment of the industrial regime, and in which France must retain the initiative.

To attain this end determined by the nature of things, one indispensable condition had first to be fulfilled. It was necessary to begin, before all else, by establishing a provisional and preparatory order: the parliamentary regime invented by the English, which experience had recognised as the best possible modification of the feudal system. The French nation had first to fulfil this condition before devoting itself to the preparation and gradual formation of the industrial system, so that it would be able to carry out this task, inevitably very slow, with all the necessary calm and maturity. This is what it has finally done, after being misled for a quarter of a century in a totally wrong direction. But this first preliminary step was still not enough; the same condition had also to be fulfilled by the other nations of western Europe. The parliamentary regime had to be adopted generally before France could proceed unhesitatingly and in complete security to the preparation of the industrial system.

That is the essential step which Spain, and subsequently Naples and Portugal, have today taken in common cause with the peoples of western Europe.[66] In this situation it is clear that you must apply yourselves without delay to the formation of the industrial system. The preliminary task which had to be executed by the other western nations has just been completed ...

[*Oeuvres,* vol. III, pt. 1, pp. 197-201, 231-3; pt. 2, pp. 3-5, 21, 25-7.]

PART IV THE TRUE CHRISTIANITY (1821-5)

It is generally believed that men are not capable of being impassioned in the religious direction, but this is a profound error. The Catholic system was in contradiction with the system of sciences and modern industry. Hence, its collapse was inevitable. It is happening, and this collapse is the signal for a new belief which, by its enthusiasm, will fill the spiritual void left by criticism; a belief which will draw its strength from all that is lacking in the old belief, as well as from all that belongs to it.

Saint-Simon to Olinde Rodrigues, *Oeuvres de Saint-Simon & d'Enfantin,* vol. II, Paris: E. Dentu, 1865, p.115.

26. ADDRESS TO PHILANTHROPISTS

(Extracts from *Adresse aux philanthropes, Du système industriel,* pt. I, 1821)

Gentlemen,
   The passion which inspires you is of divine institution, and places you in the foremost rank of Christians. It gives you the right, it imposes on you the duty to combat malevolent passions and to enter into a hand-to-hand struggle with peoples and kings who allow themselves to be dominated by those passions.
   Your forefathers commenced the social organisation of the human race. It is up to you to complete this holy enterprise. The first Christians founded general morality by proclaiming in hovels and palaces alike the divine principle: *All men should look on one another as brothers; they should love and help one another.* They organised a doctrine based on this principle, but gave it only a speculative character, and the honour of organising temporal power in conformity with this divine axiom has been reserved for you. You have been destined throughout eternity to show princes that it is in their interest and is their duty to give their subjects the constitution which can lead most directly to an improvement in the social condition of the most numerous class. You have been destined to make these national leaders subordinate their politics to the fundamental principle of Christian morality . . .
   I believe that the new spiritual power will be composed at first of all the existing Academies of Science in Europe, and of all persons who deserve to be admitted to these scientific corporations. I believe that once this nucleus is formed, its members will organise themselves. I believe that the direction of education, as well as of public teaching, will be entrusted to this new spiritual power. I believe that the pure morality of the Gospel will serve as the basis of the new public education, and that, for the rest, it will be pushed as far as possible in conformity with positive knowledge, in proportion to the time which children of different levels of wealth will be able to spend at school. Finally, I believe that the new spiritual power will settle a fairly large number of its members throughout all the communes, and that the principal mission of these detached scholars will be to inspire their spiritual charges with a passion for the public good . . .
   For six years I have been working fervently to show the scientists and industrials that:
   1. Society is now clearly moving towards the organisation most favourable to the progress of the sciences and the prosperity

of industry.
2. In order to achieve the organisation of society most favourable to the progress of the sciences and the prosperity of industry, it is necessary to give spiritual power to the scientists, and the administration of temporal power to the industrials.
3. The scientists and industrials can organise society in conformity with its desires and needs, since the scientists possess intellectual force and the industrials control material forces.

This work has brought me into contact with a large number of scientists and industrials, and has given me the opportunity to study their opinions and intentions.

This is what I have observed:

I recognised first that one may consider men to be divided in terms of morality into two different groups: those in whom feelings dominate ideas, and those in whom feelings are subordinate to the workings of the mind; those who link the hope for an improvement in their condition with a desire for the suppression of abuses, and those whose special aim in their social relations is to turn abuses to their advantage. In short, I observed that scientists and industrials, like other men, must be divided into two great classes: philanthropists and egoists.

I then observed that the number of philanthropists increases or diminishes relative to the number of egoists according to social circumstances, and that in present circumstances the number of egoists is increasing daily. But, in compensation, the philanthropists are more disposed to unite their efforts and to act energetically.

I observed, moreover, that whether a man adopts philanthropic morality or egoistic opinions depends to a large extent on the nature of his occupation; so that those men whose daily routine brings them into contact with the most individuals, and in particular with the common people, are more inclined towards philanthrophy; while those whose occupations isolate them, or who are involved mainly with the rich class, turn to egoism unless nature has endowed them with an extremely fortunate disposition.

I thus feel justified in concluding, on the basis of both my own experience and the facts of history, that it will be the philanthropists who will make the nobles and theologians support the general political consequence of the divine moral principle . . .

Preaching, both verbal and written, is the only means which the philanthropists will employ. They will preach to the kings that it is their duty as Christians, and is in their interest from the point of view of conserving their hereditary powers, to entrust the positive scientists with the direction of public education and the task of improving theories, and to give the best industrial administrators responsibility for directing temporal affairs.

To the people they will preach the need for a unanimous demonstration on their part, a demonstration to the princes of their desire to have the management of public affairs, temporal and spiritual, placed entirely in the hands of those classes most able to act in the general interest, and most interested in so acting.

The philanthropists will continue their preaching, verbal and written, as long as is necessary to persuade the princes (either through the effect of their conviction or through the all-powerful influence of public opinion) to bring about the changes in social organisation required by the progress of enlightenment, the common interest of the whole population, and the imminent and immediate interest of the vast majority.

In short, preaching will be the only means employed by the philanthropists, and the sole object of their sermons will be to make the kings use their powers, powers which they are authorised to use by the peoples, to effect the necessary political changes . . .

[*Oeuvres*, vol. III, pt. 2, pp. 85-6, 115-16, 120-24.]

27. [FROM FEUDALISM TO INDUSTRIALISM: THE ROLE OF THE LAWYERS AND METAPHYSICIANS]

(Extract from the preface to *Du système industriel,* pt. I, 1821)

... The industrial and scientific system was born and has developed under the domination of the feudal and theological system. Now, this simple juxtaposition is enough to show that between two such absolutely antipathetic systems a kind of intermediate, indeterminate system had to intervene, destined solely to modify the old system so as to permit the development of the new system, and subsequently to effect the transition. The information I have presented makes this the most obvious of general historical facts. In both the temporal and spiritual spheres all changes have to be gradual. In this case the change was so great, and, on the other hand, the feudal and theological system was naturally so resistant to all modifications, that it required the special and continuous action, for several centuries, of particular classes derived from the old system (but distinct from and to a certain extent independent of it), classes which, because of their political situation, had to establish in the bosom of society what I shall call by way of abstraction an intermediate, transitional system. These classes were the lawyers (in the temporal sphere) and the metaphysicians (in the spiritual), closely united in their political action, just as feudality and theology, industry and the sciences of observation are united.

The general fact that I have just indicated is of the greatest importance. It is one of the fundamental ideas which must serve as the basis of positive political theory; an idea which more than any other is in need of clarification today, since the vagueness and obscurity which have so far surrounded it have done more than anything else to cause the present confusion and incoherence of political ideas.

It would be absolutely unphilosophical not to recognise the utility and remarkable influence of the lawyers and metaphysicians in modifying the feudal and theological system and ensuring that it did not suppress the scientific and industrial system once it began to develop. It was the lawyers who abolished feudal justice and established a less oppressive, more regular jurisprudence. How often, in France, the action of the courts of justice has protected industry against feudality! To reproach these bodies for their ambition is to blame the inevitable effects of a useful, reasonable, and necessary cause. It is beside the point. As for the metaphysicians, they were responsible for the Reformation of the sixteenth century, and the establishment of the principle of freedom of conscience which undermined the basis of the theological power.

I would be overstepping the limits of a preface if I continued with these ideas, ideas which any sound mind can easily develop following the previous indications. For my part, I declare that I do not see how the old system could have been modified and the new system developed without the intervention of the lawyers and metaphysicians.*

On the other hand, if it is absurd to deny the special utility of the lawyers and metaphysicians in the advancement of civilisation, it is very dangerous to exaggerate that utility, or rather to misunderstand its true nature. Because of the nature of its goal, the political influence of the lawyers and metaphysicians was limited to a passing existence: it was only modificatory and transitory, and in no way organisational. Its natural function should have come to an end once the old system lost most of its power and the forces of the new system really became dominant in society, in both the temporal and spiritual spheres. If it had finished at this point, which was completely achieved by the middle of the last century, the political career of the lawyers and metaphysicians would not have ceased to be useful and honourable. In actual fact it has become a complete hindrance, since it has exceeded its natural limits.

When the French Revolution broke out, it was no longer a question of modifying the feudal and theological system, which had already lost almost all its real force. It was a question of organising the industrial and scientific system, summoned by the level of civilisation to replace it. Consequently, it was the industrials and the scientists who should have dominated the political scene, each in their natural role. But instead of that, the lawyers placed themselves at the head of the Revolution; they directed it with the doctrines of the metaphysicians. It would be superfluous to recall the strange wanderings which resulted, and the misfortunes which resulted from those wanderings. But it should be carefully noted that in spite of this vast experience the lawyers and metaphysicians have remained in charge of affairs, and that today they alone direct all political discussions . . .

[*Oeuvres,* vol. III, pt. 1, pp. 6-11.]

---

*This intermediate stage was so ordained by the very nature of things that one encounters it again even in dealing with purely scientific questions. What astronomer, physicist, chemist, or physiologist does not know that before passing, in each field, from purely theological ideas to positive ideas, the human mind availed itself of metaphysics for a long time? Is not everyone who has reflected on the advance of the sciences convinced that this intermediate stage was useful, indeed absolutely indispensable in order to effect the transition?[6,7]

28. [ON LIBERTY] [68]

(Extract from the preface to *Du système industriel*, pt.I, 1821)

... The maintenance of liberty was bound to be an object of primary concern as long as the feudal and theological system retained some of its force, because liberty was then exposed to grievous and continuous attacks. But today there need no longer be the same anxiety during the establishment of the industrial and scientific system, since this system must inevitably and automatically bring with it the highest degree of social liberty, temporal as well as spiritual. In such a situation, a great political apparatus especially designed to preserve liberty from attacks to which it can no longer be seriously exposed would be very much like Don Quixote's battle against the windmills.

Besides, the maintenance of individual liberties can in no case be the object of the social contract. Liberty, in its true perspective, is a *consequence* of civilisation — both progress together — but it cannot be its *aim*. Men do not associate in order to be free. Savages associate to hunt, to make war, but certainly not to produce liberty. In this respect it would be better for them to remain isolated. I repeat: an *active* aim is necessary, and that cannot be liberty, since liberty is a by-product of activity. True liberty is not simply a matter of keeping one's arms folded in the association, if one so desires. Such an inclination should be severely repressed whenever it arises. On the contrary, liberty means developing a temporal or spiritual capacity useful to the association, without hindrance and to as great an extent as is possible.

We may observe, moreover, that as civilisation progresses, the division of labour — both spiritual and temporal — considered from the most general point of view increases at the same rate. The inevitable result is that men depend less on each other as individuals, but that they all depend commensurately more on the mass. Now, if the vague and metaphysical idea of liberty current today continued to be taken as the basis of political doctrines, it would tend severely to impede the action of the mass on individuals. From this point of view, it would be contrary to the development of civilisation and the organisation of a well-ordered system, which demands that the parts should be firmly linked to the whole and dependent on it.

I shall not speak of political liberty, because it is all too clear that as an aim of association it is even less deserving of consideration than individual liberty. However, I will observe on this subject, as a statement of the true state of affairs, that the right to participate in public affairs irrespective of capacity, conferred in theory on every citizen as a *natural* right, and limited only in its exercise but never according to capacity, is the most complete and most obvious proof of the vagueness and uncertainty which still shroud political ideas. How else are we to explain the indirect but unambiguous declaration that political thinking requires no natural capacity?

Why is it not declared that Frenchmen who pay a thousand francs in direct taxation are qualified to make discoveries in chemistry, when exactly the same principle is established in politics, which is in fact much more difficult and important than chemistry?[69] Why? Because the kind of capacity required in chemistry is clear, while that required in politics is not. And to what is this difference due? The fact that chemistry is today a positive science, while politics is still only a conjectural doctrine which does not deserve the name of science.

It is characteristic of metaphysics, precisely because it teaches nothing real, to argue that one is qualified for everything without any need for special study. The remarkable situation which I have just indicated exists today only in politics and philosophy, its mother, because they alone, among all the branches of our knowledge, are still metaphysical. But there is an analogy with the sciences which are today the most positive, in the period when they were still plunged in the obscure realms of metaphysics. The kinds of capacity needed in order to study these sciences did not become clear and precise, nor did they cease to be the subject of universal dispute, until the sciences assumed a positive character based on observation. It must be absolutely the same in politics. Today it is not thought ridiculous when people argue that political science is innate or that to be a Frenchman by birth is sufficient proof of capacity to reason. Such language is even regarded as patriotic. But when politics has risen to the ranks of the sciences of observation, which must be before too long, the conditions of capacity will become clear and fixed, and the cultivation of politics will be entrusted exclusively to a special class of scientists who will impose silence on all twaddle.

[*Oeuvres,* vol. III, pt. 1, pp.15-17 (footnote).]

29. [CONSTITUTIONAL PROPOSALS TO THE KING]

(Extracts from the postscript to *Première adresse au Roi, Du système industriel,* pt. II, 1821)

Sire,
I think I have given sufficient proof in this Address that your ministry is proceeding in the wrong direction; and I think I have clearly established the course it ought to adopt. It remains for me to indicate what means may be employed in order to move from the present wrong path to the one you ought to be following. I shall fulfil this third task in this *Post-Scriptum.*

I advise Your Majesty to take the following measures: I advise you first to issue the ordinances whose main provisions I shall now expound:

FIRST ORDINANCE

'Considering that the political troubles which have disturbed France for more than thirty years have been caused chiefly by the people's ignorance of their own interests, and by the falsity of their ideas concerning the means to be employed by the Government to improve their existence;

'Considering also that the first duty of the Prince is to provide the children of all citizens with sound education; and seeking to ensure as far as is possible that the least well-off class has a knowledge of the principles which must serve as the basis of social organisation, as well as the laws which govern the material world, we have decreed the following:

First Article

'All Classes of the Institute will together draw up a national catechism embracing both the elementary teaching of the principles which must serve as the basis of social organisation, and a summary instruction in the principal laws which govern the material world.

Article II

'The Institute will plan its catechism so that it may be learned by the mutual method of education.[70]

'Enough elementary schools will be established to ensure that the national catechism can be taught to all children of the present generation.

Article III

'A sum of twenty millions will be employed for the education of the people. The Institute will present a plan for employing this sum.

SECOND ORDINANCE

'Considering that the strongest link which can unite the members of a society is the similarity of their principles and their knowledge, and that this similarity can only be achieved through the uniformity of education given to all citizens, we have decreed the following:

First Article

'The Institute will supervise public education. Nothing will be taught in the schools contrary to the principles established in the national catechism.

Article II

'The ministers of the various sects will be subject, in both their preaching and their teaching of children, to the supervision of the Institute.

Article III

'No Frenchman will be able to exercise the rights of citizenship until he has sat an examination on the national catechism. The Institute will regulate the method and conditions of examination.

THIRD ORDINANCE

'Considering that the most important chiefs of industrial enterprises are of all citizens the ones most interested in the maintenance of peace and internal order; considering also that more than any other class they have a personal interest in reducing taxation and employing public money sensibly; considering, finally, that more than any other citizens they have proved their capacity in administration, since it is chiefly through the exercise of this capacity that they have achieved success in their enterprises, we have decreed the following:

First Article

'A council of industrials will be formed and given the task of preparing the budget for 1822. This council will consist of: 1) the Chamber of

Commerce; 2) the General Council of Manufacturers; 3) the Bank of France's Council of Directors; 4) the twelve most important farmers from those attached to the Council of Agriculture.

Article II

'This budget will be conceived in the interest of the majority of the nation. It will aim as directly as possible to improve the condition of the people by promoting the progress and development of industry.

Article III

'The Minister of Finance will provide the Chamber of Commerce with all the information it requests and needs to prepare this project.

Article IV

'The first two items of expenditure will be: 1) the education of the people; 2) the provision of work for all persons who have no other means of existence.

FOURTH ORDINANCE

'Considering that the retention of noble titles greatly offends the nation; considering also that the retention of titles sustains the old nobles in the hope of re-establishing the feudal regime, and the new nobles in the desire to reorganise the aristocracy created by Bonaparte; considering, finally, that it is desirable, for the general good, that the chiefs of industrial enterprises should enjoy the highest degree of respect in the temporal sphere, we have decreed what follows:

First Article

'The new and old nobilities are abolished; feudal titles are annulled; no designation recalling the privileges enjoyed by the nobles will be employed in public acts, nor in the acts of the courts of justice.

FIFTH ORDINANCE

'Considering that the armies of Spain, Portugal, Naples, and Piedmont have all recently risen against the governments of their countries, because (according to their explanation) their Kings wanted to use the armed forces as an instrument for oppressing industrious and peaceful citizens; wishing to be at one with the French nation, and thereby to deprive the French army of any pretext for following the pernicious example of the military forces in those nations which have suffered military revolutions, we have decreed the following:

First Article

'We disband the whole of our military household. The individual members will be incorporated in the army of the line.

Article II

'The protection of our person will be the responsibility of the National Guard.

Article III

'The officers of the National Guard will be re-elected. The companies will elect their officers; the captains will elect their majors; the majors will choose a chief for the legion to which their batallions belong; and the chiefs of the legions will choose the general commander of the National Guard, who will be responsible for the composition of his general staff.

Article IV

'Only licensed citizens will be eligible for election as officers of the National Guard.

Article V

'Another ordinance will regulate the new organisation of the National Guard of the Realm.

SIXTH ORDINANCE

'Considering that the vast majority of members of the present Chamber of Deputies are nobles (old and new), idle property owners, and functionaries; recognising that such a majority is interested in passing laws injurious to the prosperity of industrial enterprises; and wishing to ensure that the chiefs of the most directly useful enterprises can exercise their due influence in the formation of the laws, we have decreed the following:

First Article

'The present Parliament is dissolved.

Article II

'A new election of deputies will follow immediately and the electoral assemblies will be convened for this purpose as soon as possible.

Article III

'The choice of deputies will proceed on the basis of the method established by the law of 5 February 1817.[71]

Article IV

'Since the chiefs of industrial enterprises are of all citizens the ones most interested in order and the good management of public expenditure, the electors will be invited to make their choice from licensed persons, or at least supporters of the industrial regime.

Article V

'A new electoral law will be presented in the next session.'

Sire,
    I believe that Your Majesty would be wise to publish the following proclamation at the same time as the preceding ordinances:

'THE KING, TO THE NATION

'Frenchmen,
    'Since 1789 the question of sovereignty has been discussed on three different occasions: there was a great deal of metaphysical discussion about the rights of man; than an attempt was made to establish that great military service to the nation bestowed a right to rule; finally, today, arguments are being contrived in favour of legitimacy.
    'Another question has been very much to the fore. People have tried to determine how the political powers should be divided so as to balance each other, what limits should be placed on each of these

powers, and what general restrictions should apply to the authority of the rulers over the ruled.

'An effort has also been made to distinguish the ruling class from those who are ruled, by fixing income qualifications for electors and candidates.

'As for more detailed work, innumerable things have been done: a civil code, a criminal code, a procedural code, etc., and a multitude of regulatory laws in every sphere of administration.

'Finally, eight different constitutions have been produced and implemented in succession.

'And after all these labours and efforts which have occupied us for thirty-two years, we are still in the midst of revolution, for the Government can only function with the aid of troops, and I myself have to be guarded by the Swiss.

'To what cause do you think the sterility of our management is to be attributed?

'Our failure clearly shows that we have posed the questions badly; that we have not looked at things from the right point of view; that we have been bothering about the form of the new social regime without first determining the principles on which the regime must be based.

'Europeans are presently dominated by false and vague philosophical ideas. The political system which they seek to establish and which they indifferently call the constitutional, representative, or parliamentary regime is a spurious system which tends uselessly to prolong the anti-scientific and anti-industrial existence of the theological and feudal powers.

'The hope which has existed in France since 1789, that a chamber composed of deputies from every part of the Kingdom would discover the principles on which the new social organisation must be based, and that it would implement a political system proportionate to the level of enlightenment, is completely illusory.

'The conception of a new system must be unitary, that is, it must be formulated by a single mind.

'It was not an assembly which the Athenians entrusted with the task of framing their constitution; it was Lycurgus alone who planned the social organisation of the Spartans. An assembly is good for maintaining an established constitution, but because it is a collection of individuals, it is entirely incapable of producing a system . . .

'Frenchmen!

'The greatest service which the monarchy can render the nation in the present circumstances is to assume the role of dictator for the purpose of destroying the feudal and theological regime, and establishing the scientific and industrial regime. The momentary concentration of all political powers in a single person is the quickest and easiest means of bringing about this transition. A radical change in the social system can only be effected by insurrection or dictatorship; and it is incontestable that dictatorship is a lesser evil than insurrection. The exercise of unlimited power in the present circumstances will be very much to your advantage, and will not involve any major inconvenience. Since the dictator's social purpose would be clearly determined, public opinion would not allow him to depart from the necessary course.

'One thing, above all, must be noted: The dictatorship will have a profound effect on the monarchy. It will align this institution with the interests of science and industry; it will rid it of the feudal and theological character which it still bears; and the King will become the first industrial, just as he has been the first soldier in the Kingdom.

'Frenchmen!

'Let us work with zeal, each in our own sphere, for the organisation of the true Christianity. God has shown us the route we must follow. We have only to advance.'

[*Oeuvres,* vol. III, pt. 2, pp. 236-49, 253-5.]

30. LETTER TO THE WORKERS

(Henri Saint-Simon à Messieurs les ouvriers, Du système industriel, pt. II, 1821)

Gentlemen,
   The chief aim which I set myself in my works is to improve your situation as much as possible. I hold no office, I possess no power. Thus, the only way I can be of use to you is to give you good advice. I invite you to speak as follows to the chiefs of the most important houses of agriculture, manufacture, and commerce. It seems certain to me that great advantages will result for you, and that your existence will be quickly improved. It is you who are going to speak.

'Gentlemen – Heads of the Most Important Houses of Agriculture, Manufacture, and Commerce,
   'You are rich, and we are poor. You work with your brains, we with our hands. As a result of these two fundamental differences between us, we are and we should be your subordinates.
   'Since you are our leaders, gentlemen, it is to you that we must address the grievances which we wish to reach the throne; and that is what we are going to do, by inviting you to make known to *His Majesty* what we say to you. *Henry IV* thought all the Government's energy should be directed towards making it possible for us to eat chicken every Sunday. The present Bourbons can realise the desire of this good Prince of whom they are glorified to be the descendants!

'Gentlemen,
   'Our good sense is sufficient to show us that the affairs of the French nation are very badly administered, its resources are badly employed, its activity is badly directed, or rather is paralysed through the wrong direction it has been given.
   'Again, our good sense is sufficient to show us that it would be easy to enrich the nation, to render it happier and more powerful than it has hitherto been. It is also sufficient to make us realise what means must be employed to achieve this great aim.

'Gentlemen,
   'In less than ten years the value of French territory can be doubled. To do that it would be necessary to clear uncultivated land, drain marshland, open up new roads, improve those that already exist, construct all the bridges necessary to shorten routes, and build all the canals which can be of use for shipping as well as for irrigation.

'There will be no shortage of funds with which to realise a good project for the general improvement of French territory. The capital will soon be forthcoming if the State (restricting itself to the increase in taxation which will inevitably result from the growth of wealth) grants to entrepreneurs, as far as is possible, all the benefits resulting from their enterprises.

'There will be no shortage of labour either, for in the absence of the measure which we have just recommended, which is the only one able generally to stimulate production, a large number of navvies are always unemployed. The ordinary work of agriculture provides full employment during the harvest, but once the harvest has ended, one-eighth of the population is all that is required for ploughing, seeding, harrowing, threshing, and looking after the herds; so that in those places where the population is not employed in the manufacture of wrought goods, the vast majority of workers have nothing to do for a large part of the year. It may certainly be estimated that six million navvies are without work between harvests.

'Gentlemen, trouble yourselves to fix your attention on what we have just said; think about the idea which we have just submitted to you; and you will easily recognise that if the Government announced that it would, as far as is possible, grant to the entrepreneurs of projects promoting an increase in the value of French territory all the particular advantages resulting from these projects, enterprises of this kind would be energetically pursued and quickly carried out.

'You will recognise equally that the adoption of this measure will bring, for you as well as for us, the most important advantages which society can afford. It will increase your wealth, it will give us work and consequently the comforts of life.

'Those of you and those of us engaged in agriculture will enjoy directly the advantages resulting from this operation. Those engaged in manufacturing wrought goods and in commerce will be just as well off, although for them the advantages can only be indirect, since agricultural workers, finding themselves employed all year, will receive 120 to 150 millions more in salaries each month, and will consequently consume 1,500 to 1,800 millions more per year, which will increase manufacturing and commercial activity to a degree hitherto unknown, even in England.

'The present administration of public affairs is defective on this first count: the number of administrators and their subordinates is much too large, which makes the cost of this administration exorbitant, imposing a heavy burden on the nation, which is of no use to it.

'It is defective on one even more important count: the administrators are chosen from the classes of society whose capacity is not administrative, whose interests are in many respects contrary to those of the productive class, which is the only class whose work aims directly to increase the power, comfort, and positive happiness of the nation.

'The disadvantages resulting from the poor composition of the administration are infinitely greater than those occasioned by the multiplicity of employees, and by the huge number of appointments made to staff-offices placed uselessly at the head of every administrative body.

'The economies which could be made in the cost of the present administration would amount in all to 200 millions per year at most; and one can estimate without exaggeration that France would increase its capital value (both land and moveables) by 3,000 millions per year if the administration were composed of capable men, men interested in giving the greatest stimulus to every branch of industry.

'In short, the present administration is directed chiefly by nobles, lawyers, and the military. Now, these three classes understand perfectly well how to consume the products of industry, but they are completely incapable of directing the work of producers; they even have, in certain respects, an interest in opposing the success of industry, because success of this kind tends to increase the importance of the producers and diminish that of the nobles, lawyers, and the military.

'It is our class, gentlemen, which suffers directly the disadvantages of the present maladministration. It pays most taxation and receives no salary. It proves that it alone has everything to gain. It is thus natural that we should be taxing our ingenuity to find the remedy for the evils which afflict us in particular.

'These disadvantages, gentlemen, have an even more direct and powerful effect on workers such as us than on you who are rich and able, since as a result more of us face suffering in terms of life's primary needs. It is thus up to us to take the initiative in indicating the means of bringing to an end our miseries which will obviously cease as soon as public affairs are decently administered.

'Here is what we propose to you.

'We invite you — you who are our leaders, who have become, through the progress of civilisation, the nation's most important, most useful, and most capable persons — to ask the King to give you responsibility for directing the administration of public affairs. We invite you to declare to *His Majesty* that you are certain to enrich France by more than 3,000 millions per year; that you are certain to provide us all with the means *of eating chicken every Sunday;* finally, that you are certain to establish a lasting peace by destroying all the factions that will continue to exist (whatever one does) as long as the waste of public money, which each hopes to turn to its own benefit, is allowed to go on.

'We authorise you, gentlemen, to make this demand in our name. Thus, it will be on behalf of twenty-five million men. Now, since this demand is in conformity with every principle of justice, and aims directly to improve the condition of the vast majority of the nation, we can hope that it will receive the attention of *His Majesty.*'

Gentlemen — Workers,

The only obstacle of any importance which today stands in the way of an improvement in your condition arises from the industrial chiefs' lack of confidence in their capacity to administer public affairs. I shall address to them at once a text to remove their worries on this account, and to rectify their ideas with respect to some other errors that they commit every day, and which are extremely prejudicial to them, as well as to you.

I have the honour to be,
Gentlemen, Workers,
Your most humble servant,

HENRI SAINT-SIMON
Rue de Richelieu, No. 34

P.S. All industrials who want this brochure may come to me for it. I shall let them have copies for themselves and their friends.

[*Oeuvres,* vol. VI, pp. 437-44.]

31. FIRST LETTER TO THE ELECTORS OF THE DEPARTMENT OF THE SEINE WHO ARE PRODUCERS

(Première lettre à messieurs les électeurs du département de la Seine qui sont producteurs, Du système industriel, pt. III, 1822)

Gentlemen,

So you have at last decided to place your confidence mainly in the producers, that is, your peers.

You had twelve deputies to elect, and you chose nearly all of them from the manufacturers, merchants, and bankers. This is the first election at which you have expressed an openly industrial political opinion; the first that you have conceived in your interest, which is the true national interest; it is, finally, the first at which you have adopted the course capable of bringing the revolution to an end.[72]

This resolution is certain proof that you are now more aware than ever before of your strength, your rights, and your capacity.

Thus, you have at last taken the right road. But you do not know how to advance along it at speed. Develop as quickly as possible the confidence you are beginning to show in your strength, your rights, and your political capacity: that is the best thing you can do in your own interest, and in the interest of the nation and the King.

Gentlemen, I shall now look at the distinction between landed property and moveable property, between the great owners of the soil and the proprietors of workshops. It is in this way, I believe, that I can most effectively contribute to the development of that confidence in yourselves of which I was speaking just now.

Charlemagne himself gave an account of the sale of vegetables harvested in his kitchen-gardens and of the hay gathered in the meadows. The great barons were farmers. They were the chief directors of work in the country; they attended to the rearing of animals; their wives and daughters saw to the manufacture of materials which they then made up into clothes for their families. At this time the great landowners also owned moveable property, in both agriculture and manufacturing; they were the leaders of the people in their daily work as well as the directors of the administration of public affairs. In short, in temporal affairs they were the most able as well as the richest men.

The enfranchisement of the commons gave birth to a new class of property owners: owners of moveable wealth. The new property owners made production their sole occupation; they worked relentlessly to improve every branch of industry; above all, they applied themselves to simplifying the administration and carrying it out as economically as possible. But hitherto they have been content to employ their administrative capacity in the direction of their own enterprises, and have not yet tried to apply it to the direction of public affairs.

Gentlemen, I am going to present you with a principle which will seem perfectly clear to everyone, and especially to you:

Only in enterprises whose object is production can positive capacity in administration be acquired.

Judge things according to this principle, and you will recognise that when I ask you to have confidence in your political capacity of administration, my entreaties are well founded. I shall repeat, with some minor changes, what I said to you above, because I regard this repetition as the most useful means I can employ to ensure your entire conviction in this respect.

From the conquest[73] (which was the original title to the ownership of the great domains, and therefore scarcely moral) to the enfranchisement of the commons, the owners of these domains were the foremost heads of productive enterprises. Thus, they had to be put in charge of the direction of public affairs, since they were the most able administrators.

Since the enfranchisement of the commons, the great landowners have successively ceased to concern themselves with production. They have abandoned their homes in the country; the richest were made courtiers; those belonging to the second class made their first homes in the towns. Enjoyment has become their exclusive occupation; they have inevitably lost their administrative capacity, and their incapacity in this respect has been entirely confirmed by the successive decline in the size of their lands, most of which they have been obliged to sell in order to settle the debts arising out of their extravagance. Consequently, it is clearly monstrous that they should today exert the chief influence on the administration of public affairs.

As for you, whose administrative capacity has been confirmed by the continual increase in your wealth, it is equally clear that today you would make the best administrators of the national interests. I was therefore justified in saying to you, and am justified in repeating, that you owe it to yourselves to use all your power and influence to hasten the moment when the King will select you as his first lieutenants in the administration of the national wealth.

I have the honour to be . . . etc.

[*Oeuvres,* vol. VI, pp.475-9.]

32. [HISTORICAL SURVEY OF THE PROGRESS OF FRENCH INDUSTRY]

(Extract from *Catéchisme des industriels,* bk. I, 1823)

Q... We shall ask you first what was the progress of industry, and the importance acquired by the industrials, from the settlement of the Franks in Gaul to the first crusade?[74]
A. From the settlement of the Franks in Gaul to the first crusade, a political development of the greatest importance took place, a development which paved the way for all subsequent progress in civilisation, and consequently all progress in industry, for the progress of industry is the most positive of all. This development was the amalgamation of the conquerors and the conquered to form the French nation, composed of Franks and Gauls.

The subsequent progress of industry was prepared during this period, but no progress was actually made which deserves to be mentioned.

The Franks, who were the nation's military leaders, were also the directors of industrial operations: almost all land belonged to them; they were equally endowed with moveable agricultural property, chief among which were the Gauls, who were bound to the land and who thus constituted the most important class of animal.

The manufacturers of rough agricultural implements were also in slavery, and consequently under the management of the Franks. Finally, the manufacture of fabrics for clothing was managed by the Franks' women, working under their observation in their châteaux. During this period of time, the artisans, although always in slavery, assumed importance and made money for themselves which they carefully kept secret.

Q. What happened between the first crusade and the reign of Louis XI?[75] What was the progress of industry? What were the causes of this progress?
A. For the aristocrats, that is, for the Franks, the crusades were a great expense. Their revenue was not sufficient to meet it. They were obliged, in order to procure the necessary sums of money, to sell franchises to those Gauls who were in a position to pay for them.

The Gauls who acquired most of these franchises were the artisans, who had had more opportunities and more means of saving than the others.

The Franks also sold land to the Gauls, who, by some means or other, had managed to get some money. Thus, it was the crusades which brought about the formation of the industrial class, as distinct from the military class.

Then, between the last crusade and the accession of Louis XI, the economy and activity of this class increased its importance.

It was also the crusades which brought about the improvement and the increase in scale and number of industrial operations. The nobles, who had ruined themselves through their Asiatic expeditions, brought back to France a taste for luxury and gallantry, in particular the fervent desire to possess fine arms.

The gallantry of men encouraged the coquetry of women; and the women, by becoming coquettes, developed a taste for luxury. The samples of fine materials manufactured in Asia inspired in the fair sex a desire to possess similar ones. Out of this came the origin of foreign commerce, the origin of the manufacture of high quality arms, and finally the origin of the manufacture of every satisfying object for a populaltion which was capable of enjoying the delicate pleasures.

In sum, when Louis XI came to the throne, the industrial class was quite separate from the military class. It was composed of three parts, namely:

Gauls who owned land, who were farmers of those lands and not soldiers; artisans who were free and gathered together in the towns; merchants who imported into France materials manufactured in Asia, and who put French manufactures into circulation throughout the country.

Q. *What developments took place in industry from Louis XI up to and including the reign of Louis XIV?*[76] *What caused this advance and the importance acquired by the industrials?*

A. By the fifteenth century the monarchy had already acquired a great deal of strength compared with its position at the time of the conquest of the Gauls by the Franks, when it was merely the generalship of the Frankish army, nominated by the chieftains whose troops made up this army.

When Louis XI ascended the throne he recognised that the monarchy was still only a very precarious institution with no positive and stable character. He recognised that the sovereign power still belonged collectively to the barons, that the King was in reality only the most important baron, and that those barons descended from chieftains still subscribed to the tradition that the King was a *primus inter pares,* to be appointed and dismissed according to their wishes. He recognised, finally, the need to fix his attention on the fact that in France the barons were collectively stronger and more powerful than the King, and that under the feudal constitution the monarchy could maintain its supremacy only by keeping the barons divided and attracting some of the most powerful barons to its side.

Louis XI conceived the bold plan of concentrating all sovereign power in the hands of the monarchy, destroying all the supremacy of the Franks over the Gauls, destroying the feudal system, abolishing the institutions of nobility, and making himself King of the Gauls instead of chief of the Franks.

If this plan was to be successful, the King had to merge his authority with the interests of a class strong enough to support him and ensure the success of his enterprise. He united with the industrials.

The industrials wanted the sovereign power to be concentrated in the hands of the monarchy, because this was the only way of destroying the impediments to commerce in France, which resulted from the division of the sovereign power. They also wanted to become the first class in society, as much to satisfy their self-esteem as to achieve the material advantages involved in making the law (the law always favouring its makers). Consequently, the industrials accepted the alliance proposed by the monarchy, an alliance which they have maintained ever since.

Louis XI may thus be regarded as the founder of the league formed in the fifteenth century between the monarchy and industry against the nobility, between the King of France and the Gauls against the descendants of the Franks.

This struggle between the King and the great vassals, between the chiefs of industrial enterprises and the nobles, lasted for more than two hundred years before the sovereign powers were concentrated in the hands of the monarchy, and before the direction of industrial enterprises by the nobles had completely ceased. But in the end Louis XIV saw the descendants or successors of the most important chieftains (who had subsequently become barons) fill his antechambers in their efforts to obtain household posts. And at last the numerous class of workingmen had no other leaders, in their work, but men drawn from their ranks and whose capacity or wealth had enabled them to become entrepreneurs of some industrial enterprise.

It is curious to observe in this struggle the direct action of the industrials against the nobles, and the means which they employed to deprive them of all the influence they exerted over peaceful labour. This observation explains the radical difference between the political character of nobles and industrials, between the civil conduct of the Franks and the Gauls.

The industrials, the Gauls engaged in agriculture, went to the gentlemen in their castles, and spoke to them in the following terms: You live a very sad life in this state of isolation in the country. The job of managing the cultivation of your land is not worthy of your high birth. Lease your land, so that you can spend the winter in the towns and the summer in the country, without ever having to bother with anything except your pleasures. In the towns our colleagues, the manufacturers, will hasten to make the most expensive and most comfortable furniture for you; our colleagues the merchants will show you materials in their warehouses to set off the charms of your spouses; and our colleagues the capitalists will lend you money when you need it. In summer, when you return to your castles, you will be able to concentrate on the pleasures of the hunt, while your wives keep themselves amused by looking after their flower-beds.

The nobles were seduced by this proposal. They accepted it, and henceforth ceased to have any political importance in the State, since they ceased to be the leaders of the people in their daily work.

In our view, what is most noteworthy in this change brought about by the industrials is the nature of their conduct, which was quite different from the way things proceeded in society before the formation of their class.

Before the formation of the corporation of industrials, only two classes existed in the nation: those who commanded and those who obeyed. The industrials appeared with a new character: from the beginning of their political existence they did not seek to command and did not wish to obey. They introduced a system based on private contract between themselves and their superiors or inferiors. The only masters they recognised were the calculations which reconciled the interests of the contracting parties.

We shall move on now, if you wish, to an examination of what happened from the century of Louis XIV to the establishment of the credit system.

Q. You are going too quickly. One very important point needs to be clarified. It would seem that Louis XIV, after reaping the benefits arising from his alliance with the industrials and converting the great vassals into men who passed his shirt and served at his table, completely abandoned the industrials; that he was concerned only with acquiring a great reputation as a soldier and conqueror, with building superb palaces and having his courtiers devour all the products of industrial labour. What do you have to say on this subject?

A. Louis XIV was certainly too extravagant. He loved war too much. But it would be wrong to conclude from this that he rendered no great services to industry. It was he who ordered Colbert to provide the manufacturers with capital for building large workshops. Financial assistance from his treasury enabled Van Robais to develop his fine manufacturing, which gave an impetus to the entire industry in beautiful woollen fabrics.

Finally, it was he who arranged the alliance between the positive scientific and manufacturing capacities. He created the Academy of Sciences and gave it the special task of guiding and promoting industrial enterprise.

May we remind you that this recapitulation must be as quick as possible. We therefore suggest that you do not ask us to go into the greatest detail, but proceed immediately to an examination of the progress of industry and the importance acquired by the industrials from the reign of Louis XIV up to and including the establishment of the credit system.

Q. To meet your request, we would like you to tell us how the industrials were able to raise themselves from their very subordinate social position relative to the nobility under Louis XIV to their present attitude of rivalry with all non-industrial classes. In short, we would like you to explain why the Antin embankment today dares to struggle against the Faubourg Saint-Germain. [77]

A. Before the eighteenth century the farmers, manufacturers, and merchants were still only separate corporations. It was at the end of Louis XIV's reign that these three great branches of industry were linked financially and politically through the creation of a new kind of industry whose particular interests are in perfect harmony with the common interests of the industrials. It was the formation of this new branch of industry which gave the industrials the means of establishing the credit system.

It is extremely important to pay the greatest attention to the development of the industrials' financial and political organisation; only through a knowledge of the way in which this organisation has operated is it possible to conceive, clearly and firmly, what the industrials must do today to improve their social condition. We request you to follow what we are going to say very attentively.

The protection granted to manufacturing and commerce by Louis XIV gave a great impetus to those two branches of industry. But this great benefit had one disadvantage: having expanded their operations the manufacturers and merchants had to arrange their payments and receipts in many different places, with the result that the task of settling both sides of their accounts employed a large part of their time.

Needs give rise to resources. It was not long before a new branch of industry was formed, banking industry. These new industrials sought the manufacturers and merchants, and said to them: 'You spend a lot of time and make great sacrifices collecting your revenue and making your payments. We suggest that you give us this task. Seeing that this will be our sole occupation, and that all transactions of this kind will be made by us, we will be able to settle your payments and revenue much more economically than you can, since the material transfer of money will thereby be considerably reduced, etc.'

The bankers' proposal was accepted by all manufacturers and merchants, so that henceforth all movements of money were undertaken by the bankers.

The bankers soon obtained a lot of credit. This was the inevitable result of the fact that all movements of money were undertaken by them.

In order to put their credit to good use, the bankers lent it at interest to the merchants and manufacturers.

With more credit the merchants and manufacturers were able to expand their operations and produce a greater stock of wealth.

So the general result for industry and society of the establishment of banking was a very large increase in capital and the development of a taste for comfortable things. It also meant that the industrial class now began to possess a much greater financial power than that of all other classes put together, greater even than the Government's.

While the industrials were making great progress in terms of capacity, importance, and real power, the non-industrial classes declined in every respect. Yet the monarchy continued to choose the administrators of the national wealth from these classes.

Bad administration of the national wealth resulted in a continually increasing deficit. Finally, in 1817 the public treasury was in such an embarrassing position that its non-industrial administrators could no longer think of any way of solving the problem and keeping the agreements made by the King with foreigners – agreements resulting from the bad financial transactions which caused revolution and then anarchy in the Kingdom, and which finally made the French nation dependent on foreign nations.

In these circumstances the bankers offered the Government all the money it needed, but they laid down the following conditions:

1. The Government must completely abandon its barbarous conduct in financial affairs; it must renounce bankruptcy for ever; it must adopt the industrial, that is, the loyal course; it must pay all creditors in full, whatever the origin of their credit.
2. This affair must be treated as a private matter between the bankers and the Government; discussion of the terms of the loan must be regarded as a simple matter between private individuals, between the bankers and the ministers.

The bankers' proposal was accepted. In this way public credit was born, and public credit gave the monarchy more strength than it had ever had before.

Here ends our promised recapitulation of the progress of industry and the importance acquired by the industrials from the settlement of the Franks in Gaul to the present day ...

[*Oeuvres*, vol. IV, pt. 1, pp.16-31.]

33. [ON THE INTERMEDIATE (BOURGEOIS) CLASS]

(Extract from *Catéchisme des industriels*, bk. I, 1823)

Q... There is one thing you have not mentioned: that there is an intermediate class between the nobles and the industrials; that it is this valuable class which is the true social link, and which reconciles feudal and industrial principles. What do you think of this class?
A. The division which you have just established is very fine in metaphysics, but we do not want to practise metaphysics; on the contrary, we want to fight against it. The aim of our work is to replace metaphysical reasoning with facts. Consequently, we shall summarise the formation, existence, and most recent achievements of that intermediate class which you consider to be so valuable.

For a long time the Franks dispensed justice to their vassals personally — by themselves and without the help of any experts. But when social relations multiplied and became more complicated, when written law was introduced, the descendants of the Franks, who could not even write their names, were no longer competent to do judicial work. Thus, a body of lawyers was formed. The barons employed these lawyers as advisers. At audiences they placed them at their feet and consulted them on the legal questions they had to resolve. Later they relieved themselves completely of the task of settling disputes between their vassals: the lawyers held audiences by themselves, and dispensed justice in the name of the descendants of the Franks. That is how one section of the intermediate class originated.

Until the discovery of gunpowder the army was composed mainly of men-at-arms, that is, descendants of the Franks. After the discovery of gunpowder the army's strength rested on fusiliers and artillerymen. It was mainly descendants of the Gauls who became engineers, artillerymen, and fusiliers, while the descendants of the Franks always retained command of the troops. That is how another section of the intermediate class originated.

The whole of French territory was originally divided among the Franks. Sovereign power was then attached to landed property. When the descendants of the Franks mounted the crusades and were obliged to sell some of their land for the money they needed, they found they had thereby alienated a part of their sovereignty; for no matter what efforts they made to divest the land they sold of sovereign rights, all the land was so imbued with feudalism that the new owners, although originally commoners, became minor nobles. That is how the third section of the intermediate class originated.

It can be seen that these three sections of the intermediate class were created and engendered by descendants of the Franks. We shall see below that as soon as they seized power, they acted in conformity with their original nature. But let us first examine their conduct from their origin until 1789.

The lawyers, common soldiers, and landowners who are neither nobles nor farmers have usually played the role of protectors of the people against the claims and privileges of the descendants of the Franks.

In 1789, considering itself to be sufficiently strong to shake off the supremacy of the descendants of the Franks, the intermediate class incited the masses to rise against the nobles. Through popular force it succeeded in massacring some descendants of the Franks, and forced those whom it did not massacre to flee abroad. The intermediate class then became the first class, and it is very curious to observe its conduct after it seized supreme power:

It chose from amongst its ranks a bourgeois whom it made King. To those members who had played the chief role in the Revolution it gave the titles of prince, duke, count, baron, chevalier, etc. It created majorats[78] in favour of the new nobles. In short, it reconstituted feudalism to its advantage.

There you have the conduct of the intermediate class whose existence you regard as so useful to the industrials. The bourgeoisie has certainly rendered services to the industrials, but today the bourgeois and noble classes both burden the industrial class. The bourgeoisie has no more social existence than that of minor nobles; and the industrials are interested in ridding themselves simultaneously of the supremacy exercised over them by the descendants of the Franks and by the intermediate class which was created by the nobles, and which will consequently always be inclined to constitute feudalism in its own interests. The industrial class must form no other alliance except the one contracted with the monarchy under Louis XI. It must combine its efforts with the monarchy in order to establish the industrial regime, that is to say the regime under which the most important industrials will form the first class in the State, and will be given the task of directing the administration of the national wealth.

Q. You are too trenchant, too absolute, too exclusive. You want to see only one class, the industrial class. This is absolutely impracticable, since the industrials themselves need soldiers, lawyers, etc. Can you vindicate our reproach?

A. To produce a system is to produce an opinion which is naturally trenchant, absolute, and exclusive. That is our reply to the first part of your objection. You then say that we want to see only one class in society, the industrial class. You are mistaken: What we want, or rather what the progress of civilisation wants is to see the industrial class made the first class, with the other classes subordinate to it.

In the age of ignorance the character of national activity was chiefly military and secondarily industrial. All social classes then had to be subordinate to the military class. This was, in effect, the social organisation of the time, and it would have been bad had it not been trenchant, exclusive, absolute. The progress of civilisation has brought about a situation in which the character of the French population is essentially industrial. Thus, the industrial class must be made the first class, with the other classes subordinate to it. Certainly, the industrials need an army. Certainly they need courts of justice. Certainly, the property owners should not be forced to invest their capital in industry. But in the present state of civilisation it is monstrous that the military, the lawyers, and the idle property owners should be the chief directors of the national wealth.

Q. Stop! You are going too far for the moment. You are discussing the essence of the question, and you are forgetting that the purpose of the present investigation is to specify the character of the present political situation. Give us your résumé in this respect.

A. Here, in a few words, is the résumé you require: *The present age is an age of transition . . .*

[*Oeuvres,* vol. IV, pt. 1, pp.35-41.]

34. [COMPARISON OF THE ENGLISH AND FRENCH POLITICAL SYSTEMS]

(Extracts from *Catéchisme des industriels*, bk. II, 1824)

Q. . . . Give us, in a few words, a clear idea of how the great political change which the human race must undergo, from the governmental system to the industrial regime, will be brought about.
Tell us in which two nations this change will begin.
A. The first nation to undergo this change will be the one in which a movement arises, a peaceful movement, resulting in the most important institution, the institution which exerts the greatest influence over the administration of national wealth, assuming an industrial character and ridding itself of its governmental character.
Q. In which nation, out of all the nations in Europe, in the world, can this change be brought about most easily?
A. The French nation.
Q. What gives the French nation this advantage over the others?
A. It is the fact that the nobility, the only institution interposed between the King of France and the industrials, no longer possesses any real strength, since it is no longer dominant through its property, and since public opinion no longer favours it. In France, therefore, there is no important obstacle to the union between the monarchy and the industrial class, and this union will inevitably be brought about, because it is in the interest of both the King and the industrials to join together immediately.
Q. But will the union of the King of France with the industrials result in the French monarchy assuming an industrial character and ridding itself of its governmental character?
A. Most certainly. For directly following the union of the King of France with the industrials, His Majesty will form his Supreme Council chiefly from industrials, and the budget will be drawn up mainly by the industrials, etc.
Q. After France, which will be the next nation to pass from the governmental to the industrial regime?
A. The English nation.
Q. Tell us why the English nation will not bring about the political change required to pass from the governmental to the industrial regime until after the French nation. And remember that you cannot justify your reply too firmly, since your outlook in this respect is in direct opposition to public opinion in France, England, and the whole world, which regards the French nation as being very much behind England in political terms.

A. The Lords have succeeded in dominating the monarchy. They have left the King with just the decorum of monarchy; but in reality it is they who exploit the royal power to their advantage, that is, to the advantage of feudalism. Thus, the preponderant political institution in England, the one which exerts the greatest influence over the administration of the national wealth and which gives the impetus to the whole political structure, is the peerage. Now, it is much more difficult to change the character of the Lords, from feudal to industrial, than it is to bring about such a change in the monarchy. It follows that the French Government must assume an industrial character before the English Government.

When the King of France becomes industrial, that is, when he gives the most important industrials the task of preparing the budget, he will lose nothing personally, none of his individual pleasures will be diminished. The reform will only affect his incapable or useless courtiers and functionaries. In England, on the other hand, because the peerage is the most important political institution, and because the peers exploit the royal power, reform would affect the very people who possess power, and who have a very great interest in opposing the change.

By virtue of their rank, and all capacity apart, the Lords take away from the nation, that is, from the productive or industrial class, an enormous amount of money in the form of sinecures, appointments, pensions, gratuities, etc. If one adds to this financial cost imposed by the Lords on the industrial class, the cost in terms of power, esteem, social importance, it will be recognised that the English industrials are still suffering, in a very positive and important way, the disadvantages of the governmental or feudal regime.

From what we have just said, we conclude that the industrial regime must be established in France before being adopted in England, because the French industrials are working much more actively for its establishment, and the members of the feudality can offer less resistance in France than in England. Our opinion in this respect will become clearer when we compare the means which France and England must employ to establish the industrial regime.

Q. When will the change from the governmental regime to the industrial regime, which the French nation must undergo, begin to take effect?
A. It is not possible to give the exact date. But it is clear that it cannot be very far away now, and that the means of establishing a calm and stable political situation in France has been found. For upright men (who, whatever one might say, form the vast majority of the rulers and the ruled) are tired of revolution. They ardently desire to leave the reefs in which the Ship of State has been sailing for more than thirty years, and are prepared to make the greatest sacrifices to establish a

calm and stable situation which will be the ruin of intriguers, and which will force them to become labouring and peaceful men.

Q. Even if we admit that the means you propose for establishing a calm and stable situation is good, is indeed the best for achieving this aim, is, in short, guaranteed success, it is nevertheless bound to be a long time before it is understood, appreciated, assessed, and before the interested parties have become sufficiently convinced to actually put it into effect.

A. The means can be stated so simply that there is not one working man who could not explain it to his fellow workers. Pure and simple good sense is all that is required to assess it thoroughly. Thus, we maintain the view stated above: that it cannot be long before the change from the governmental to the industrial regime, which the French nation must undergo, begins.

Q. Now tell us how the change will begin to take effect. Tell us who will instigate it, and who will clothe it in legal form.

A. The industrial class will instigate it; the King will clothe it in legal form. The King will in fact carry it out through a simple ordinance . . .

Q. Let us go on to examine the case of England. Tell us how the English can establish the industrial regime.

A. If the English are to establish the pure industrial regime without violence, their Parliament will have to pass one law abolishing entail, and another converting land into moveable property.

Q. It seems impossible to us that the English Parliament would agree to pass these two laws, for, as you have established, it is subject to the influence of the peerage. The Lords dominate both the royal power and the House of Commons, and since these laws are contrary to their feudal interests, which are important and more precious to them than their industrial interests, the Lords will inevitably prevent them from being passed.

In short, it seems as though the industrial regime cannot possibly be achieved through loyal and peaceful means, since the Lords have the power to oppose it, while at the same time only they have sufficient authority to allow it. We therefore conclude that England cannot achieve the industrial regime except through insurrection.

A. It is undoubtedly easier for the French to establish the industrial regime than it is for the English, since a simple ordinance of the King is all that is required in France. But we do not conclude from this that insurrection is absolutely necessary in England.

The English nobility is the most educated in Europe. It shows the greatest appreciation of industry's importance. There is not one Lord without some financial interest in industrial enterprises. Add to this the fact that the English people have a national pride which does not allow them to be surpassed by any other people, and you will agree that shortly after the example provided by France in establishing the industrial system, all the English — almost without exception — will then put their individual interests to one side and work together to establish the system themselves . . .

[*Oeuvres,* vol.IV, pt. 1, pp.107-13, 139-41.]

35. [THE FAILURE OF EUROPEAN LIBERALISM]

(Extract from *deuxième appendice sur le libéralisme et l'industrialisme, Catéchisme des industriels*, bk.II, 1824)

We invite all industrials who are zealous for the public good and who understand the relationship between the general interests of society and those of industry, not to tolerate any longer the designation *liberals*. We invite them to unfurl a new flag and inscribe on their banner the emblem: *Industrialism.*

We address the same invitation to all persons, whatever their estate or profession, who share our profound conviction that the only way to establish a calm and stable order is to entrust the high administration of national wealth to those who contribute most to the public treasury and who take out the least. We invite them to declare themselves *industrialists*.[79]

It is mainly to the true royalists that we address this invitation, that is, we address it especially to those who want to base the peace and happiness of the House of Bourbon on national prosperity.

Q. What benefit do you expect from this change of name? What advantage do you see in substituting the word industrialism *for* liberalism? *What, therefore, are the disadvantages attached to the word* liberalism *which make you stress the importance of abandoning it?*

A. You are asking too many questions at once. Which one do want us to answer first?

Q. Tell us what disadvantages attach to the word liberalism, *and what benefit can result from its abandonment by the party which wants to improve social organisation by using only loyal, legal, and peaceful means.*

A. In our view the designation *liberalism* has three great disadvantages for all well-intentioned men who march under this banner.

Q. What is the first of these disadvantages?

A. The word *liberalism* designates an order of sentiments; it does not denote a class of interests, with the result that this designation is vague and consequently defective.

Q. What is the second of these disadvantages?

A. Most of those who allow themselves to be known as *liberals* are peaceful men, men inspired by the desire to put an end to revolution by establishing through loyal, legal, and peaceful means a calm and stable order proportionate to the state of enlightenment and civilisation. But the leaders of this party are men who have maintained the critical, that is, revolutionary character of the eighteenth century.

All who played a role in the Revolution, first as *patriots,* then as *Bonapartists,* today claim to be *liberals.* Thus, the party which is reputedly *liberal* is today composed of two classes of men with different, even contrary opinions. The founders of this party are men whose principal aim is to overthrow every possible government so that they can take over themselves; whereas the majority of this same party are inclined to establish the most stable and most powerful government, provided that it clearly acts in the national interest.

The designation *liberalism,* having been chosen, adopted, and proclaimed by the remnants of the *patriotic* and *Bonapartist* parties, is most inconvenient for the men whose essential aim is to constitute a sound order by peaceful means.

We are not suggesting that the patriots and Bonapartists have been of no service to society. Their energy has been useful, for it was necessary to demolish in order to be able to construct. But today the revolutionary spirit which inspired them is in direct opposition to the public good. Today, a designation which does not denote a spirit absolutely opposed to the revolutionary spirit cannot be right for enlightened and well-intentioned men.

Q. What is the third disadvantage involved in the name liberalism?
A. The party which is called *liberal* has been defeated not only in France, but also in Naples, Spain, and England.[80] The members of the extreme Left in France cut no better a figure than MM. Brougham and Robert Wilson in England.[81] The repeated defeats of the *liberals* have proved that nations as well as governments did not wish to adopt their political opinions. Now, when sensible men are shown that they have followed the wrong road and chosen bad guides, they hurry to change direction.

We conclude from the three reasons just given that peaceful men whose opinion favours a calm and stable state of affairs must hasten to proclaim their desire no longer to be designated *liberals,* and must inscribe a new emblem on their banner . . .

[*Oeuvres,* vol. IV, pt. 1, pp. 178-82.]

36. [THE REORGANISATION OF FRENCH SCIENCE]

(Extract from *Catéchisme des industriels,* bk. IV, 1824)

... We are going to tell you how the scientists should be organised, and how they can most usefully serve the industrials, to whom they owe their very existence.

The most able scientists should be divided into two classes, that is, they should form two separate Academies. The general aim of one of these Academies should be to formulate the best code of interests; the aim of the other should be to improve the code of sentiments whose principles were established by the famous Plato and applied and developed by the Fathers of the Church.

Louis XIV founded one of these Academies, the Academy of Physical and Mathematical Sciences, which has already contributed a great deal to the improvement of observations and reasoning. With a few minor additions it would be equipped to establish the code of interests.*

The other Academy, the one which should work to improve the code of sentiments, did exist in embryo for some time under the title Class of Moral and Political Sciences.[82] The establishment of this Academy would be just as useful as that of the Academy of Sciences. It would in fact be even more useful under present circumstances, because for 1,200 years, since the time when the Arabs began to cultivate the sciences of observation as well as mathematics, the study of morality has been increasingly neglected, so that this branch of our knowledge is today very much behind the various parts of physics and mathematics.

The Academy of Moral Sciences should be composed of the most distinguished moralists, theologians, lawyers,** poets, painters, sculptors, and musicians.

It will be no more extraordinary to see musicians, painters, and sculptors in the Academy appointed to improve sentiments, than it is today to see opticians, clockmakers, and toolmakers in the Academy of Physical and Mathematical Sciences. Theorists should not be

---

*Most importantly, a class of political economists needs to be added to the Academy of Sciences.

**A class of lawyers should also be included in the Academy of Sciences because society needs to be subject to fixed rules governing the relations between its members' interests as well as the relations between their mutual sentiments. In both cases the making of good rules requires ability and special study. Thus, as they have received a special education in this area, lawyers are best equipped to deal with all the regulatory aspects of the task.

separated from those who distinguish themselves in the chief applications. We shall prove later that the Academy of Sciences should call upon a much greater number of practical mechanics.

Q. Who will nominate the Academy of Sentiments?

A. The King should make the first nomination, and after the initial formation he should replace members on the advice of the Academy of Sentiments, as is the case today with the Academy of Sciences.

Q. The establishment of these two Academies, independent of one another and with the same political importance, seems to us to be good and useful. It is certainly necessary for society to have both its sentiments and its ideas well coordinated and subject to good general rules, that is, good laws. But these two Academies will be rivals, and it is in the nature of things that the one in charge of improving the code of sentiments will work to subject the code of interests to the code of sentiments, and vice-versa. *Who is to maintain the balance between these two Academies? Is not the formation of a supreme scientific institution necessary to attain this end?*

A. Certainly, the establishment of a Supreme Royal Scientific College is indispensable. The function of this College will be to coordinate the work of the Academy of Sentiments with that of the Academy of Reason. This College will work to bring together in a single doctrine the principles and rules produced by the two Academies. It will first form and then improve the general doctrine which will serve as the basis of public education for all classes of society, from the lowest proletarians to the richest citizens. It will also be engaged in framing the code of general laws most advantageous to the majority.

The Royal Scientific College will certainly be the most important of all social institutions, since it will exercise supreme direction over the general activity of society. It might therefore seem that this College ought to be established before all other institutions. But the Academy of Sentiments and the Academy of Reason must naturally be formed before the Supreme Scientific College, because only the men most capable in the elaboration of sentiments and the coordination of reasoning are able to judge which scientists possess these two kinds of capacity to the highest degree. It is evident, therefore, that the members of the Supreme College can be chosen only by the Academy of Sentiments and the Academy of Reason, joined together in a single assembly to give effect to that nomination.

The scientists nominated by the Academy of Sentiments and the Academy of Reason to compose the Supreme Scientific College will co-opt the most able lawyers, and will give them the task of developing the general doctrine they produce into a framework of rules. They will also co-opt those practical politicians they consider capable of providing useful advice, chosen from all branches of public administration, to enlighten them on all points and supply them with information of all kinds. These will therefore be chosen from the Departments of the Interior, War, the Navy, Finance, Police, etc.

Once the industrials obtain the King's assurance that he is willing to entrust the task of preparing the budget to the most important of them, and that he has ordered the establishment of the three scientific colleges which we have just discussed, society will be organised in accordance with its present level of enlightenment and civilisation; it will be organised as well as the human race can be for the satisfaction of all its moral and physical needs, for these four institutions constitute the fundamental arrangements of that social order most favourable to the production and coordination of what can be most useful to men in every moral or physical respect.

Finally, when this social organisation is established in France, the famous prediction made by the Fathers of the Church will soon be realised: the entire human race will share the same social doctrine; one by one every people will adopt the principles proclaimed and put into practice by the French . . .

[*Oeuvres,* vol. V, pt. 1, pp.26-33.]

37. FRAGMENTS ON SOCIAL ORGANISATION

(Extracts from *De l'organisation sociale. Fragments d'un ouvrage inédit, Opin. litt.*, 1825)

SECOND FRAGMENT
Proof that the French proletariat is capable of successfully administering property

It is a question of proving here that the most numerous class, in short, the people, today consists of men who no longer need to be subject to any special supervision, men whose intelligence is sufficiently developed, and whose capacity for prudence* is great enough to enable them, without inconvenience, to establish a system of organisation which admits them as members.

First of all, let us examine the case of the farmers.

At the time of the sale of national lands[83] several thousand proletarians, availing themselves of the limitless facilities offered to those with enough character to speak out in the face of the entire European aristocracy, purchased those properties and suddenly joined the class of landowners. Now, the way in which this mass of proletarians, having suddenly become property owners, directed the administration of their property has proved and established a great political fact: that the nation's largest class is today composed of men whose intelligence is sufficiently developed, and who have acquired sufficient prudence to enable the law, without any threat to public order, to put an end to the tutelage hitherto exercised over them; and that henceforth, since one must consider the nation to be composed of individuals who are all capable of administering property, the law must establish the political system in which the direction of common interests will be entrusted to the most distinguished men, men with capacities of the most general and most positive utility, so that governmental, controlling action will be exercised only over those men whose conduct tends to disturb public order.

We shall cite a fact which we witnessed personally, and which proves how the capacity for administering property is today generally shared by men who, through accident of birth, belong to the proletarian class.

A small province, Cateau-Cambrésis, belonged in its entirety to the Archbishopric of Cambrai and other ecclesiastical establishments. The population of this province was so thoroughly proletarian, in respect of immoveable property, that there was not a single person who

*See the note at the end of the fragment.

could not be expelled from the manor he occupied.

What happened when the land in this province was put up for sale?

By mutual agreement all the inhabitants formed an association. They made themselves adjudicators of the land of their communes, and they divided it up between them, so that one whole section of the population, quite an important section, suddenly moved out of the proletarian class and into the class of landowners.

Well! This sudden change did not cause the least disorder in agriculture. The new owners proved themselves to be much more capable than the old ones, for the very next year the lands began to produce much better crops than they had ever produced before.

It clearly follows from what happened during the sale of national lands, and from a local fact which we have just cited in support of the general fact, that the French nation (considering the present stage in the development of its intelligence) can be governed much better and much more economically than at present; and that a stable social social situation will not be achieved until governmental action is surpassed by the activity of those men whose capacities are of the highest degree and the most general and positive utility.

Let us go on now to consider the working men employed by manufacturers and merchants, and the proof they have provided of their capacity.

At the beginning of the Revolution many entrepreneurs in manufacturing and commercial industry were ruined by the pillage which followed the insurrections. Those entrepreneurs who escaped pillage were crushed by the law of the *maximum*;[84] while those who were fortunate enough to escape these two industrial calamities and survive financially saw their wealth wiped out by requisitions and the burning of English merchandise.

What would have happened, after such widespread misfortune, if a large number of the working men employed by the ruined and morally destroyed manufacturers and merchants had not been capable enough to replace them?

For a long time the factories and commerce of France would have lost much of their importance, and France would today be paying an industrial tribute to foreigners much greater than the one it had to bear before the Revolution. In short, production in France would have declined.

In actual fact, production of all kinds has increased greatly since and even during the misfortunes of the Revolution. In all the manufacturing and commercial workshops men who used to be employed as ordinary workers have become entrepreneurs and directors of these enterprises, and have shown themselves to be more intelligent and energetic than their predecessors. Consequently, France is today much more prosperous, more productive, and more important in agricultural, manufacturing, and commercial industry than it was before the Revolution, although the present directors of these kinds of enterprise have come very largely from the class of common people.

Could there be surer and more complete proof that the common people, that is, the majority of the nation are now sufficiently intelligent to enable French society to be organised directly for the public good, without any threat to public order, and, on the contrary, with great advantages for all social classes?

Note to the second fragment

The education of all classes is divided into two parts: education properly speaking and instruction.

The improvement of education properly speaking is more important than the improvement of instruction from the point of view of increasing social welfare.

It is education properly speaking which forms habits, develops feelings, and fosters general prudence. It is education which teaches each person to apply principles and to use them as sure guides to conduct. Education may be regarded as the continual teaching of knowledge which is absolutely necessary for the maintenance of social relations.

Let us suppose that children receive the most thorough instruction but are entirely deprived of education. Let us assume for a moment the existence of an establishment in which children follow courses given by the best teachers in every subject, and are separately shut away between classes to prevent them from being distracted. These children would consequently be deprived of all education. What would happen to them when their studies came to an end? What would become of them when they went out into the world?

Those children would be ignorant of all knowledge which might help them to live a good social life. They would have no experience of relationships. They would have to serve a very long apprenticeship before being able to perform any social function. And if a population brought up in this way was left to fend for itself, it would not be very much more civilised than the first human societies.

We may add, in support of what we have just said, that in every generation some of the knowledge acquired by previous generations becomes so common that the fathers or guardians of children inevitably possess this knowledge, and are therefore qualified to teach their children in this respect. Now, such unstudied teaching of these rudiments develops children's intelligence so that they are much more able to grasp the more abstract knowledge given to them by their real teachers.

It is chiefly in and for the proletarian class that education is much more important than instruction ...

People still fail to appreciate just how civilised the lowest class is in France, and how much positive improvement in intelligence there has been among the proletarian class ...

It is mainly because of the superiority in civilisation of its most numerous class over the most numerous classes of other nations — unquestionably the most positive superiority of all — that the French nation excels over all others.

If one compares the French proletariat with the English, one finds the latter inspired by sentiments which incline them to commence the war of the poor against the rich as soon as the right circumstances arise, whereas the attitude of the French proletariat towards the wealthy industrials is generally one of attachment and goodwill ...

THIRD FRAGMENT
Since the proletarian class are fundamentally as civilised as the class of property owners, the law should recognise them as full members of society.

The mechanism of social organisation was inevitably very complicated as long as the majority were too ignorant and imprudent to administer their own affairs. As long as their intelligence was still not fully developed, they were ruled by brutish passions which urged them towards insurrection and consequently every kind of disorder.

In such a state of affairs, which had to precede a better social situation, it was necessary (in order to hold the majority in check and exert a strong hold over the nation) for the minority to be organised along military lines, to claim an exclusive right to the law-making power, and to frame the law so as to give themselves a monopoly of power. Thus, the chief forces in society have hitherto been employed simply to maintain society as a society, and work directed towards improving the moral and physical well-being of nations has had to be regarded as subordinate.

Today this situation must change completely, and the most important work must be directed towards improving our moral and physical well-being. This can be done, since a small amount of force is sufficient to maintain public order, now that the majority have acquired a taste for work (which eliminates every tendency towards disorder) and have recently proved themselves to be capable of administering moveable and immoveable property.

The minority no longer need force to keep the proletarian class in subordination, so they must now concentrate on arranging things so that 1) the proletariat has the greatest possible interest in maintaining public order; 2) the transmission of immoveable property is made as easy as possible; 3) the workers are given the highest degree of political importance.

The right arrangements should be very simple and very quick to find, once people have taken the trouble to apply their own intelligence to the situation, and have entirely shaken off the mental bondage imposed by the political principles of our fathers, principles which were good and useful in their time, but which are no longer applicable in present circumstances.

Since the population today consists entirely of men who (apart from some exceptions which occur more or less equally in all classes) are capable of administering moveable or immoveable property, we can and must work directly for an improvement in the moral and physical well-being of the social body.

Now, the most direct way to bring about an improvement in the moral and physical well-being of the majority of the population is to give priority in State expenditure to the provision of work for all fit men, so as to assure their physical existence; to disseminate as quickly as possible among the proletarian class the positive knowledge which has been acquired; and finally to ensure that the individuals composing this class have forms of leisure and interests which will develop their intelligence.

In addition, measures must be taken to ensure that national wealth is administered by the men who are most capable in administration, and who have the greatest interest in good administration, that is, the most important industrials.

And society, by means of these fundamental arrangements, will be organised in a way which will completely satisfy reasonable men of every class. Then there will no longer be any fear of insurrections, and consequently no need to maintain numerous permanent armies to oppose them. It will no longer be necessary to spend enormous sums on the police department; and there will be nothing to fear from abroad, for thirty million happy men could repel a combined attack by the entire human race.

To that we may add that neither princes nor peoples will ever take extravagance to the point of attacking a nation composed of thirty million men who are in no way offensive to their neighbours, and who are united through good management of their interests.

We may add further that there is no need for espionage in a society where the vast majority are interested in maintaining the established order . . .

* * * *

FOURTH FRAGMENT
On the administration and government of public affairs

People may say to us:

'Your most important view on politics, the view to which you relate all your ideas, is that calm and stability can best be established in Europe by superimposing administrative power on governmental power. Your first duty, therefore, must be to trace a clear dividing line between the administrative and governmental capacities. You must show exactly what each of them involves, so that you will be in a position to explain clearly why the administrative capacity should be superimposed on the governmental capacity.'

The high administration of society embraces the invention, examination, and execution of projects useful to the people.[85]

The high administrative capacity thus involves three capacities: the capacity of the artists, the capacity of the scientists, and the capacity of the industrials, whose collaboration fulfils all the conditions necessary for the satisfaction of society's moral and physical needs.

In the great enterprise of working directly for the establishment of the system of public good, the artists, the men of imagination, will lead the way. They will proclaim the future of the human race. They will take the age of gold out of the past and offer it as enrichment to future generations. They will inspire society to increase its well-being by presenting it with a rich picture of new prosperity, and by showing that all members of society will soon share the pleasures which have hitherto been the prerogative of a very small class. They will sing of the benefits for civilisation, and in order to achieve their aim they will put to work every means offered by the fine arts, oratory, poetry, painting, music. In short, they will develop the poetical part of the new system.

The scientists, the men whose chief occupation is to observe and reason, will demonstrate the possibility of a great increase in well-being for all classes of society, for the most hard-working class — the proletariat — as well as for the richest class. They will show what are the most certain and most rapid means of guaranteeing continuity of work for the mass of producers. They will lay the foundations of public education. They will establish laws of hygiene for the social body, and in their hands politics will become the complement of the science of man.

The most important industrials, relating all ideas to production, will judge what is immediately practicable in the projects of public utility conceived and elaborated in concert by the scientists and artists. They will plan methods of execution to be directed by the bankers, who are always at the head of financial movements.

That is the administrative course — firm, frank, and loyal — which the scientists, artists, and industrials will follow when they are entrusted with the direction of general interests.

Let us compare it with the course adopted by the present Government. Let us see what miserable arrangements the governmental capacity has been reduced to by the progress of enlightenment and civilisation.

Trapped in a circle of antiquated feudal doctrines, the rulers, whose intentions for the public good are generally the best, make vain efforts to organise a calm and stable situation.

Believing that they cannot maintain themselves without a large staff in every branch of administration, and a great apparatus of governmental power, they are ultimately reduced to extracting as much money as possible from the nation, whether it be through taxes or loans, while at the same time they are careful not to arouse any obvious discontent. They thus exhaust themselves in subtle arrangements for improving and collecting taxes.

They are reduced to using the greatest part of the nation's money to cover the costs of official business, while a tiny portion goes on expenditure which is really useful to the producers.

They are reduced to maintaining the nobles and courtiers in positions of great political importance, and they tax their ingenuity to provide them with enough money to keep them in the luxury which they consider so indispensable.

Let us examine the conduct of the Minister-President,[86] who is still the person who has best understood the importance of industry and the state of society. Let us examine the way he has used governmental power.

We have seen him use all the ministerial influence at his disposal to get a large number of nobles and idle rich into the Chamber of Deputies, and to carefully keep out the most notable industrials, the scientists, and the most capable artists.

He has made Parliament septennial,[87] but has done nothing to change the age requirement of forty years for entry to the Chamber. In this way he has considerably diminished its energy, has made it dependent on the ministry, and has made it subject at the same time to the influence of the high nobility.

He has concentrated the supreme direction of national interests in the hands of nobles, bishops, soldiers, lawyers, and bureaucrats. They are undoubtedly all quite honourable in terms of their private characters or the services they or their ancestors have been able to render the nation; but they have learned administration only at the expense of the public (who have always had to pay for their mistakes) and never at their own expense, as the industrials do every day.

At the Ministry of the Interior, out of respect for ministerial dignity, he maintains a distinguished barrister, but one who is very ignorant of everything concerning industry, the sciences, and the fine arts; a man who, unaware of their importance and the respect due to them, forgets himself to the point of having his clerks maltreat in every way the men whose work brings most honour to France.

The same Minister-President also believes, out of deference to the old doctrines, that he must allow the Jesuits to have a great influence over public education, their ultimate aim being to inculcate in youth the idea that mediocre capacities should surpass and direct capacities of the highest order, and that vague knowledge should be superimposed on useful and positive knowledge.

Finally, in an attempt to promote industry, M. de Villèle has established a Supreme Council of Commerce, but he has composed it chiefly of men who have never practised in any branch of industry. Only through human respect, apparently, has he actually admitted two or three retired industrials.

These are the sad remnants of the governmental capacity. Swept along by the torrent of civilisation it tries in vain, by clinging to the past, to maintain the predominant role attributed to it in previous societies . . .

FIFTH FRAGMENT
Continuation of the subject dealt with in the previous fragment

. . . It is a question of deciding what means should be employed to superimpose administrative action on governmental action.

Should this change be brought about all at once through direct measures, or slowly through a succession of measures?

Our opinion is that the change should be brought about all at once through direct measures.[88]

We base this opinion, first of all, on the following great and unique fact.

Let us examine the only change of social system of which history has preserved an exact and detailed record, and see how this change was brought about. Let us remind ourselves whether it was slowly and through a succession of operations that men passed from polytheism to theism, from the regime of the Greeks and Romans to the social organisation adopted by the Europeans of the Middle Ages.

We recognise that the first Christians substituted directly a belief in one single God for the belief in a multitude of divinities, and that they did not undertake to reduce the thousands of acknowledged divinities to hundreds and then to tens before arriving at the idea of a single God. Thus, we are justified in saying that men passed all at once from polytheism to theism.[89]

It was also all at once that the powers of the Chieftains, Goths, Visigoths, Ostrogoths, Danes, English, Franks, Saxons, Germans, etc. replaced the powers of the consuls and proconsuls.

Finally, the nature of slavery also changed all at once, when slaves ceased to depend directly on their masters and became bound to the soil.

Another fact, essentially different from the first, lends further support to our opinion.

The natural consequence of the first fact is that changes of system are brought about all at once; and the consequence we shall draw from the fact we are now going to discuss is that half-measures, however powerful, cannot produce a change of system.

Could there be anything more powerful, more decisive, more severe than the measures taken at the beginning of the Revolution against the priests and nobles? They were nearly all plundered, massacred, or banished. At the same time they were deprived of their moveable and immoveable property as well as their political powers so that the common people found themselves in exclusive control of the public interest.

What was the result of all these atrocities?

Nothing of real importance. The feudal system was not destroyed. It was soon reborn out of its ashes, and within a few years, with some slight modifications, it had reproduced itself. It was the re-establishment of this system which destroyed anarchy. Most importantly, it was the common people themselves who actually reconstructed the feudal system, who created a new nobility, and who established majorats, that is, entailed estates. Foreigners therefore found France completely *refeudalised* when they were in the position of having to make the laws there.

We shall give a very simple explanation of this fact, which at first seems inexplicable, and which has not yet been properly analysed.

The massacre, expulsion, and pillage of the nobles was, despite all its atrocity, only a half-measure. It placed power in different hands, but did not change the nature of power.

Society has always remained subject to governmental action. During the Revolution governmental action continued to reign supreme over administrative action.

Now, it is in the nature of governmental action to maintain or establish hereditary political rights, just as it is a consequence inherent in administrative action to establish the greatest political equality in respect of rights of birth, and to base political rights on superiority in positive capacities.

From what we have just said we conclude, in support of our opinion, that:

1. The only change of social system of which history has preserved an exact and detailed record was brought about all at once and through a radical change of principles.
2. The Revolution, in spite of all its violence, did not result in the change required by the progress of enlightenment, because it did not alter the principles on which the feudal system was based . . .

[*Oeuvres,* vol. V, pt.1, pp.116-29, 136-42, 151-5.]

38. PHYSIOLOGY APPLIED TO THE IMPROVEMENT OF SOCIAL INSTITUTIONS: SUPPLEMENTARY NOTES[90]

(Extracts from *De la physiologie appliquée à l'amélioration des institutions sociales. Continuation, Opin. litt.*, 1825)

The idle man is a burden upon himself, just as he is a weight upon society.

Idleness is the father of all vices.

Idleness constitutes a state of sickness in man.

Thus, according to the principles of politics and morals, as well as those of physiology and hygiene, the legislator must create a social organisation calculated to encourage all classes to do work, particularly the work most useful to society.

Social organisation at present, which accords the highest degree of respect to idleness and to the kind of work that is least useful to society, is thus essentially and radically defective.

The nobles first of all, then the bourgeoisie, are the two most respected classes. But their work is the least useful to society, and it is in these classes that the greatest number of idlers are to be found.

The direction of society's interests is entrusted chiefly to the nobles, and after them to the rich bourgeoisie.

This political arrangement is monstrous, since the nobles and the bourgeoisie are precisely the classes which contribute least to national prosperity, are inevitably ignorant of the means needed to increase society's well-being, and, finally, have an interest in opposing the rapid development of industry, which tends to increase the respect accorded to workers and diminish that given to idlers.

The defect of the present social organisation is all the greater, in that the very basis of the system leads workers to aspire to enter or enable their children to enter the class of idlers; so that the whole of the present population is incited to use its maximum energy in seeking to enter a state of idleness...

Physiological observations have shown that societies as well as individuals are subject to two moral forces of equal intensity and acting alternately: one is the force of habit, the other the force that is born of the desire for new sensations.

After a certain time, habits inevitably become bad, because they were acquired in circumstances which no longer correspond to society's needs. It is then that the need for something new is felt, and that need, which amounts to a true revolutionary situation, inevitably lasts until the social order has been changed in accordance with the level of civilisation. Once it has been suitably reorganised, new habits are contracted, and the force of habit again becomes dominant.

The European population has been dominated by the revolutionary force since the fifteenth century, and this force will continue to dominate until a social system radically different from the theological and feudal system has been established in its place. To check the action of the revolutionary force, the first need was to conceive and present clearly the social system appropriate to the present level of enlightenment. That first operation has now been completed.

It is clear that in the system which will overcome the force of revolution, the most important influence must be that of men with peaceful occupations and habits, and that the ablest of these men ought to be in charge of national interests. Now, the ablest men, since it is their work that contributes most to social prosperity, are the artists, scientists, and industrials . . .

Whenever a man or a society has passionately adopted the wrong course, it is not the language of reason that must be used to lead the man or society on to the right road, it is the language of passion.

There are only two ways of passing from a state of exaltation to a state of calm: by achieving the aim that has aroused one's passions, or by recognising the impossibility of achieving that aim. But it is fairly easy to pass from a badly directed enthusiasm to a beneficial one.

During the Revolution the French nation often went astray, although at the beginning its passions were directed to the public good. It was guilty of many acts diametrically opposed to morality, physiology, public hygiene, and most injurious to its interests.

As a result of the Revolution the French nation became accustomed to strong feelings. So, the Government acts in an entirely anti-physiological manner when it tries to make the nation more reasonable without allowing it to achieve the goal that has aroused its passions.

It is not to apathy that the French nation needs to be subjected.

All its citizens must be stirred to work as energetically as possible for the progress and applications of the sciences and the fine arts; and it is not under the direction of the nobility, to whom the greatest respect is paid and to whom almost exclusively the direction of public interests is entrusted, that the fine arts, the sciences, and industry can rise to the greatest heights of which they are capable, for nobody strives passionately for a subordinate position.

Physiologists have observed that the moral and physical forces of society act and react on each other, so that a great physical disturbance experienced by a nation is always followed by great moral productions, and conversely a great moral ferment always leads to great physical effort.

And in fact, it was after the physical crisis of the Fronde[91] that the great men appeared who gave the century of Louis XIV its glory.

Shortly after the English Revolution, Milton, Newton, and Locke published their immortal works.

The philosophers of the eighteenth century underwent and produced a great ferment; and it was the excitement they aroused in everybody's mind that caused the Revolution and set in motion all the physical forces of the French nation.

The physical activity of the French nation has lost its former excitement, and has taken a more measured road, that of industrial labour. After physical efforts as prodigious as those of the French nation during the last forty years, moral productions of the greatest importance can, must be expected. Thus, there should be nothing surprising in the appearance of a new system of social organisation, a system which will respect religion and vanquish superstition, a system which will strengthen the monarchy while nevertheless destroying all rights originally based on conquest, that is, on the law of the strongest.

According to the observations of physiologists, peoples experience two kinds of political need which are quite distinct: they also possess two kinds of means for satisfying these needs.

One part of these needs and means is common to all peoples. These common needs and means are derived directly from the organisation of the human race and from its general tendency to improve its social system.

To satisfy these general and common needs, different peoples can employ only the same means. It is through moral exaltation and reasoning that they can achieve their aim; it is the capacity of the artists combined with that of the scientists that must produce new principles, demonstrate their superiority over those adopted by previous generations, and bring about their adoption by the present generation.

Every people also has different secondary needs and means, peculiar to itself, which have as their cause or foundation the nature of the soil and the climate in which it lives, its geographical position, and the habits it has acquired.

We shall limit ourselves for the moment to applying this observation to the two peoples which are unquestionably the most enlightened and the most advanced in practical civilisation, that is, we shall consider first together and then separately the English and French nations.

Since the fifteenth century, the period in which the human mind made its greatest effort to move towards things of direct and positive utility, the English and French nations have been the two peoples which have worked most consistently and energetically for the improvement of their social existence and the establishment of a political system organised directly for the public good.

Let us look at the political conduct of these two peoples.

We shall examine separately the individual efforts of each of them, and shall then say what has been common to their work in the field of politics.

Let us speak first of the particular efforts made by the English nation to free itself from the theological and feudal yoke.

In order to rid themselves of the theological yoke, the English made their King head of the Anglican Church.

In order to make the feudal yoke which they continued to bear less burdensome and less painful, the English forced their lords to exercise their governmental action only in combination with the commons in Parliament.

In France, in order to achieve the same aim in respect of theology, the people acted on behalf of royal power against papal power. Since the fifteenth century they have refused to recognise papal bulls unless they have been given royal sanction.

In order to curtail feudal powers and to prepare the complete destruction of the nobility, the French people became royalist and supported the efforts of kings to abolish all sovereign rights in the hands of the nobles.

Independently of these particular efforts made by the English and French nations to rid themselves of theological and feudal supremacy, the philosophers of these two nations worked together towards the same end.

Their work consisted of scientific research which sought to establish a new political theory, quite distinct from the theological and feudal theory, a theory which would as far as possible direct the peoples' work towards the improvement of their moral and physical existence.

These theoretical studies have not yet produced clear, positive, and satisfactory results.

The debate on the constitution of spiritual power and its prerogatives began in the fifteenth century. Philosophers have not yet managed to bring about an agreement between Protestants and Catholics. All they have done is to establish a truce between them which must last until the discovery of the principles by which these two Christian sects can be led to adopt the same doctrine.

The debate on the constitution of temporal power and its prerogatives has been vigorous ever since the English Revolution, which gave it a positive character. One of the two parties in that country is called *Whigs*, the other *Tories*. In France these two parties have taken the names *constitutional royalists* and *theological and feudal royalists*.

In France the first of these parties wants the King to entrust the direction of the national interests to the men who have shown the greatest capacity in matters of positive utility. The other maintains that the nation should be directed above all by the clergy and the nobility.

The slow pace of scientific work on the theory of politics has made society tired, and as a result of its weariness it has adopted as a principle the very false idea that politics is by nature a purely practical branch of knowledge, so that in that field theoretical considerations should be seen only as dreams of varying ingenuity.

This error, generally accepted by the mass of the ruled, and especially adopted by the rulers, who have an interest in propagating it, should in no way astonish philosophers; it should not be taken by them as a pretext for working less zealously to fulfil their task. The truth is that it took three centuries of preliminary and preparatory studies to place the human mind in a condition to conceive clearly a new social system. It was only when two great revolutions, those of England and France, had brightened the political horizon with regard to theological beliefs and feudal principles that the eye of the philosopher was able to discover the system of public good.

Now that these two conditions are at last completely fulfilled, philosophy can today begin to speak in clear, firm, and satisfactory language about the social organisation which suits the enlightened peoples of the nineteenth century.

English and French philosophers will now immediately combine their efforts in order to bring about the adoption in England and France of the basic institutions of the social system of public good.

These philosophers will make the practitioners of the two nations aware of the fact that in politics, just as in other sciences, theory and practice must lend each other mutual support. They will point out to them that the experience of England and France, in the course of their revolutions, has clearly shown that the most enthusiastic practitioners, the most energetic revolutionaries, were quite unable to bring about a radical change in social institutions without the intervention and cooperation of theorists.

Their doctrine will be quite different from the one professed in the eighteenth century by Voltaire, Diderot, d'Alembert, and all the other Encyclopaedists. They will not set themselves the same goal; they will not employ the same means, and will bring about totally contrary results.

The Encyclopaedists of the eighteenth century worked to overthrow the old system. These philosophers will work to establish a new system in harmony with the needs of society in the present state of its enlightenment and civilisation.

Instead of rousing the ruled against the rulers they will show that it is possible, in fact easy, to have persons directing public affairs whose interests are identical with those of the people.

Far from considering religion to be an obstacle to the progress of civilisation, as in the eighteenth century, they will regard Christianity as providing the best weapons with which to fight the prejudices introduced into the minds of the multitude by the Catholic and Anglican clergies. They will remind the faithful that it is chiefly to the Christian religion that men are indebted for the destruction of slavery, and that the spirit of Christianity today urges society towards the establishment of the regime which can improve as quickly as possible the moral and physical existence of the poorest class. Finally, they will show that lay scientists are today, by virtue of their sentiments and their enlightenment, very much better Christians than the professional theologians, and that consequently the clergies of the various Christian sects should be subject to the direction of the body of lay scientists.

The philosophers of the eighteenth century decried monarchy by showing it to be inevitably allied with theology and feudalism; those of the nineteenth century will be essentially royalist, and will show that monarchy must have as its support and close advisers the most distinguished scientists and artists (in the spiritual sphere), and the most important industrials (in the temporal sphere) . . .

Why do doctors at present lead such a pitiful and inferior existence, when among the Greeks that class of scientists enjoyed great respect and exerted a great political influence over the rulers?

What means must doctors employ to recover their former importance?

The answers to those two questions will lead to enormous progress for civilisation. We shall limit outselves for the moment to giving a first outline of our opinion on the subject.

We say then: As a result of the establishment of Christianity the science of man was divided into two parts. Priests were given special responsibility for the study of spiritual man and the direction of social conduct in the realm of sentiment.

And from that time onwards it was with physical man that doctors were principally concerned. They directed their studies above all towards the preservation of man's material health.

The religions which existed before Christianity were essentially applications of the fine arts.

The study of the science of man was not divided. Doctors cultivated this science to the full, in all its aspects. Hippocrates gave prescriptions for both moral and physical illnesses; he gave them to peoples as well as to individuals.

Now that these facts have been established, and a reasoned judgement has been offered as the basis of our opinion, we shall reply to the first question:

Among the Greeks Hippocrates practised the science of man in all its aspects; this is why he enjoyed such enormous respect, and why he exerted such a great influence over the rulers of his time.

Doctors today are concerned above all only with physical man; and the *subordinate* moral role accorded to them in society is the inevitable result of the *subordination* of the functions they perform in society.

It can be seen that the answer to the second question is to be found in the answer to the first; for it is clear that in order to recover their former importance doctors must again see observations on spiritual or moral man as a part of their province, and they must satisfy society's greatest need at present by giving it, in the form of a medical prescription, the system of social organisation best suited to the present state of its enlightenment and civilisation.

[*Opin. litt.*, pp.246-64, 268-70.]

39. THE ARTIST, THE SCIENTIST, AND THE INDUSTRIAL: DIALOGUE – by Saint-Simon and Léon Halévy[92]

(Extracts from *L'Artiste, le savant et l'industriel: dialogue, Opin. litt.*, 1825)

Several conversations took place between an artist, a scientist, and an industrial, on matters of great importance. They complained to each other about their social position, and reflected on ways of improving it. They agreed to have one final meeting in order to sum up their previous discussions and, if possible, to reach some positive conclusion. Here is the conversation that took place when they met:

THE ARTIST

Gentlemen,
   None of us is satisfied with his position. Well! It is within our power to change it. To succeed we have only to redirect our labours and change the nature of the relations between us . . .
   Does it not seem to you, as it does to me, gentlemen, that all the force in society resides in us; the Government owes all its strength to us; that we are, in short, the support, the life of the social body? Can you see it existing if it were deprived of our labours? Who could satisfy man's needs or provide him with pleasure if the arts, industry, and the sciences were suddenly to disappear? Would it be the rulers, who are neither artists, scientists, nor industrials, and who would consider it beneath their dignity to be ranked among the producers – would it be the rulers whom the father of the family would then ask for bread, clothes, and shelter for his children; whom the farmer would ask for agricultural implements or advice on how to get a good harvest; whom the rich man would ask for paintings and statues to charm both his eye and his mind, for sublime songs to please his ear and his soul? Amidst such general distress what could the rulers do in response to the public's entreaties? What could they give to society? Ordinances are the only thing in the world they are fit to produce, and they would not even be able to do that if the arts, sciences, and industry – which always have to bear the brunt of ordinances – if they were to deny society the fruits of their ingenuity and the assistance of their labours and vigilance.
   I do not, however, regard the rulers as useless. God forbid! Responsible for giving society a framework of rules, they will render very important and very real services to society as soon as they recognise that their functions are secondary to the high administration of public affairs

through positive capacities, and that they should stand in the same relation to men of industry, science, and fine art as college supervisors stand in relation to teachers . . .

European society is no longer composed of children who, in their own interest, need to be subject to strict and active supervision. It is composed of men whose education is complete and who are only in need of instruction.[93] Politics should now be nothing more than the science of providing the people with as many material goods and as much moral satisfaction as possible. The rulers, although dominated by the old prejudices and labouring under delusions, nevertheless generally behave with respect for the force of opinion. They are beginning to show, if not through their actions then at least through the form in which they clothe them, that they realise they are dealing with reasonable men who do not wish to live in order to be ruled, but who consent to be ruled in order to live more comfortably. I know that they help the arts, sciences, and industry as much as they can under present circumstances; but why should these three great capacities, which can look after their own development, and without which nothing else could develop, why should they need help? They could say to the rulers: 'What do you have in common with us? Why are we indebted to you? To whom does the nation owe its well-being? Is the throne supported by you or by us? All that is useful to society comes from our bosom, from the heart of our studies, our workshops, our factories, and not from the heart of your offices and dining-rooms . . .'

If one of us were to say this to a ruler, his reply would be quite simple: 'I have only one thing to say to you. You are divided and we are united.'

It is a reproach, gentlemen, which is well founded. Unity, the virtue and protector of the weak, is also one of the requirements of strength. Far from there being harmony between us, there is, on the contrary, a kind of permanent hostility between scientists, industrials, and artists. I do not pretend that the faults are on one side only; they are mutual.

Because of the nature of his work and his ability, the scientist tends to value only rigorous demonstration and positive results, and therefore considers the artist to be too exalted. He does not believe in the artist nor in the power of the fine arts. He readily imagines that reasoning alone can convince, while sensations persuade and seduce.

The industrial also, generally speaking, fails to do justice to the artist, of whom he has a false impression. He regards the talent of the author, the poet, the painter, the musician as slight. He considers these men to be lacking in bearing and consistency. With their emphasis on cold calculation, a result of their preoccupation with material production, the industrials tend to belittle intellectual labour which does not lead to concrete results. Some, who have not remained immune to feudal influences, and who all too often forget their plebeian origins and the hard work which is the honourable basis of their wealth, prefer to open their splendid drawing-rooms to personages who are useful by virtue of their great name or their wealth, afraid of treating as equals those men who can do without esteem based on titles and honours. In short, they all consider their social supremacy over the artists as obvious and incontestable.

As for us (I shall be just as frank), we are perhaps even more exclusive and unjust. The ideal world in which we live often inclines us to cast a pitiful and scornful eye over this earthly world. Imagination, the source of our sweetest pleasure and purest consolation, seems to us to be the only human faculty worthy of esteem and praise. We do not attach any great value to the work of scientists, whose importance we do not appreciate. We do not think much of their dealings, which fail to satisfy our sensations. Their minds seem to us to be dull, and to our eyes their work is purely material. With all the more reason we underrate the work of industry, and the unfavourable opinion several of us have of such an honourable and necessary class of men is further reinforced by our conviction that industrials are dominated exclusively by a passion for money, a thoroughly terrestrial passion which is detested by poets, painters, and musicians, for whom money has neither dignity nor value, and who, since time immemorial, have only ever been good at spending it . . .

Let us recognise our mutual worth: then we shall have the dignity which becomes our position. Let us combine our forces, and mediocrity, which triumphs from our disunion, will be ashamed of its own feebleness, and will take its place beneath us, overshadowed by our peaceful power and our triple crown.

Let us unite. In order to reach the same goal each of us has a different task to fulfil.

We — the artists — will be your vanguard. The power of the arts is in effect the most immediate and most rapid of all powers. We have all kinds of weapons. When we wish to spread new ideas among men, we inscribe them on marble or canvas; we popularise them in poetry and song; we use, in turn, the lyre or the tabor, the ode or the ballad, the story or the novel; the drama is open to us, and through it, above all, we are able to exercise an electric and victorious influence. We address ourselves to man's imagination and sentiments; consequently we are always bound to have the sharpest and most decisive effect . . .

That is the task, the mission of the artists. The scientists' mission is no less honourable or momentous. It is the scientists, according to the excellent definition of one of the most eminent men of the present age,* *who demonstrate the practical utility of knowledge, who increase man's power over the external world, who multiply and spread the pleasures of human life.* It is their task completely to destroy any influence which uncertain ideas might still have, to support with sound demonstrations artistic conceptions and industrial enterprises, to ensure, through the great results of their studies and their powerful action, the triumph of intelligence, genius, and moral force over animal force and numerical superiority...

The industrials, who are the physical force of the social body, and who can become a moral force whenever they wish, must impress upon themselves the idea of their importance and the duties which that importance imposes, and must strive to spread these sentiments throughout the class of producers. This mission is reserved, above all, for the bankers, who are the agents of all industrials. It is up to them to propagate, in all classes of workers, the firm opinion that the most advantageous organisation for society would be that in which the management of general interests was entrusted to the most capable producers in both the industrial and moral-scientific fields . . .

THE SCIENTIST

The ideas you have just expressed are, it seems to me, of undeniable merit and clarity, and are obviously oriented towards the public good. But I have some observations to make. First, it seems to me that in the system you are proposing everyone will benefit except the artists. I see clearly that the new order would be favourable to industry and science, but it seems to me that it would be fatal for the fine arts, and that on this point you are deceiving yourself . . . The fine arts provide noble and ardent pleasures for those whose intelligence has been developed by education; but, if they are to be active and flourish, there has to be a class of rich and idle men in society. Even despotism favours the arts, if the despot enjoys delicate sensations. In short, I have always believed that the regime most suitable for the arts, most favourable to their development and success, is an absolute monarchy, surrounded by an opulent nobility, an idle and magnificent aristocracy.

THE ARTIST

I can easily reply to your objection, which is the result of a widespread prejudice that you yourself acknowledge, in spite of your honest mind.

*Humphrey Davy, President of the Royal Society of London . . .

enlightened philanthropy of your sentiments will sooner or later win the esteem and support of those persons who, like me, are engaged in industrial works. I have only become convinced of this today. You have, in effect, clarified a number of points which were still obscure to my mind, and you have presented your principles so clearly and with such good faith that if others react in the same way as me, I can certainly foresee the future success of your opinions.

However, I must not hide the fact that there are obstacles preventing their immediate adoption by the industrial class. Eventually, the individuals of this class will undoubtedly appreciate your ideas and support their development. And the chiefs of industry undoubtedly have all-powerful means to promote an enterprise of general utility. But you must first release them from the grip of habit and remove them from their accustomed sphere, and you must, above all, show them a positive advantage to be gained through the working of your system.

It is chiefly the industrials involved in a continuous series of labour who are burdened by the *yoke* of *routine*. It is only with difficulty that they become accustomed to general ideas . . . When they hear that civilisation summons them to manage their own general affairs just as they manage their individual affairs, they are amazed, they treat anyone who declares such a paradox as a madman . . .

A man has recently appeared who is the first to realise and prove the *political* importance of industry, and who has surmounted the barren land of ordinary discussion and adopted a sufficiently elevated viewpoint to perceive all the relations of the social body, to study its organisation at different periods, to discover its present needs and proclaim its future state. What has happened to him? This philosopher is still not understood, and to certain superficial minds he appears to be *deranged*. Some industrials, it is true, have appreciated his good intentions and have seemed to realise the value of his doctrine and his works. Others, fewer in number, are at last beginning to be inspired by ideas whose development and success are daily being prepared with astonishing rapidity by the progress of enlightenment and the needs of the time.

His philosophy, the nature of which should have guaranteed its rapid popularity, is still known only to a few minds, and has only a very limited number of supporters. The only trace which his doctrine has left in the nation is the frequent use of the word 'industrial' *['industriel']*, a word created by him to express a new idea, and which his writings have certainly popularised.

However, that is not all: after frankly explaining the inevitable and involuntary wrongs of industry towards   M. Saint-Simon,[94] let us not conceal those of the philosopher himself. He addressed himself principally only to the industrials, and secondarily to the scientists and artists. He wanted the industrial body to engage directly in political activity. This attempt was impracticable, and will remain so as long as public opinion is not strongly influenced by the sciences and the fine arts. Also, he took his investigation of the relations between the noteworthy industrials and the *non-producers* too far. He offended those self-respecting persons who were anxious to judge for themselves the propriety of their relations; and besides, he should have seen that the industrials, who today benefit enormously from their dealings with governments, have an interest in treating with respect (up to a certain point) those men who are still useful to them in their individual and personal affairs.

By avoiding such errors, and by adopting a more natural and wiser course, you may hope to see your ideas have a rapid and powerful influence on the industrials. In order to release them from the yoke of their habits, and launch them in a new direction, it is first of all necessary to set the men of imagination and the scientists to work; for only science and the fine arts can form and develop a new political opinion . . .

THE ARTIST

We have succeeded, gentlemen, in giving a clear and precise account of our position and our duties. By a common hearth we have imbibed a new philosophy. We feel the need to develop and propagate it, and to contribute — each according to our faculties and means — to the successful application which we believe to be possible.

I propose that we first of all publish a first volume of our works. Later, in a second volume, we shall complete the exposition of the most general points of our doctrine . . .

For the literary and philosophical development of our doctrine, for its application to all the events of the day, we shall publish a journal . . . a new journal, capable of bringing together all the elements of the public mind and reconstituting them according to the moral needs of our age.

That is what we should strive to do if our first works are received with interest, but we shall not limit our task to that.

It was through an encyclopaedia that the French were able to overthrow the theological and feudal system; and it will be through an encyclopaedia that Europeans will be able to establish the scientific and industrial system . .

We shall therefore endeavour to bring together the most important scientists and artists of France and England to prepare an encyclopaedia of the nineteenth century. . .

[*Oeuvres,* vol. V, pt. 1, pp.201-11, 216-23, 226-31, 234-49, 251, 253, 256-7.]

40. NEW CHRISTIANITY: FIRST DIALOGUE

(Extracts from *Nouveau christianisme. Dialogues entre un conservateur et un novateur. Premier dialogue*, 1825)

Conservative. Do you believe in God?
Innovator. Yes, I believe in God.
Con. Do you believe that the Christian religion is of divine origin?
Inn. Yes, I believe that.
Con. If the Christian religion is of divine origin, it cannot possibly be improved. Yet in your writings you urge the artists, the industrials, and the scientists to improve this religion. You therefore contradict yourself, since your opinion and your belief are in opposition.
Inn. The opposition which you think you see between my opinion and my belief is only an apparent one. A distinction must be made between what God himself has said and what the clergy have said in his name.

What God has said certainly cannot be improved, but what the clergy have said in God's name forms a science which can be improved, just like all the other human sciences. There are times when the theory of theology must be brought up to date, just like the theory of physics, chemistry, and physiology.
Con. What part of religion do you consider divine? What part do you consider human?
Inn. God has said: *Men should treat one another as brothers.* This sublime principle embraces all that is divine in the Christian religion.
Con. What! You reduce the divine content of Christianity to a single principle!
Inn. God has naturally reduced everything to a single principle, and has naturally deduced everything from that principle. Otherwise his will towards men would not have been systematic. It would be blasphemous to suggest that the Almighty has founded his religion on several principles.

Now, according to this principle which God has given to men to guide them in their conduct, they must organise society to the greatest advantage of the greatest number, and must direct all their work and all their activity towards the aim of improving as quickly and as completely as possible the moral and physical condition of the most numerous class.

I say that it is this, and this alone, which is the divine part of the Christian religion.
Con. I admit that God has given men one single principle. I admit that he has commanded them to organise their society so as to guarantee

to the poorest class the most rapid and most complete improvement in its moral and physical existence. But I would remind you that God provided the human race with guides. Before ascending to Heaven, Jesus Christ gave his apostles and their successors the task of directing the conduct of men, by showing them how to apply the fundamental principle of divine morality, and by enabling them to deduce the proper consequences from this principle.

Do you recognise the Church as a divine institution?

Inn. I believe that God himself founded the Christian Church. I am filled with the deepest respect and the greatest admiration for the conduct of the Fathers of the Church.

These leaders of the early Church preached sincerely to all peoples of the need for unity. They urged them to live at peace with one another. To the men of power they declared positively and most vigorously that their first duty should be to employ all their resources for the quickest possible improvement in the moral and physical condition of the poor.

These leaders of the early Church produced the best book ever published, *the first catechism,* in which they divided men's actions into two classes: good and evil, that is, those that conform to the fundamental principle of divine morality, and those that are contrary to it.

Con. Explain your idea further, and tell me if you regard the Christian Church as infallible.

Inn. If the Church is led by the men who are best qualified to direct the forces of society towards the divine goal, I believe that it may conveniently be called infallible, and in such circumstances society is wise to let itself be guided by the Church.

I consider the Fathers of the Church as infallible for the age in which they lived, whereas it seems to me that the clergy of today is, of all established bodies, the one which commits the greatest errors, the errors most harmful to society, the one whose conduct is most directly opposed to the fundamental principle of divine morality.

Con. The Christian religion is thus, according to you, in a very bad state?

Inn. On the contrary. There have never been so many good Christians; but today they nearly all belong to the laity. Since the fifteenth century the Christian religion has lost its unity of action, and there has no longer been a Christian clergy. All the clergies who are today trying to graft their opinions, their morals, their cults, and their dogmas onto the principle of morality given to man by God are heretics, because their opinions, their morals, their dogmas, and their cults are all more or less opposed to divine morality. The most powerful clergy is also the most heretical.

Con. What will become of the Christian religion if, as you think, those men responsible for teaching it have become heretics?
Inn. Christianity will become the universal and only religion. The Asians and Africans will be converted. The members of the European clergy will become good Christians; they will abandon the various heresies which they profess today. The true doctrine of Christianity, that is to say, the most general doctrine which can be deduced from the fundamental principle of divine morality, will be produced, and immediately the differences between religious opinions will come to an end.

The first Christian doctrine only provided society with a partial and very incomplete organisation. The rights of Caesar remained independent of the rights attributed to the Church. *Render unto Caesar the things which are Caesar's:* such is the famous saying which separated these two powers. The temporal power has continued to base its power on the law of the strongest, while the Church has taught that society should only recognise as legitimate those institutions which aim to improve the existence of the poorest class.

The new Christian organisation will base both temporal and spiritual institutions on the principle that *all men should treat one another as brothers.* It will direct all institutions, whatever their nature, towards increasing the well-being of the poorest class . . .

I have, then, a clear conception of the New Christian doctrine, and I shall produce it. I shall then review all the spiritual and temporal institutions in England, France, northern and southern Germany, Italy, Spain, Russia, and North and South America. I shall compare the doctrines of these different institutions with the doctrine deduced directly from the fundamental principle of divine morality, and I shall easily convince all men of good faith and good intentions that if all these institutions were directed towards the aim of improving the moral and physical well-being of the poorest class, they would bring prosperity to all classes of society and all nations with the greatest possible speed . . .

I shall begin by examining the different religions which exist today. I shall compare their doctrines with the doctrine deduced directly from the fundamental principle of divine morality . . .

THE CATHOLIC RELIGION

The Catholic, Apostolic, and Roman association is the largest of all European and American religious associations, and . . . is unquestionably still very powerful, although it has declined considerably since the pontificate of Leo X, who was its founder.[95] But the force which this association possesses is only a material force, and it only manages to maintain itself by trickery. Spiritual force, the force of morals, the Christian force, based on frankness and loyalty, is entirely lacking. In short, the Catholic, Apostolic, and Roman religion is nothing but a Christian heresy...

I challenge the Pope, who calls himself Christian, who claims to be infallible, who assumes the title of Vicar of Jesus Christ, to reply clearly and without employing any mystical expressions to the four accusations of heresy which I shall bring against the Catholic Church.

I accuse the Pope and his Church of heresy on this first count: The teaching given by the Catholic clergy to their lay communicants is at fault, because it fails to guide their conduct along the path of Christianity.

The Christian religion teaches the faithful that their aim on earth should be to improve as quickly as possible the moral and physical condition of the poor. Jesus Christ promised eternal life to those who worked with the greatest zeal to increase the well-being of the most numerous class.

The mission of the Catholic clergy, as well as of all other clergies, should therefore be to direct the ardour of all members of society towards work of general utility.

Thus, all clergies should use all their intellectual resources and all their talents, in their sermons and more intimate conversations, to show laymen that an improvement in the existence of the lowest class will inevitably lead to an increase in the real and positive well-being of the higher classes: for God regards all men, even the rich, as his children.

Thus, in the teaching they give to children, in their sermons to the faithful, in the prayers they address to Heaven, as well as in every part of their cults and dogmas, the clergies should fix their audience's attention on this important fact: that *the vast majority of the population could enjoy a much more satisfying moral and physical condition than the one they have enjoyed hitherto, and that the rich, by increasing the happiness of the poor, would improve their own condition.*

That is the conduct that true Christianity prescribes for the clergy. It will now be easy for us to show the defects of the teaching given by the Catholic clergy to those who accept their creed.

If one looks through all the works written on Catholic dogma with the approval of the Pope and his Sacred College, and examines all the prayers authorised by the leaders of the Church for recital by the faithful, both laity and ecclesiastics, nowhere will one find a clear statement of the Christian religion's aim. There are few moral ideas in these writings, and these do not form a body of doctrine. They are thinly scattered among this vast number of volumes which mainly consist of tiresome repetitions of a few mystical conceptions, conceptions which cannot possibly serve as a guide, and which are contrary to nature because they make us lose sight of the principles of Christ's sublime morality.

It would be unfair to bring the accusation of incoherence against the vast collection of Catholic prayers authorised by the Pope. One recognises that this choice of prayers has been based on a systematic conception, and that the Sacred College has directed all the faithful towards one goal. But it is clear that this goal is not the Christian goal; it is an heretical one. It is to persuade the laity that they are not capable of conducting themselves according to their own enlightenment, and that they must allow themselves to be directed by the clergy, *even though the clergy are not obliged to show any greater capacity than their own.*

The clear aim of every part of worship and every principle of Catholic dogma is to make the laity absolutely dependent on the clergy.

The first accusation of heresy which I bring against the Pope and his Church, concerning the poor teaching they give to Catholics, is thus well founded.

I accuse the Pope and the Cardinals of being heretics on this second count: of lacking the knowledge which fits them to guide the faithful towards their salvation.

I accuse them of giving a bad education to seminarists, of failing to insist that new members of the priesthood receive sufficient instruction to become worthy pastors, capable of looking after the flocks placed in their care.

Theology is the only science taught in the seminaries, the only science which the Pope and the Cardinals feel obliged to pursue. Theology is the science which the leaders of the clergy require of those who, as vicars, bishops, archbishops, etc. are destined to guide the conduct of the faithful.

Now, I ask, what is theology? And I find that it is the science of argument on questions relating to dogma and worship.

It is unquestionably the most important science of all for the heretical clergies, since it enables them to fix the attention of the faithful on minutiae, and to make Christians lose sight of the great earthly aim which they must set themselves in order to obtain eternal life, that is, the quickest possible improvement in the moral and physical condition of the poor class.

But theology should not be of great importance for a truly Christian clergy, which should consider worship and dogma only as religious accessories, should regard morality as the only true religious doctrine, and should use dogma and worship simply as means which may often be useful for fixing the attention of all Christians upon morality.

The Roman clergy were orthodox until the accession of Leo X to the papal throne, because until that time they were superior to the laity in all the sciences whose progress helped increase the well-being of the poorest class. They have since become heretical, because they have only pursued theology, and have allowed the laity to surpass them in the fine arts, the exact sciences, and in terms of industrial capacity.

The accusation of heresy which I bring against the Pope and the Cardinals, on account of their misuse of their intelligence and the bad education they give to seminarists, is thus well founded.

I accuse the Pope of heretical behaviour on this third count:
I accuse him of ruling in a way more opposed to the moral and physical interests of the temporal subjects belonging to the destitute class than the rule of any lay prince over his poor subjects.

If one surveys the whole of Europe, one will see that it is in the Papal States that the administration of public interests is most at fault and most anti-Christian.

Large areas of land belonging to the domain of St. Peter, which at one time yielded abundant harvests, have turned into pestilent marshes through the negligence of the Papal Government.

A large part of the territory, if it has not been overrun by water, is still uncultivated, not because of the barrenness of the soil, but because so little importance is attached to the profession of farming in the Papal States. Because the profession offers neither esteem nor adequate profits it is rarely sought after. Men with ability or capital avoid it. The Pope has reserved for himself the monopoly not only of all important agricultural products, but also of all the primary necessities, and he allows his favourite Cardinals to exercise this monopoly.

Finally, there is no manufacturing in the Papal States, although the cheap cost of labour could make manufacturing very profitable. This is due solely to faults in the administration.

Every branch of industry is paralysed. The poor are without work, and would die of hunger if the ecclesiastic institutions, that is, the Government did not feed them. Because the poor are fed through charity, they are badly fed; thus, their physical existence is miserable.

Their moral condition is even more miserable, since they live in idleness, which is the mother of all vices of all the brigandage infesting this unfortunate country.

The third accusation of heresy which I bring against the Pope, on account of the faulty and anti-Christian way in which he rules his temporal subjects, is thus well founded.

I accuse the Pope and all the present Cardinals, indeed all the Popes and all the Cardinals since the fifteenth century, of being and having being heretics on this fourth count:

I accuse them first of having consented to the formation of two institutions diametrically opposed to the spirit of Christianity: the Inquisition and the Jesuits. Next, I accuse them of having protected these two institutions ever since, almost without interruption.

The spirit of Christianity is gentleness, goodness, charity, and above all honesty. Its weapons are persuasion and demonstration.

The spirit of the Inquisition is despotism and greed. Its weapons are violence and cruelty. The spirit of the company of Jesuits is egoism, and it is through trickery that they strive to attain their end, which is to exercise general domination over both ecclesiastics and laity.

The idea of the Inquisition is radically faulty and anti-Christian. Even if the Inquisitors had put to death in their *auto-da-fé* only those persons guilty of opposing the improvement of the moral and physical condition of the poor class, even in this case (which would have condemned the entire Sacred College to the stake), they would have been heretics, for Jesus allowed no exceptions when he prohibited his Church from using violence . . .

THE PROTESTANT RELIGION

. . . The Protestant religion, as conceived by Luther, is still only a Christian heresy. It was certainly right of Luther to say that the Court of Rome had departed from the path selected by Jesus for his apostles, and to proclaim that the form of worship and the dogma established by the Popes were not suitable for fixing the attention of the faithful on Christian morality, but could, on the contrary, only be considered as accessories to religion. But, on the basis of these two unquestionable truths, Luther did not have the right to conclude that morality should be taught to the faithful of his time in the same way that it had been taught by the Fathers of the Church to their contemporaries. Nor did he have the right to conclude that worship should be stripped of all the beauty with which the fine arts could enrich it.

The dogmatic part of Luther's reform was a failure. This reform was incomplete, and is itself in need of reform.

I accuse the Lutherans of being heretics on this first count: I accuse them of adopting a morality which is much inferior to the morality appropriate to Christians in their present state of civilisation.

Public opinion in Europe is favourable to Protestantism, and opposed to Catholicism. I must therefore demonstrate the Protestant heresy very strictly, which means I must deal with this question in a very general manner.

Jesus gave his apostles and their successors the mission of organising the human race in the way most favourable to the improvement of the condition of the poor. At the same time he requested his Church not to use any means other than gentleness, persuasion, and demonstration to attain this great goal.

The fulfilment of this task required a great deal of time and effort. Thus, we should not be surprised to find that it is still unaccomplished.

What part of this task fell to Luther? How did Luther acquit himself in it? These are the two points I have to clarify.

To do this, I shall examine successively four major questions:

1. What was the state of social organisation when Jesus gave his apostles the mission of reorganising the human race?
2. What was the state of social organisation at the time when Luther introduced his reform?
3. What was the complete reform needed by the Papal religion in order to resume the direction which Jesus gave to his apostles, when Luther revolted against the Court of Rome?
4. In what does Luther's reform consist?

The analysis of these four major questions will naturally lead to the conclusion that the Lutherans are heretics.

1. At the time when Jesus gave his apostles the sublime mission of organising the human race in the interest of the poorest class, civilisation was still in its infancy.

Society was divided into two great classes: masters and slaves. The class of masters was divided into two castes: the patricians who made the law and occupied all important posts, and the plebeians who had to obey the law, even though they had not made it, and who generally occupied only subordinate posts. The greatest philosophers could not conceive of any other basis for society.

There was as yet no moral system, since no one had yet found the means of relating all the principles of this science to one single principle.

There was as yet no religious system, since all official creeds recognised a multitude of gods, inspiring men with a variety of contrary sentiments.

The human heart had not yet risen to philanthropic sentiments. Patriotism was the broadest sentiment felt by the most generous minds, but it was an extremely limited sentiment, because the nations of antiquity were so small in terms of territory and population.

One nation, the Roman nation, dominated all others and ruled them arbitrarily.

The size of the planet was not known, so it was impossible to conceive any general plan for improving the territorial property of the human race.

In short, Christianity, its morality, its form of worship and dogma, its followers and ministers, found themselves at first completely outside the organisation, customs, and morals of society.

2. By the time Luther introduced his reform, civilisation had made great progress. Since the establishment of Christianity society had changed completely, and social organisation was now based on new foundations.

Slavery was almost entirely abolished. The patricians no longer had exclusive control over law-making, and no longer occupied all the important posts. Temporal power, which was essentially unholy, no longer dominated spiritual power, and spiritual power was no longer under the control of the patricians. The Court of Rome had become the foremost court in Europe. Since the establishment of the papacy, all the Popes and nearly all the Cardinals had come from the plebeian class. An aristocracy of talent had surmounted the aristocracy of wealth, as well as the aristocracy founded on the rights of birth.

Society had a combined system of religion and morality, since the love of God and of one's neighbour gave unity to the most general sentiments of the faithful.

Christianity had become the basis of social organisation, and had replaced the law of the strongest. The right of conquest was no longer considered the most legitimate right of all.

America had been discovered; and because the human race now knew the full extent of its territory, it was in a position to draw up a general plan of work to be undertaken in order to make the best use of the planet's resources.

Peaceful capacities had developed and acquired precision. The fine arts had just been revived; the sciences of observation, as well as industry, had just started to advance.

The philanthropic sentiment, which is the true basis of Christianity, had replaced patriotism in all generous hearts. If all men did not treat one another as brothers, at least they all acknowledged that they should regard one another as children of the same father.

3. If Luther's reform could have been completed, Luther would have produced and proclaimed the following doctrine, saying to the Pope and Cardinals:

'Your predecessors have sufficiently perfected and propagated the theory of Christianity. The Europeans are sufficiently imbued with it. You must now concentrate on the general application of this doctrine. The true Christianity should make men happy not only in heaven, but on earth.

'No longer should you keep the attention of the faithful fixed on abstract ideas. You will succeed in establishing Christianity as the general, universal, and sole religion only by making proper use of sensual ideas, and combining them so as to achieve the highest degree of felicity attainable by the human race during its earthly life.

'It is no longer enough to preach to the faithful of all classes that the poor are the cherished children of God. You must make bold and energetic use of all the powers and methods acquired by the militant Church in order quickly to improve the moral and physical condition of the most numerous class. The preliminary and preparatory work of Christianity is complete. You have a task to fulfil which is much more satisfying than the one accomplished by your predecessors. It consists in establishing the general and definitive Christianity, in organising the whole human race according to the fundamental principle of divine morality.

'To fulfil this task you must make this principle the basis and aim of every social institution.

'The apostles had to recognise the power of Caesar. They had to say: *"Render unto Caesar the things which are Caesar's"* because they were not strong enough to fight against it, and therefore had to avoid becoming its enemy.

'But today the respective positions of the spiritual and temporal powers have changed completely, thanks to the work of the militant Church, and so you must declare to the successors of Caesar that Christianity no longer recognises their right to command men, a right founded on conquest, that is, on the law of the strongest.

'You must declare to all kings that the only way to make monarchy legitimate is to consider it as an institution for preventing the rich and powerful from oppressing the poor. You must declare to them that their sole duty is to improve the moral and physical condition of the most numerous class, and that every unnecessary expense ordered by them in the administration of the national wealth is a crime which makes them enemies of God.

'You possess all the strength necessary to compel the temporal power to accept this application of Christianity; for your supremacy is recognised by all the powers, and you control the clergy spread across the whole of Europe. Now, the clergy will always exert a preponderant influence over the temporal institutions of every people, if they work in a positive manner to improve the condition of the poorest class, which is everywhere the most numerous class . . .

'Most Holy Father, the human race is presently going through a major intellectual crisis. Three new capacities are emerging: the fine arts are reviving, the sciences are about to surpass every other branch of our knowledge, and great industrial establishments are doing more to improve the condition of the poor class than any measure taken hitherto by the temporal or spiritual powers.

'These three capacities are of a peaceful nature. It is consequently in your interest, and in the interest of the clergy, to unite with them. Through this union you will soon, and without too much difficulty, be able to organise the human race in the way most favourable to the improvement in the moral and physical condition of the most numerous class; and the power of Caesar, which is unholy in its origin and in its claims, will be completely destroyed.

'If, on the other hand, you regard the fine arts, sciences, and great industrial establishments as unholy, or at least as disagreeable to God; if you try to prolong your domination of the species by the means which your predecessors used to acquire it in the Middle Ages; if you continue to present mystical ideas as the most important ideas of all for the happiness of the human race, then the artists, scientists, and the heads of industry will unite with Caesar against you. They will open the eyes of the common people to the absurdity of your doctrines, to the monstrous abuses of your power, and you will then be able to maintain your social existence only by becoming the instruments of temporal power. Caesar will use you to oppose the progress of civilisation by continuing to fix the people's attention on mystical and superstitious ideas, and by diverting them as far as possible from all education in the fine arts, the sciences of observation, and industrial enterprise. Your chief concern will be to induce respect for temporal power, which you have hitherto been fighting against. You will preserve your honours and your wealth by preaching passive obedience to kings, and by laying down that they are accountable only to God for their actions, and that, in any case, their subjects cannot refuse to obey them without committing a crime . . .'

4. Luther was a very powerful and able critic; but it is only in this respect that he demonstrated any great ability. Thus, he proved in a most vigorous and thorough manner that the Court of Rome had left the path of Christianity; that on the one hand it was trying to establish itself as an arbitrary power, and that, on the other, it was striving to unite with the powerful against the poor, so that the faithful must compel it to reform.

But that part of his work relating to the reorganisation of Christianity was much worse than it should have been. Instead of taking the necessary measures to increase the social importance of the Christian religion, he made this religion revert to its point of departure. He put it back again outside the social organisation, thus recognising the power of Caesar as the source of every other power. He reserved for his clergy only the right of humble petition to temporal power. Through these arrangements he delivered the peaceful capacities into a state of eternal dependence on the men of violence, the military.

In this way he confined Christian morality to the same narrow limits which the state of civilisation had imposed on the first Christians.

The accusation of heresy which I bring against the Protestants, on account of the morality which they have adopted, a morality which is very much behind the present level of our civilisation, is thus well founded.

I accuse the Protestants of heresy on this second count:
I accuse them of adopting a bad form of worship.

The more society improves morally and physically, the greater the division between intellectual and manual work. Thus, in the course of their daily lives, men find their attention fixed on an increasingly specialised interest, as the fine arts, sciences, and industry progress.

It follows from this that the more society progresses, the more necessary it is for the form of worship to be improved; for the purpose of worship is to direct the attention of men, in their regular assemblies on the day of rest, to the interests common to all members of society, to the general interests of the human race.

Luther the reformer, and since his death the ministers of the reformed Churches, should therefore have tried to find a way of making worship as suitable as possible for directing the attention of the faithful to their common interests.

They should have tried to find the means and circumstances most favourable for completely developing in the faithful the fundamental principle of the Christian religion: *all men should treat one another as brothers.* They should have done this so as to familiarise the minds of the faithful with this principle, and accustom them to applying it in all their social relations. In this way they would be prevented from completely losing sight of it in the course of their lives, however specialised their daily occupations might be.

Now, there are two main ways of drawing men's attention to a particular set of ideas, and stimulating them in a particular direction: they must be filled with terror by the sight of the terrible evils they will have to face if they disregard the established rules of conduct; or they must be enticed by the pleasures which will inevitably result if they follow the prescribed course.

In both cases, in order to achieve the most decisive and most useful effect, it is necessary to combine all the methods, all the resources offered by the fine arts.

The preacher, who naturally makes use of eloquence, the first of the fine arts, should make his audience tremble by depicting the awful state of the man who, in this life, brings public disgrace upon himself. He should even show the arms of God raised against the man whose sentiments are not predominantly philanthropic.

Or else he should imbue the souls of his audience with the most generous and most powerful sentiments, by convincing them that the pleasure which comes from public esteem is much greater than any other pleasure.

The poets should assist the preachers in their work. They should provide the religion with pieces of poetry suitable for recital in unison, so that all the faithful may preach to one another.

The musicians should enrich the religious poetry with their harmonies, and give them a musical character which will move the faithful to the depths of their souls.

In the temples, the painters and sculptors should remind Christians of those deeds which are most outstandingly Christian.

The architects should build temples so that the preachers, poets, musicians, painters, and sculptors can, at will, fill the souls of the faithful with feelings of terror or joy and hope.

Clearly, this is the basis on which the form of worship should be established, and the means by which it may be made useful to society.

What did Luther actually do in this respect? He reduced worship in the reformed Church simply to preaching. He *vulgarised* Christian sentiments as much as possible. He banned from his temples all painted and sculptured decoration. He suppressed music, and gave preference to the dreariest religious buildings, which were consequently most unsuitable for inspiring the faithful with a feeling of passion for the public good . . .

I have clearly stated what the form of worship should have been if, on the day of rest, it was to succeed in fixing the attention of the faithful on Christian morality.

I have clearly proved that Protestant worship lacks the most effective secondary means of filling the souls of the faithful with a passion for the public good. I have thus proved that this second accusation of heresy against Protestantism is well founded.

I bring a third accusation of heresy against the Protestants: I accuse them of adopting a false dogma.

In the early days of religion, when the people were still steeped in ignorance, they had little inclination to study natural phenomena. Man's ambition had not risen to the point where he wanted to master his planet and transform it to his greatest advantage. At that time men had few needs of which they were clearly aware; but they were swayed by the most violent passions, reflecting their vague desires and whims, in particular the presentiment of the power they were destined to exercise over nature. Commerce, which has since civilised the world, still only existed in rudimentary form. Every small tribe was in a state of hostility towards the rest of the human race, and citizens had no moral links with any men who were not members of their city. Thus at this time philanthropy could still only exist as a speculative idea.

At the same time all nations were divided into two great classes: masters and slaves. Religion could only have a powerful effect on the masters, since they alone were able to act according to their own free will. Morality was bound to be the least developed part of religion, since there was no reciprocity of common duties between the two great social classes. Worship and dogma were bound to appear much more important than morality. Religious practices, and reasoning on the utility of these practices and of the beliefs on which they were founded, were inevitably the parts of religion of chief concern to the priests and the mass of believers.

In short, the material part of religion originally played a much more important role; whereas the spiritual part has acquired increasing importance as man's intelligence has developed.

Today, worship should be regarded only as a means of drawing men's attention, on the day of rest, to philanthropic ideas and sentiments; and dogma should no longer be conceived as anything but a collection of commentaries aimed at the general application of those ideas and sentiments to major political events, and seeking to make it easy for the faithful to apply morality in their daily relationships.

I shall now examine what Luther thought of dogma, what he said about it, and what rules he laid down for Protestants.

Luther considered that Christianity, in its original form, was perfect, but that after its foundation continual deterioration set in. This reformer concentrated all his attention on the errors of the clergy in the Middle Ages, completely disregarding both the enormous progress in civilisation which the priests achieved, and the great social importance they helped peaceful workers to acquire by diminishing the power and standing of temporal power, that unholy power whose natural tendency is to subject men to the rule of physical force, and to govern nations for its own profit. Luther ordered Protestants to study Christianity in the books written at the time of its foundation, and particularly in the Bible. He declared that he did not recognise any dogmas which were not expounded in the Holy Scriptures.

This declaration was as absurd as if the mathematicians, physicists, and chemists, and all other scientists maintained that their subjects should be studied in the earliest scientific works . . .

Four major disadvantages have resulted from the excessive emphasis placed by Protestants on studying the Bible:
1. Such study has made them lose sight of positive ideas, the ideas of current interest. It has given them a taste for aimless research, and has strongly inclined them towards metaphysics. In fact, in northern Germany, which is the home of Protestantism, vagueness of ideas and feelings dominates all the writings of the most famous philosophers and the most popular novelists.

2. Such study soils the imagination by its reminders of several shameful vices which have disappeared with the progress of civilisation, such as every conceivable kind of bestiality and incest.
3. Such study fixes the attention on political desires contrary to the public good. It encourages the governed to establish in society an equality which is absolutely impracticable. It prevents Protestants from working for the formation of that political system in which the general interests are managed by the most capable men in the sciences of observation, the fine arts, and industrial enterprises — the best social system to which the human race can attain, since it is the one which would contribute most directly and most effectively to the moral and physical improvement in the condition of the poor.
4. Such study encourages those who pursue it to regard it as the most important kind of study. This has resulted in the formation of biblical societies, which distribute millions of copies of the Bible to the public each year.

Instead of using their energy to promote the production and diffusion of a doctrine suited to the state of civilisation, these so-called Christian societies give a false direction to philanthropic feelings, a direction contrary to the public good. Thinking they are serving the progress of the human mind, they would prefer to push it backwards if that were at all possible.

On the basis of these four major facts I conclude that my third accusation of heresy against Protestants, on account of the dogma they have adopted, is firmly established ...

Con. I have followed your speech with careful attention. While you were speaking my own ideas became clearer, my doubts disappeared, and I felt a growing love and admiration for the Christian religion. My devotion to the religious system which has civilised Europe has not prevented me from understanding that it can be improved, and on this point you have convinced me completely.

It is clear that the moral principle, *all men should treat one another as brothers,* given by God to his Church, embraces all the ideas which you include in the precept that *the whole of society should work to improve the moral and physical condition of the poorest class; society should be organised in the way most suitable for achieving this great aim.*

It is equally certain that when Christianity originated the first formula had to be used to express this principle, and that today the second formula should be used.

At the time of Christianity's foundation, you have said, society was divided into two great classes which were, politically, absolutely different: masters and slaves, forming, in one respect, two distinct human races, and yet closely interrelated. It was then absolutely impossible to establish complete reciprocity in the moral relations between the two races, so that the divine Founder of the Christian religion had to restrict his moral principle to an obligation on all the individuals belonging to each human race. He was not able to establish it as a link uniting the masters and the slaves.

We are now living at a time when slavery is completely abolished; when all men share the same political character; when classes are only separated by slight differences. You therefore conclude that the fundamental principle of Christianity should be formulated so that it becomes a mutual obligation for the people as a whole, without ceasing to be an obligation for men in their individual relations. I find your conclusion legitimate and of the greatest importance; and henceforth, New Christian, I shall join in the propagation of New Christianity . . .

[*Oeuvres,* vol. III, pt. 3, pp. 107-16, 118-30, 141-50, 154-62, 164-74.]

NOTES

1. The original text has 'astrological' here, not 'astronomical'; but the sense of this paragraph makes it clear that it is the latter term which is intended.
2. i.e. one mathematician, one physicist, one chemist, one physiologist, one author, one painter, one musician.
3. Saint-Simon is obviously thinking of Napoleon here.
4. Marie-Jean-Antoine-Nicolas de Caritat, marquis de Condorcet, 1743-94, mathematician and philosopher. Outlawed by Robespierre's Revolutionary Government in 1793, he went into hiding and wrote his *Esquisse d'un tableau historique des progrès de l'esprit humain*, in which he outlined a theory of mankind's unlimited perfectibility. (This is 'the idea' to which Saint-Simon refers.) Arrested on 27 March 1794, he died in prison two days later. After the fall of Robespierre many of his works were published, including the *Esquisse* in 1795. Both Condorcet and Saint-Simon came from Picardy, and it is possible that the two men knew each other at one time. In some of Saint-Simon's manuscripts there is mention of meetings between them during 1791-2. See *T.c.*, p.15 (fn.4).
5. i.e. England.
6. René Descartes, 1596-1650, presented his 'system of vortices' in *Principia philosophiae* (1644). According to this system, the movement of matter is due to the effect of 'vortices' or 'whirlpools' of fluid ether which fill all space and which propel matter in a circular movement around the planets, the planets themselves moving round the central vortex of the sun.
7. i.e. The French scientific school.
8. Institut de France, founded in 1795 to replace the French Academies. It was originally divided into three classes: physical and mathematical sciences, moral and political sciences, literature and the fine arts — each subdivided into sections. A reorganisation took place in 1803 (under Napoleon): the class of moral and political sciences was abolished, and the class of literature and the fine arts was divided into three new classes — French language and literature, ancient history and literature, fine arts. In 1816 Louis XVIII introduced another series of changes, abolishing the system of classes and re-establishing the Academies as component parts of the Institute.
9. *Novum Organum,* the title of a major work (published 1620) by Francis Bacon, 1561-1626.
10. In the original text the date of Bacon's birth is given incorrectly as 22 January 1565. I have adjusted all the figures accordingly.
11. *Théorie des fonctions analytiques* (1797) by Joseph-Louis, comte de Lagrange, 1736-1813. This work contains the texts of lectures given by Lagrange at the École Polytechnique (founded 1795).
12. *Traité de mécanique céleste* (5 vols., 1798-1827) by Pierre-Simon, marquis de Laplace, 1749-1827. This work established Laplace's reputation as 'the Newton of France'.
13. *Traité des sensations* (1754) by Étienne Bonnot, abbé de Condillac, 1715-80. Condillac also wrote an important study on political economy which may have influenced Saint-Simon: *Le Commerce et le gouvernement considérés*

305

relativement l'un à l'autre (1776).
14. See Note 4.
15. Richard Price, 1723-91, and Joseph Priestley, 1733-1804. Authors of philosophical and theological works. Priestley also achieved fame as a chemist, through his discovery of various gases, including oxygen. As philosophers the two men did not always agree: Priestley's uncompromising materialism and denial of free will were strongly opposed by Price.
16. Denis Diderot, 1713-84, and Jean Le Rond d'Alembert, 1717-83, co-edited the great *Encyclopédie ou Dictionnaire raisonné des sciences, des arts et des métiers*, which was published in 28 vols. (17 vols. text, 11 vols. plates) between 1751 and 1772. The *Discours préliminaire* to vol. I was by d'Alembert.
17. Académie des Sciences, founded 1666.
18. The Sorbonne (named after its founder Robert de Sorbon) was established as a theological college in Paris in 1257.
19. Louis-Gabriel-Ambroise, vicomte de Bonald, 1754-1840, Catholic counter-revolutionary philosopher, Ultra-Royalist politician during the Restoration (first as a deputy, then as a peer). Author of *Théorie du pouvoir politique et religieux dans la société civile* (1796), *Essai analytique sur les lois naturelles de l'ordre social* (1800), *Recherches philosophiques sur les premiers objets des connaissances morales* (1818), and other works.

François-René, vicomte de Chateaubriand, 1768-1848, author of the acknowledged masterpiece *Le Génie du christianisme, ou beautés de la religion chrétienne* (1802). His philosophy was, like Bonald's, fundamentally Catholic and royalist. Under the Restoration he held a number of important political and diplomatic posts, including the Ministry of Foreign Affairs (1823-4). In numerous Restoration writings he sought to show how monarchical and parliamentary institutions could be combined. See, for example, *De la monarchie selon la charte* (1816).
20. Two schools of philosophy in Greece. The Academicians were followers of Plato, the Peripatetics followed Aristotle. See further *S. W.*, p.121.
21. Jacques-Bénigne Bossuet, 1627-1704, theologian, Bishop of Meaux, author of an important *Discours de l'histoire universelle* (1681).
22. This article follows the section *On Religion* in the *Introduction aux travaux scientifiques du XIXe siècle*. See *Oeuvres*, vol. VI, pp.172-5. An English translation has been provided by Felix Markham in his edition of Henri de Saint-Simon, *Social Organization, the Science of Man and Other Writings*, New York, 1964, pp.19-20.
23. Cf. *S. W.*, pp.269-70, where Saint-Simon describes this transition in somewhat different terms, suggesting in fact that it was accomplished very quickly.
24. Under the Restoration Saint-Simon changed his attitude towards the Gospel's moral principle. See in particular *S. W.*, chs. 18, 26, 40.
25. Alexandre (Alessandro) Farnèse, 1468-1549, Pope from 1534 until his death (Paul III).
26. See Note 16.
27. Saint-Simon is referring to Catholic demands for religious freedom through the disestablishment of the 'United Church of England and Ireland' (created by an Act of Union in 1800). Disestablishment was eventually achieved in 1871.
28. William Pitt, the Younger, 1759-1806. Entered the House of Commons 1781, Chancellor of the Exchequer 1782-3, Prime Minister 1783-1801, 1804-6.

29. Saint-Simon is here referring to meetings with Ellis during the late 1790s, in particular at the time of the Anglo-French peace negotiations. See Introduction, p.17.
30. Félix Vicq-d'Azyr, 1748-94, anatomist, author of *Traité d'anatomie et de physiologie* (1786).
   Pierre-Jean-Georges Cabanis, 1757-1808, author of *Rapports du physique et du moral de l'homme* (1802), which includes a number of memoirs presented by Cabanis to the Institute during 1796-7 on the subject of the relationship between man's physical and moral constitution.
   Marie-François-Xavier Bichat, 1771-1802, founder of general anatomy (see *Anatomie générale,* 1801) and embryology. Undertook important investigations on the structure of the body's organs, showing that certain tissues and membranes are common to all organs.
   For Condorcet see Note 4.
31. Jean Burdin, 1777-1858, author of a five-volume *Cours d'études médicales,* published with Saint-Simon's financial assistance in 1803.
32. Charles-François Dupuis, 1742-1809, published his *L'Origine de tous les cultes ou religion universelle* in 1795.
33. 'Organisation' here means 'organic structure'. See Introduction, p.30.
34. Charles-Joseph-Julien Bougon, 1779-1851. When, in 1825, he was appointed to a chair at the Ecole de Médecine, a number of his critics pointed out that he had not written a single medical work. Five years later a major work did appear: *Anatomie élémentaire et descriptive de toutes les parties du corps humain.*
35. Konrad Engelbert Oelsner, 1764-1828, German historian and philologist who wrote in French. His study *Des effets de la religion de Mohammed pendant les trois premiers siècles de sa fondation* won a prize at the Institute in 1809.
36. According to Saint-Simon, the 'savage' was a male (he does not give the exact age) who had been abandoned in early infancy and had subsequently led an isolated existence. Recently captured by peasants (presumably in Aveyron − a department in the south of France), he had been taken to Paris for medical examination. See further *O.c.,* vol.II, pp.90-97.
37. Saint-Simon here seems to be suggesting that the Institute was divided into just three classes. In fact, in 1803 Napoleon reorganised the Institute into four classes. See Note 8.
38. Université Impériale, founded by Napoleon in 1808.
39. Napoleon had posed this question to the Institute in 1802, and a report was duly presented to the Emperor by the class of physical and mathematical sciences in 1808.
40. This treaty brought the Thirty Years' War to an end in 1648.
41. Louis XVIII's Constitutional Charter of 1814.
42. During the Revolution a vast amount of property belonging to the Church and the nobility was confiscated by the Government and put up for sale. After the restoration of the Bourbon monarchy, many of the original owners of these *biens nationaux* demanded the return of their property. Louis XVIII was not willing to meet these demands, as Article 9 of his Charter made clear; but he had to recognise that there was a strong current of public opinion opposed to his policy.
43. The Minister was Lazare Carnot. He knew Saint-Simon and found him a job at the Bibliothèque de l'Arsenal during the 'Hundred Days'.
44. To the best of my knowledge this is the first occasion on which Saint-Simon used the term *'industriel'.*

45. See further *S.W.*, ch.14.
46. See Introduction. pp.14-15.
47. Jean Baptiste Say, 1767-1832, published his *Traité d'économie politique* in 1803.
48. Book I, Chapter I of *Inquiry into the Principles of Political Economy* (1767) by Sir James Denham Steuart, 1712-80. A French translation of this work was published in Paris in 1792.
49. The 'economists', as the name suggests, were in many respects the founding fathers of political economy. Also known as the 'physiocrats', their 'master' was François Quesnay, 1694-1774, whose chief work, *Tableau économique,* was published in 1758. The school included Victor Riqueti, marquis de Mirabeau, 1715-89; Pierre-Samuel Dupont de Nemours, 1739-1817, who was the first economist to be admitted to the Institute, in 1803; Pierre-Paul Lemercier de La Rivière de Saint-Médard, 1720-92?; Nicolas, abbé Baudeau, 1730-92.
50. Jean-Jacques Rousseau, 1712-78, author of the well-known *Du contrat social* (1762), contributed an article on *Économie politique* to the *Encyclopédie* of Diderot and d'Alembert (1755).
51. Adam Smith, 1723-90, author of *An Inquiry into the Nature and Causes of the Wealth of Nations* (1776).
52. Pierre Bayle, 1647-1706, presented a brilliant critical survey of the philosophical and theological knowledge of his time in the *Dictionnaire historique et critique* (1695-7).
53. *Vues sur la propriété et la législation* is the title given to this part of *L'Industrie* by Olinde Rodrigues in his *Oeuvres complètes de Saint-Simon* (1832).

    In the Goldsmiths' Library (University of London) there is a rare first edition of *L'Industrie,* vol. IV, pt.2 (ref. A.817) which contains a manuscript note by Saint-Simon, at p.4, explaining that he did not approve of the printer's frequent use of italics in the text. This was due, he explains, to a copyist who prepared his manuscripts for publication. In view of this note, I have though it unnecessary to maintain the original heavy italicising.
54. Saint-Simon is here arguing that in agriculture it should be the farmer, rather than the landlord (the lessor), who decides how to employ capital, just as in commerce and manufacturing it is the entrepreneur rather than the financier.
55. The electoral law of 1817 abolished the system of indirect election through local (arrondissement) colleges consisting of the chief taxpayers in each particular area, and gave the vote to all men who had reached the age of twenty-five and who payed 300 francs or more each year in direct taxation. These new provisions went some way towards meeting the demands of the liberals for a more representative system.
56. As outlined in *S.W.*, ch.14.
57. In 1825 Saint-Simon rejected gradualism in favour of more rapid change. See *S.W.*, pp.269-71.
58. The marquis de Barthélemy proposed, on behalf of the Ultra-Royalists, an abrogation of the 1817 electoral law (see Note 55) and a return to the system of electoral colleges, the intention being to ensure that only the country's wealthiest class — the chief taxpayers — had the vote. The proposal failed, but some months later, in 1820, the 'Ultras' made another attempt to secure reform, and this time they were successful.
59. The electoral law of 1817 had implemented provisions contained in the charter of 1814.

60. This text has become well known as the *Parabole politique* – a title provided by Rodrigues in 1832. (See Note 53).
61. i.e. engineers from the Bridge and Roads Service *(Service des Ponts et Chaussées).*
62. Académie Française, originally founded in 1635, abolished in 1795, re-established in 1816 as part of the Institute. (See Note 8.)
63. 'Ultras' and 'Ministerials': the names given to the two major political parties that emerged during the early years of the Restoration. The Ultras (Ultra-Royalists) advocated a new Catholic monarchical regime. The Ministerial or Constitutional party supported the Charter of 1814. They achieved a majority in the Chamber of Deputies in 1816, and retained power until 1820 when, after the assassination of the duc de Berry, a royalist reaction set in and the Ultras gained seats. The Liberals (or Independents), originally members of the Ministerial party, formed their own distinct group after the elections of 1817, when their numbers increased to 25. By 1820 they had made considerable gains in electoral support, but, like the Ministerials, their fortunes declined with the royalist reaction that began in that year. In 1823 they suffered a disastrous electoral defeat, their representation in the Chamber going down from 110 to 19.
64. *Sur la loi des élections,* a pamphlet published in 1820.
65. See *S.W.,* ch.23.
66. A liberal constitution was first established in Spain in 1812, but it quickly gave way to the authoritarian rule of King Ferdinand VII. The King was in turn overthrown in 1820, and the constitution of 1812 re-established. King Ferdinand I of Naples was forced by the army to grant a new constitution in 1820. (In 1821, however, supported by Austrian troops, he was able to withdraw it.) 1820 also saw liberal reforms in Portugal which the King (John VI) willingly accepted.
67. This statement clearly foreshadows Auguste Comte's celebrated 'law of the three states', according to which all human knowledge passes through three theoretical stages: theological/fictitious, metaphysical/abstract, scientific/positive.
68. This text was originally printed as a footnote to the Preface of *Du système industriel,* pt.I.
69. To be a deputy under the Bourbon Restoration one had to be at least forty years of age and pay 1,000 francs or more in direct taxes.
70. See Introduction pp.42-3.
71. See Note 55.
72. The Charter of 1814 provided for annual partial elections to the Chamber of Deputies (one-fifth of the seats to be contested each year). Saint-Simon is referring to elections held in October 1821 at which, over France as a whole, there was a clear move to the Right.
73. i.e. The conquest of Gaul by the Frankish kings in the first half of the sixth century.
74. On the settlement of the Franks in Gaul see Note 73. The first crusade against the Muslims began in 1096.
75. Louis XI, King of France 1461-83.
76. Louis XIV, King of France 1643-1715.
77. Saint-Simon is referring to two contrasting districts of Paris: the wealthy, aristocratic Saint-Germain quarter and the industrial Antin embankment.
78. Majorat: entailed estate, that is, an estate settled upon a fixed line of descendants.
79. 'Industrialistes'.

80. Cf. *S. W.*, p.222.
81. Two English Whigs.
82. This class was part of the Institute from 1795 to 1803. (See Note 8.) An Académie des Sciences Morales et Politiques was founded a few years after Saint-Simon's death, in 1832.
83. See Note 42.
84. This law was issued by the ruling Convention in the autumn of 1793. It introduced price- and wage-controls in an attempt to promote *maximum* productivity.
85. Cf. *S. W.*, pp.202-6.
86. The comte de Villèle, Ultra-Royalist. Became *de facto* head of the Government at the end of 1821; formally appointed Minister-President (president of the Council of Ministers) in 1822. Retired from politics after electoral defeats in November 1827.
87. This measure was approved by Charles X, who succeeded to the throne in 1824 on the death of Louis XVIII.
88. Cf. *S. W.*, pp.179-80, where Saint-Simon advocates *gradual* change.
89. Cf. *S. W.*, p.103, where Saint-Simon suggests that this transition was a slow process.
90. See Preface, p.8, for a note on this text. For further discussion see M.H. James, 'A Bibliographical Mistake in the Study of Henri de Saint-Simon', *Political Studies,* vol.XX, No. 2, June 1972, pp.202-5.
91. The name given to a series of uprisings against the Regency between 1648 and 1653.
92. This text was published anonymously. In the past it has frequently been attributed to Olinde Rodrigues. (See, for example, *Oeuvres,* vol. V, pt.1, p.199.) However, to the best of my knowledge, no evidence has ever been produced to confirm this judgement. On the other hand, we do have a clear statement by Léon Halévy that he and Saint-Simon were the authors. See 'Souvenirs de Saint-Simon', *La France littéraire,* March 1832, p.539.
93. See *S. W.*, pp.264-5, for an explanation of the distinction between education and instruction.
94. The reader may consider this discussion of Saint-Simon's ideas, in a work jointly written by Saint-Simon, to be out of place. However, it must be remembered that the text was published anonymously.
95. Leo X, Pope from 1513 to 1521, responsible for the excommunication of Martin Luther (1521).

BIBLIOGRAPHY

This bibliography is offered as a guide to further reading for the English-speaking student of Saint-Simon's thought. There is, in addition, a vast amount of material available in French and other languages for which the student should consult Jean Walch's *Bibliographie du Saint-Simonisme*, Paris, 1967. A number of additional titles are listed in the bibliographies to Rouchdi Fakkar, *L'influence internationale de Saint-Simon et de ses disciples. Bilan en Europe et portée extraeuropéene*, Geneva, 1967; and Georg G. Iggers, *The Cult of Authority. The Political Philosophy of the Saint-Simonians*, 2nd ed., The Hague, 1970.

Bernstein, Samuel. 'Saint-Simon's Philosophy of History', *Science and Society*, vol. XII, no. 1, Winter 1948, pp.82-96. Reprinted with revisions in the same author's *Essays in Political and Intellectual History*, New York, 1955.

Booth, Arthur John. *Saint-Simon and Saint-Simonism. A Chapter in the History of Socialism in France*, London, 1871.

Bowle, John. *Politics and Opinion in the Nineteenth Century. An Historical Introduction*, London, 1954.

Cole, G.D.H. *A History of Socialist Thought*, vol. 1, London, 1953.

Dondo, Mathurin. *The French Faust. Henri de Saint-Simon*, New York, 1955.

Durkheim, Émile. *Socialism and Saint-Simon*, ed. Alvin W. Gouldner, trans. Charlotte Sattler, London, 1959. Reissued under the title *Socialism*, New York, 1962.

Germino, Dante. *Modern Western Political Thought: Machiavelli to Marx*, Chicago, 1972.

Gide, Charles, and Rist, Charles. *A History of Economic Doctrines*, 2nd English ed., trans. R. Richards, Ernest F. Row, London, 1948. Reissued London, 1961.

Gooch, G.P. *French Profiles. Prophets and Pioneers*, London, 1961.

Gray, Alexander. *The Socialist Tradition, Moses to Lenin*, 4th imp., London, 1963.

Grossmann, Henryk. 'Evolutionist Revolt Against Classical Economics. I. France: Condorcet, Saint-Simon, Sismonde de Sismondi', *Journal of Political Economy*, vol. LI, 1943, pp.381-96.

Halévy, Elie. *The Era of Tyrannies, Essays on Socialism and War*, trans. R.K. Webb, note by Fritz Stern, London, 1967.

Hart, David K. 'Saint-Simon and the Role of the Elite', *Western Political Quarterly*, vol. XVII, no.3, September 1964, pp.423-31.

Hayek, F.A. 'The Counter-Revolution of Science', Part I, *Economica*, vol. VIII (New Series), no.29, February 1941, pp.9-36; Part II, *Economica*, vol. VIII, no.30, May 1941, pp.119-50; Part III, *Economica*, vol. VIII, no.31, August 1941, pp.281-320. Reprinted in *The Counter-Revolution of Science, Studies on the Abuse of Reason*, Glencoe, Ill., 1952.

Iggers, Georg G. (ed. and trans.). *The Doctrine of Saint-Simon: An Exposition. First Year, 1828-1829*, 2nd ed., New York, 1972. (This contains the texts of the series of public lectures given in Paris by Saint-Simon's disciples during 1828-9.)

Ionescu, Ghita. 'Saint-Simon and the Politics of Industrial Societies', *Government and Opposition*, vol.8, no.1, January 1973, pp.24-47.

James, M.H. 'A Bibliographical Mistake in the Study of Henri de Saint-Simon', *Political Studies*, vol. XX, no. 2, June 1972, pp.202-5.

Jenks, Leland Hamilton. 'Henri de Saint-Simon', in *Essays in Intellectual History* (various authors), dedicated to James Harvey Robinson by his former seminar students, New York, 1929.

Larrabee, Harold. 'Henri de Saint-Simon at Yorktown. A French Prophet of Modern Industrialism', *Franco-American Review*, vol. II, 1937, pp.96-109.

Lichtheim, George. *The Origins of Socialism*, London, 1969.

A Short History of Socialism, London, 1970.

Lukes, Steven. 'Saint-Simon', *New Society*, no.225, 19 January 1967, pp.90-92.

Lyon, Peyton V. 'Saint-Simon and the Origins of Scientism and Historicism', *Canadian Journal of Economics and Political Science*, vol. XXVII, no.1, February 1961, pp.55-63.

Manuel, Frank E. 'From Equality to Organicism', *Journal of the History of Ideas*, vol. XVII, no.1, January 1956, pp.54-69.

The New World of Henri Saint-Simon, Cambridge, Mass., 1956. reissued Notre Dame, Ind., 1963.

'The Role of the Scientist in Saint-Simon', *Revue internationale de philosophie*, vol.14, nos. 3-4, 1960, pp. 343-56.

The Prophets of Paris, Cambridge, Mass., 1962.

Freedom from History and Other Untimely Essays, London, 1972. (This includes reprints of the two articles: 'From Equality to Organicism' and 'The Role of the Scientist in Saint-Simon'.)

Markham, F.M.H. 'Saint-Simon. A Nineteenth-Century Prophet', *History Today*, vol. IV, no.8, August 1954, pp.540-47

Mason, E.S. 'Saint-Simonism and the Rationalisation of Industry', *Quarterly Journal of Economics*, vol. XLV, no.4, August 1931, pp.640-83.

Plamenatz, John. *Man and Society*, vol. 2, London, 1963.

Polinger, Elliot H. 'Saint-Simon, the Utopian Precursor of the League of Nations', *Journal of the History of Ideas*, vol. IV, no.4, October 1943, pp.475-83.

Saint-Simon, Henri Comte de. *Selected Writings*, ed. and trans. F.M.H. Markham, Oxford, 1952. Reissued under the title *Social Organization, the Science of Man and Other Writings*, New York, 1964.

Simon, Walter M. 'History for Utopia: Saint-Simon and the Idea of Progress', *Journal of the History of Ideas*, vol. XVII, no.3, June 1956, pp.311-31.

'Ignorance is Bliss: Saint-Simon and the Writing of History', *Revue internationale de philosophie*, vol.14, nos. 3-4, 1960, pp.357-83.

Soltau, Roger. *French Political Thought in the Nineteenth Century*, London, 1931.

Stark, W. 'Saint-Simon as a Realist', *Journal of Economic History*, vol. III, no. 1, May 1943, pp.42-55.

'The Realism of Saint-Simon's Spiritual Program', *Journal of Economic History*, vol. V, no.1, May 1945, pp.24-42.

Talmon, J.L. *Political Messianism. The Romantic Phrase*, New York, 1960.

Taylor, Keith. 'Henri de Saint-Simon: Pioneer of European Integration', *European Community*, June 1972, pp.22-3.

Wilson, Edmund. *To the Finland Station. A Study in the Writing and Acting of History*, London, 1941. Reissued London, 1960.

Zeitlin, Irving M. *Ideology and the Development of Sociological Theory*, Englewood Cliffs, N.J., 1968.